Polish Refugees and the Polish American
Immigration and Relief Committee

ALSO BY JANUSZ CISEK
AND FROM MCFARLAND

*Kosciuszko, We Are Here!
American Pilots of the Kosciuszko Squadron
in Defense of Poland, 1919–1921* (2002)

Polish Refugees and the Polish American Immigration and Relief Committee

JANUSZ CISEK

Foreword by Janusz Krzyżanowski

McFarland & Company, Inc., Publishers
Jefferson, North Carolina, and London

Translated from the original Polish by Albert Juszczak

LIBRARY OF CONGRESS CATALOGUING-IN-PUBLICATION DATA

Cisek, Janusz.
  Polish refugees and the Polish American Immigration and Relief Committee / Janusz Cisek ; foreword by Janusz Krzyzanowski.
     p.   cm.
  Includes bibliographical references and index.

  ISBN 0-7864-2294-7 (softcover : 50# alkaline paper)

  1. Political refugees — Poland — History — 20th century.
  2. Political refugees — United States — History — 20th century.
  3. Polish Americans — History — 20th century.   4. Polish American Immigration and Relief Committee — History.
  5. United States — Emigration and immigration — History — 20th century.   6. Poland — Emigration and immigration — History — 20th century.   7. Poland — Politics and government —1945- .
  8. World War, 1939–1945 — Refugees — Poland.   I. Title.
  HV640.5.P66C57   2006
  362.87'57630899185073 — dc22   2005026336

British Library cataloguing data are available

©2006 Janusz Cisek. All rights reserved

No part of this book may be reproduced or transmitted in any form or by any means, electronic or mechanical, including photocopying or recording, or by any information storage and retrieval system, without permission in writing from the publisher.

On the cover: Polish children living in refugee camps, UNHCR/M. Benamar; PAIRC Logo by Waclaw Perkowski, Zirndorf, Germany, 1958

Manufactured in the United States of America

McFarland & Company, Inc., Publishers
  Box 611, Jefferson, North Carolina 28640
     www.mcfarlandpub.com

Contents

Foreword by Janusz Krzyżanowski   1
Introduction   9

I	The Genesis of the Polish American Immigration and Relief Committee in New York	11
II	A Survey of U.S. Immigration Law	14
III	The Polish American Community and the Problem of Aid for the Polish Republic During World War II	18
IV	The Committee's Founding and the First Period of Activity	38
V	Other Engagements in the Years 1948–1957	71
VI	A Who's Who in the Initial Years	83
VII	The Conclusion of the First Phase of Activity: A Summation of the Years 1947–1958	94
VIII	Enlarging the Scope of Operations: The Field Offices	103
IX	The Branches Abroad	115
X	The Committee Fights to Amend Immigration Laws	126
XI	Swimming with the Tide: Scaling Down, and Transformations	133
XII	Activity in the Years 1980–1990	187
XIII	A Review of Immigration Law in the Years 1980–1990	204

XIV	Political Changes in Poland: The Committee's Activity in the Years 1990–2000	207
XV	A Summing Up and Conclusions	215
Notes		219
Bibliography		231
Index		239

Foreword
by Janusz Krzyżanowski

This is the story of an American organization, based in New York City, known as the Polish American Immigration and Relief Committee (PAIRC). Although the idea to help Polish immigrants had taken practical shape in various organizational forms well before World War I, its greatest incarnation, in the shape of the PAIRC, focused on the alleviation of the misery of Polish people who, through the inscrutable hand of history, had become displaced persons and refugees after World War II. The mission of the PAIRC reflected Emma Lazarus' famous phrase: "Give me your tired, your poor, your huddled masses yearning to breathe free..." with the paramount aim of integrating the newcomers into American life and getting them quickly resettled so that they could become self-sufficient and productive members of their adopted country, as were their predecessors (the preceding waves of Polish immigrants to American shores).

In order to understand the Polish emigration–refugee issue immediately after World War II, particularly as it related to the United States, one must look at it from the perspective of its historical background. There were five major waves of Polish immigration to the United States: the colonial immigration in the years 1608–1776; the political immigration, 1776–1870; the economic (hardship) immigration, 1870–1939; the second political immigration, 1948–1989; and since then what might be called a humanitarian immigration, facilitated through the Family Unification Program and the Visa Diversification Program.

Each of the periods saw the influx of different sorts of people. The colonial period brought courageous and pioneering people, with initiative and skills. The first political immigration brought people who were mostly well educated in the arts and sciences, or who had professional degrees; the economic wave of the late 1870s through 1914 brought hard-working people desperate to make a better life than the miserable existence they had suffered in a Poland partitioned and occupied by Prussia, Austria, and Tsarist Russia. The second political immigration, prompted by Soviet Russia's reoccupation of Poland after World War II, brought refugees who were a cross-section of Polish society from blue collar to intellectual and professional, as is also true of the Poles coming to America since 1989.

Ironically, since the Middle Ages, Poland had been a nation that was itself open to immigrants and refugees from countries that did not practice religious or political tolerance, or that were going through great economic hardship. In some ways, Poland from the medieval period to the end of the eighteenth century was a European America, where Emma Lazarus' "tired ... poor ... huddled masses, yearning to be free" could come and live under conditions that they could not even dream of in their own countries, such as France, Spain, Germany, and even England, which at various times were bloodied by religious wars or political turmoil. Poland went even one step further than the United States as a haven for the underprivileged of the world. The Polish Commonwealth at times invited various groups to come to Poland to enjoy her freedoms and hospitality. It is enough, even today, to look through a phone book in Warsaw, in Krakow, or in any other Polish city to note the ethnic diversity of names. Scots, Jews, Englishmen, Frenchmen, Armenians, Tartars, and even Russians and Ukrainians after the 1917 Bolshevik Revolution, and many others streamed into Poland by the thousands and even tens of thousands. A striking example was German citizens of Jewish heritage fleeing Nazi Germany and seeking refuge in Poland prior to World War II.

It does not at all require a stretch of the imagination to state that Poles and those of Polish ancestry have figured prominently in American history from its very beginning, from the very first English settlement at Jamestown, and continue to do so today. In 1608 a number of Polish craftsmen, recruited by the Virginia Company of London at the request of Captain John Smith, came to Jamestown to manufacture glassware, tar, pitch and other goods. In character with their Polish sense of justice and civil rights, when the English did not want to treat them on a par with the English settlers, they went on strike and stopped manufacturing their goods. The British merchant ships had to return empty to England, and the English capitulated. The first fight for equal rights in America was won by the Poles. Poles were prominent in the Revolutionary War, fighting for the freedom of America; they were prominent in the Civil War on the Union side, fighting for the freedom of all Americans regardless of race or creed; and they were American soldiers and allies in the two world wars, fighting on the side of freedom and opportunity for all.

During the period between the two world wars (1919–1939) there was an uninterrupted movement of people between the United States and Poland. Some returned to Poland with their savings while others migrated to America. But the quota system introduced in 1921 allowed only 6,500 Poles per year to enter the United States.

From the end of World War II to 1989, when Communism began toppling in Poland, some 250,000 Poles reached America. This massive movement was made possible by the Displaced Persons Act of 1948 and its subsequent amendments, and by the Immigration and Nationality Act of 1980. This wave of immigrants-refugees was mostly composed of well-educated people who were strongly anti-communist. They had either chosen not to return to Poland at the close of the war due to the effects of the Yalta Agreement, or in the later years, wanted to get out from under the repressive Communist yoke in Poland.

Together with the immigrants of prior generations, Polish Americans contributed to the growth and development of the United States in many areas of national activity, including industry, civil service, the major professions, the arts, music, science, education, politics, and the military.

Polonia, as the Polish American community often refers to itself, and which at the beginning of the twenty-first century counts about fifteen million people, is very proud of her sons and daughters who have served their country honorably over the last four centuries. Over time, that service has been conducted on ever higher levels. During President Carter's administration, for instance, three Polish Americans helped guide the course of U.S. foreign policy: Secretary of State Edmund Muskie, National Security Adviser Zbigniew Brzezinski, Congressman Clement Zablocki, chairman of the House Foreign Affairs Committee.

Lieutenant General Edward Rowny served several presidents in an advisory capacity on disarmament. The citation on the Presidential Citizens Medal awarded him by President Reagan reads: "Edward L. Rowny has been one of the principal architects of America's policy of peace through strength. As an arms negotiator and a presidential advisor, he has served mightily, courageously and nobly in the cause of peace and freedom."

America is called the country of immigrants, and how true that is. Immigrants have built this country with their hard work and blood. They knew that to better themselves and to be able to send money to help the family back in the old country they had to start with any job they could get — a job nobody else wanted. Polish immigrants, and immigrants of other nationalities that came to America, love their adopted country and are ready for the ultimate sacrifice. The best proof of it is the list of immigrant volunteers in military service, and the list of immigrant soldiers who have been casualties in the most recent conflicts in Afghanistan and Iraq.

Left to right: Secretary of State Edmund S. Muskie, National Security Adviser Dr. Zbigniew Brzezinski, and Congressman Clement Zablocki, chairman of the House Foreign Affairs Committee.

Thank God, Poland is now free and there are no more Polish refugees. But in this world of constant turmoil there are always others, in other regions, who yearn for freedom. The United States, which for decades has been in the forefront of humanitarian aid that has helped oppressed people without regard to their national origin or religion, should continue to help people in need even in economically difficult times. Refugee-immigrants are an asset to this country, and the initial cost of resettlement is later repaid manifold by them.

During our work with refugees since 1948, and in our day-to-day contacts with the State Department's Refugee Program Bureau and other departments and agencies of the federal government, we had the opportunity to experience their best intentions. So, as the last executive officer of this organization, I would like to express our gratitude to all the departments of the United States government involved in the refugee programs. Our words of heartfelt gratitude also go to the USCC Migration and Refugee Services for the initial help with paperwork, received at the beginning of our work with refugees, and for helping out on a constant basis with ICM/IOM travel-loan accounts for needy refugees resettled by this committee.

In our work over the years, we dealt with displaced persons and refugees. The former consisted of people who spent World War II in German camps or were virtual slaves in Germany. They yearned for their own living space, and were thankful for any help and advice given to them by our office personnel, whom they considered their best friends. The latter, the refugees, consisted of people who spent the war in Poland and lived under the Communist regime. They were used to being lied to in the offices of the Communist government and to having their requests ignored if they asked meekly. From time to time, a refugee with exaggerated expectations would bring that baggage of bad feelings to the office of an organization that tried its best to resettle him or her in America, within existing budgetary restraints and refugee program regulations. A typical example is when a refugee would refuse to take an offered job, and, despite advice to the contrary, would voluntarily sign up for a tuition loan to study in a technical school for which he or she had no qualifications. The refugee would quit after a month or two, thus finding himself or herself on the outside of the resettlement program.

People who choose to work with refugees are the most dedicated people, and that is especially true for people working in a small organization like the Polish American Immigration and Relief Committee where, due to constant budgetary constraints, staff gave more of themselves than they would have in a larger organization that paid better. Our day's work is never done.

I want to thank our board of directors, but especially the president of the board, the Rev. Msgr. Joseph A. Marjańczyk, P.A., M. Div., who constantly preached to us all about the need to leave some written record of this committee's fifty years of work with refugees. Much to my dismay, whenever he told us that, he would always look in my direction. So, like it or not, one by one I began to consider people who might have a "feel" for the bygone era of political betrayal, human misery and devotion rendered to destitute people at the end of the Second World War and the communist period. Eventually, I proposed Dr. Janusz Cisek to the board. I had had a chance to observe him, and to hear his opinions expressed at board meetings of the Józef Piłsudski Institute here in New York, where he served as the executive director. As a young historian educated in Poland during the Communist regime, he had firsthand knowledge of the two worlds, and that was what was needed to understand the work of the Polish American Immigration and Relief Committee. But that was only one half of the problem. The other half was finding a translator for the benefit of English-speaking readers of the

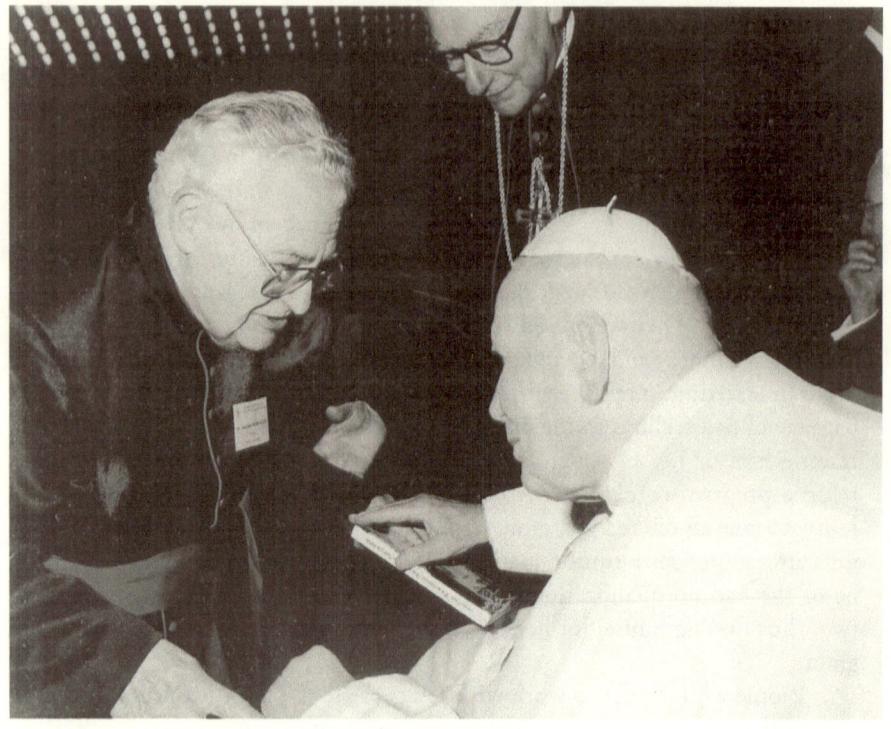

Left to right: The Rev. Msgr. Joseph A. Marjańczyk, P.A., M. Div.; Archbishop Szczepan Wesoły, chairman of the Administrative Council of the Pope John Paul II Foundation, and His Holiness, Pope John Paul II, at an audience with the pope at the Vatican in Rome, November 4, 2003. The pope is holding a gift from Msgr. Marjańczyk: the just-published Polish language edition of the present book.

book written by Dr. Cisek in Polish for the libraries and educational institutions in Poland.

Here, again after many considerations, my choice was Dr. Albert Juszczak, whom I knew when he served as president of the Kosciuszko Foundation in New York and later as the executive director of the Polish and Slavic Center in Brooklyn, a 50,000-member social services organization founded in the early 1970s by Polish World War II refugees in New York. Dr. Juszczak had the needed competence for this translation. He had a feeling for the subject, and he understood the nuances of all the situations because his parents were both members of the underground Polish Home Army and became refugees after World War II because they would not and could not safely return to Soviet-controlled Poland. My thanks go to both of them for agreeing to help PAIRC with their talents.

As this final chapter of our organization is being written, we also want to thank all the people who worked for the PAIRC in the United States and in all our European offices. The work was difficult and demanding, but it was done with the full awareness that precious human life was involved. And last but not least, our thanks go to the thousands of benefactors for their financial and moral support, which made the life of PAIRC's personnel easier.

As with every coin, refugee work also has its other side: not only exhaustion, but also pleasant and joyous moments, such as receiving a Christmas card from a former refugee, a positive response to a fund-raising letter or, above all, when suddenly — after the passage of some time — someone greets you on the street and tells you about the good job they now have, or when they proudly mention the great progress their children have been making in school. Suffice it to say, it was worth it.

"...The homeless Pole arriving here knows that he has no government and no country of his own to protect him. Washington and the United Nations recognize representatives of Poland who are his enemies, whose enemy he is. He is not only homeless — he is also stateless. We are his Poland. We are his representative and protector, who speaks for him..."

—*The Reverend Monsignor Feliks Burant,*
Founder of the Polish American Immigration
and Relief Committee, In Search of Milestones

Introduction

The Polish American Immigration and Relief Committee is one of the oldest and most distinguished Polish American organizations in the United States. Founded in 1947, for over fifty years it has provided aid to Poles who had been cast outside the borders of their nation, who had suffered loss due to war, who had been persecuted by both the brown and the red totalitarianisms, and to the needy of other nations in Europe and other regions of the world. The Committee has capably weathered political change and effectively survived the entire Cold War period up to the moment when the Polish Republic regained its sovereignty, which essentially resolved the problem of political refugees, and to a great degree also resolved the problem of economic refugees. In this period the Committee was able to secure entry to the United States for about 50,000 Poles, helped them gain employment and eased their adjustment to a new life in America. Moreover, about 20,000 persons were resettled to other countries thanks to the Committee's efforts. It effectively fought for changes in immigration law and for a justly proportioned participation of the Poles in the benefits flowing from every law pertaining to this matter. Thanks to a high work standard, the selflessness of the membership, and capable management and leadership by its presidents and volunteers, the Committee was blessed with high regard both in its own community and outside it.

This monograph drew on the archives of the Committee and on consultations with its prominent members, assisted by a review of accessible literature on the subject, and also on materials extant in the József Piłsudski Institute in New York. The structure of the monograph, its contents and its size are the result of the framework established together with Janusz Krzyżanowski, the Committee's executive vice president. The basic premise was to supply the data for a full picture of the Committee's work together with reference to and citation of archival sources and information from prominent Committee members.

The aim of this study is to make the story of the Polish American Immigration and Relief Committee accessible to the general reader while maintaining the rigors of a historical treatise.

Janusz Cisek
New York
February 2006

I

The Genesis of the Polish American Immigration and Relief Committee in New York

The emigration of Poles to the American continent has a history that is over four centuries long. To the end of the 19th century only a small, basically insignificant number of emigrants arrived in the States in an organized manner. The situation changed dramatically as a result of World War II, which bore fruit in the form of new, specialized agencies, both federal and civic (private and religious), which took an interest in emigration to the United States. One of the organizations that helped Poles was the Polish American Immigration and Relief Committee (referred to later as the Committee, or simply PAIRC).

The Committee was founded in 1947, but its genesis reaches back, though not under the same name, to at least the last fifteen years of the 19th century. In view of the fact that other ethnic groups founded immigrant relief committees, Polish American leaders in New York founded the Central Welfare Committee in 1885. Its soul was Erazm Jerzmanowski, a philanthropist and vice president of the Equitable Gas Light Company in New York. Also worthy of mention are Dr. Wincenty Żółtowski, Ignacy Pawłowski, and the Reverend Hieronim Klimecki, the pastor of St. Stanislaus Parish on the lower East Side of Manhattan.

The Committee's first office was located in an immigrant employment agency at 34 East Third Street. The Committee's first activity report, published one year after the commencement of work, stated that $4,202.19 had been expended on behalf of immigrants. This amount, large for those times, was the sum of a $1,025 donation from Jerzmanowski, and individual donations from other sources. According to a report printed in *Zgoda*, the organ of the Polish National Alliance, Poles arriving in the United States were provided for, received help in finding jobs, and received advice in difficult life situations. Soon thereafter the Committee merged with the Polish National Alliance, which had a positive effect on the scope of the Committee's activities but at the cost of its exclusive character, and caused it to dissolve into the much larger organization. In addition, it became the object of an unsubstantiated attack by Chicago's *Gazeta Katolicka* (*Catholic Gazette*), which undermined its existence. Despite this, efforts did not cease to have an independent organization in New York acting on behalf of immigrants. Those efforts were centered around St. Stanislaus Bishop and Martyr Parish, which in the years 1874–1900 was located on Stanton Street.

There was an enormous influx of Polish immigrants during the last decade of the 19th century, much larger than in the prior period. These were mostly people who did not know English, had no knowledge of living conditions in America, had no money, and had no place to live. Cognizant of these conditions, a group of Polish American priests in New York decided to found St. Joseph's Charity Organization — Society for Polish Immigrants. The Society was incorporated on February 18, 1891, and a building was rented to accommodate it. The following priests were the founding members: the Rev. Jakub Wójcik, the Rev. Jan Patrzycki, the Rev. Mieczysław Barabasz, the Rev. Hieronim Klimecki, and the Rev. Jan Golcz. The founders set themselves the following goals:

1. To open a home in New York where Polish immigrants could find shelter during the initial phase of their stay in America.
2. To supply information to immigrants on housing, settlement, and employment.
3. To provide help in obtaining U.S. citizenship.

Activity was financed by donations from parishioners. The first house was rented in Brooklyn, but subsequent ones were in Manhattan. The Society was located, in turn, on Rector Street, Morris Street, and Greenwich Street. Finally, in 1904 a building was purchased at 171 Broad Street, which was called St. Joseph's Home for Polish Immigrants. The Felician Sisters managed it to 1913, after which their duties were assumed by the Sisters of the Congregation of the Immaculate Conception, from New Britain, Connecticut. Pastoral care was provided by these priests: the Rev. Wincenty Bronkowski, the Rev. Jan Golcz, the Rev. Józef Dworzak, the Rev. Jan Strzelecki, the Rev. Zygmunt Świder, the Rev. Piotr Baciński, the Rev. Józef Klucz and the Rev. Stanisław Nowak. They and their associates maintained contact with the immigration authorities. They combed lists published by transportation companies for Polish names, participated in the Immigration Service's processing on Ellis Island as translators, and gave legal assistance to arriving Poles. The Society also developed an employment search operation, ran a shelter for the homeless, and gave spiritual support. In the period 1900–1913 the Society helped 114,577 immigrants. At first, during the years 1901–1907, some 3,000 to 6,000 persons annually availed themselves of the Society's aid; however, from 1908 to 1913 an average of 16,000 persons per year were helped.

In 1914–1915, St. Joseph's Home suspended operations due to disputes with the municipal authorities over fire security requirements. The Home was reopened in 1916, but its development was ever more limited by the war, which halted the stream of immigrants, and after the war ended, by the introduction of immigration quotas, and to a certain degree by the reverse emigration of Poles from America to the "old country." These factors contributed to the demise of the Society and St. Joseph's Home.[1]

The Society's objectives were resumed only several years later, to a limited extent, by other Polish American organizations. This happened at the beginning of World War II, which confronted the nations of the world with an immigration problem of unprecedented proportions.

II

A Survey of U.S. Immigration Law

It has become customary to consider the United States a land of immigrants. Indeed, this nation was built with the effort of successive generations of citizens hailing from all over the world, a fact reflected in U.S. legislation. Immigration law was an essential element in the regulation of the influx of millions of people, and it is as old as the nation itself. To get an idea of the genesis of the problem and the framework within which the Polish American Immigration and Relief Committee maneuvered, it is necessary to present at least a thumbnail sketch of the basic legislation enacted up to the moment of the Committee's founding in 1947.

Before March 26, 1790, immigration was regulated by individual states. On that date, Congress introduced a residence requirement of two years in the United States, before a person could become naturalized. This was the first federal immigration act. In 1795 the requirement was increased to five years. The Alien Enemy Act of July 6, 1798, gave the president the right to deport men over 14 years of age in case of war, with a guarantee of safekeeping for personal property. This law coincided with serious upheavals in Europe, such as the French Revolution and the Napoleonic campaigns that followed, which caused an exodus from many European countries to America. Several laws later, on July 4, 1864, the post of commissioner of immigration was established, appointed by the president and under the control of the secretary of state. In 1875 (the Act of March 3, 1875), direct federal control of the immigration process was introduced. It denied right of entry to persons convicted of felonies or prostitution. It was forbidden to import persons from Oriental countries without their agreement, thus making forced "coolie" labor illegal.

Moreover, the control of immigrants was placed in the hands of special port officials. The Chinese Exclusion Act of May 6, 1882, suspended, for 10 years, the right of laborers from China to immigrate, forbade the naturalization of the Chinese, and secured the right to deport them if they gained illegal entry into the United States. This law was not suspended until December 17, 1943.

A big breakthrough came with the introduction of the Immigration Act of March 3, 1891, which was the first comprehensive law controlling immigration. It established the formation of a Bureau of Immigration within the Department of the Treasury, to administer the entire scope of immigration matters with the exception of the Chinese Exclusion Act of 1882. Added to the category of persons denied immigration were those who could be a threat to public order, the carriers of certain infectious diseases, criminals, persons convicted of misdemeanors, and those accused of polygamy. Also defined were the methods of inspection that officials of the Department of the Treasury could use regarding persons traveling across or along the U.S. borders with Mexico, Canada, and British Columbia. Finally, every immigrant who entered the United States illegally was ordered deported. From 1907 on, every person entering the United States had to declare permanent or temporary residence, which permitted an appropriate classification into immigrants and non-immigrants. Moreover, a tax of $4 per person was established. Also denied entry were children without parental care, persons infected with tuberculosis, and women seeking entry for immoral purposes. The president was given the right to deny entry to specified individuals if labor market conditions demanded such a decision. In this instance, it concerned the denial of entry to workers from Japan. The aforementioned act also established a congressional committee to do a comprehensive review of immigration law. In 1917, this committee presented its conclusions, which became the basis for the passage of the Immigration Act of February 5, 1917.

The Quota Law of May 19, 1921, had enormous significance for Poles, and for the efforts of the Polish American Immigration and Relief Committee in later years. It limited entry on the basis of nationality to 3 percent of the number of residents of that ethnic group in the United States as of 1910. On the basis of that law, on average, 350,000 persons were admitted annually, mainly from Europe. From the Polish point of view, the problem was that in 1910 the Republic of Poland was not represented as a nation-state on the map of Europe. As a result, an enormous number of emigrants from Polish territories that were controlled by the three occupying powers (Russia, Germany, and Austro-Hungary) were not documented as Polish nationals. On one hand, the number of entrants could have been tremendous, as the absolute number of Poles in America at that time was considerable; on the other hand, there was no way to formally verify it, as they declared their country of origin as Austro-Hungary, Russia, or Germany. That was in line with the contemporary political situation and that is how those immigrants were treated in the official statistics. That drastically lowered the 3 percent threshold which was the basis of the quota for Polish nationals. Fortunately, Poland was already a sovereign state in 1921, which allowed the Polish quota to be defined in administrative terms.

In 1924, additional immigration restrictions were introduced based on a national quota. The threshold was lowered to 2 percent of the total number of persons of a given nationality living in the United States (with the exclusion of overseas territories) as of 1890. Coupled with the weaker national consciousness of Poles at that time, this system was even less favorable than the Law of 1921. The overall immigration quota for all nationalities in light of the Law of May 26, 1924, was set at 164,667 persons; thus it was less than half of what it had been under the Quota Law of May 19, 1921. Also in 1924, preferential categories were created within the quota (for example, spouses of U.S. citizens, children under the age of 21, or specified professions) that established a non-quota status. It was decided that no immigrant could enter the territory of the United States without a visa issued by the appropriate consular office in the country of residence. This meant that the consular corps was given control over selection, and that the obligation to qualify immigrants was moved outside U.S. borders.

Immigration law went through a serious revolution during World War II. As of June 28, 1940, all immigrants 14 years old and over had to be fingerprinted. Also, the categories of persons liable for deportation were expanded to include a wider scope of subversive organizations (including communist ones). The Public Safety Law of June 20, 1941, permitted a consular office to deny a visa to any foreign national suspected of subversive activity. In several successive bills (the Act of June 21, 1941, and the Act of December 8, 1942) the president's and attorney general's right to deport or deny entry to foreigners as national security risks was affirmed and enlarged. On the other hand, the period immediately after World War II saw an increase in stipulations permitting certain categories to immigrate, such as the fiancées of members of the armed forces. As a matter of fact, attention was turned to resolving the burgeoning problem of refugees, displaced persons, and victims of war, among them hundreds of thousands of Poles.[1]

Generally speaking, Congress spent a significant amount of time codifying immigration issues, but there was a lack of close scrutiny of the problems of particular nationalities, except for a series of restrictions on citizens or residents of certain Asian countries. The problem of East European immigration was not a priority item because it was by nature strictly of an economic character. Simultaneously, it ought to be noted that with the exception

II—A Survey of U.S. Immigration Law

of the war period the problem of political immigration did not exist, in the present understanding of that term. Nor was there a massive refugee immigration problem, though there undoubtedly were larger waves of emigration from several European and Asian nations. But this was not reflected in existing legislation. Characteristic, however, were the frequent adjustments of existing law to suit the moment, and the avoidance of comprehensive solutions of the kind represented by the quota system.

It is evident even from this brief analysis that immigration law went through a series of twists and turns—from a period of relative liberalism, even openness, to periodic restrictiveness that reflected isolationist moods. Notably, immigration law after World War II went through similar contortions, to which the representatives of many nations, including the Poles, were to be subjected.

III

The Polish American Community and the Problem of Aid for the Polish Republic During World War II

In 1939 no one was able to anticipate the degree of destruction and the enormity of human loss, or the demographic shifts that were soon to occur on a European and global scale. It is impossible, therefore, to unequivocally prove that any Polish American organization consciously prepared itself to handle a massive refugee problem. However, the activation of volunteerism and charitable giving at the outbreak of the war was very essential. First, it prepared the ground for the handling of tasks that emerged after 1945. Second, it aroused civic awareness and charitableness to match the scale of the entire mass of refugees, and it lifted Polish American communities out of their regionalism and parochialism, characterized by the concentration of efforts solely within the local community. Finally, it was highly significant that the Polish cause was positioned as the central issue of international relations during the war. Both the Polish Republic, with its government in exile in London, and the Polish American community gained by this in terms of promotion and public relations. This situation undoubtedly contributed to the unification of the Polish American community's efforts through the Polish American Congress, established in 1944. The political scientist John L. Snell accurately described this international aspect of the Polish cause. He wrote in his book on diplomacy in the years 1939–1945:

> Poland was to become the alpha and omega of diplomacy during World War II — a cause which became the reason for war between Germany and the Western democracies in 1939 and the key element in the dispute between

Soviet Russia and the West, when the war began to wind down. Both in 1939 and in 1944 the Polish question served as a litmus test for the true intentions of the West, on the one hand reflecting the enormity of Hitler's ambitions, and on the other Stalin's will to possess all of Central Europe. Thus the Polish question was more important than the Polish Republic itself, it was a litmus test of relations between the great powers.[1]

The issue of Polish refugees in vanquished Germany after 1945 became, to a certain degree, a beneficiary of this situation. For they represented the first army that took up arms in the conflict with Hitler, and the hundreds of thousands of forced laborers who were compelled to leave their homes to work as slaves for the Third Reich. This problem was also connected with Soviet Russia's withdrawal from cooperation with Great Britain and the United States, in the sense that Stalin's breach of promise concerning free elections and the character of the Polish nation-state made a return home impossible for tens of thousands of people who in 1945 found themselves within the three Allied occupation zones in Germany.

At the outbreak of war, the Polish American community was largely caught off-guard by the development of events. The American and Polish American press reported on the looming conflict; nonetheless, the outbreak of the war itself, and even more its course, shocked the Polish American community. These moods are well reflected in the reaction at the Polish National Home, on St. Mark's Place in lower Manhattan, to the first news of Germany's invasion of Poland. There was an outbreak of enthusiasm at the first news of war. A *Nowy Świat* (*New World*, a Polish American New York daily) correspondent related "great animation and enthusiasm that it had finally begun. We will sure give that Hitler hell."[2]

On the other hand, there was a pervasive feeling of surprise and uncertainty as to the outcomes of the conflict and the directions of action. This mood was enhanced by a lack of directives from Polish diplomatic-consular delegations and by a lack of decisiveness on the part of the Polish American leadership.[3] One of the largest organizations, the Rada Polonii Amerykańskiej (American Relief for Poland — ARP), published a proclamation on September 1, 1939, titled "Countrymen — to Action!" which said:

> In this historic moment the American Relief for Poland calls on all who have Polish blood in their veins, to unleash the full power of their spirit, to direct their thoughts and will in one direction — Poland's victory. The entire Polish American Community ... stands by its Motherland in this decisive conflict. We appeal to all our countrymen to unite in heart and mind.[4]

The proclamation of the Second District of the Polish Falcons Society in America (Sokolstwo Polskie w Ameryce), whose leadership had convened in Milwaukee, Wisconsin, did not differ much from the one above. On September 3, 1939, the Polish Falcons sent the Polish Army an encouragement to fight the eternal foe and wished it success and made an offer to help.[5]

The cited proclamations lacked a call to arms for the Polish American community, a call for political demonstrations on behalf of the Polish Republic, and a call to help Polish refugees. The press reacted differently. Many headlines called for sacrifice on behalf of the Fatherland, tried to organize collections, even called to arms. But there was, in all this, no unifying element that could organize and direct the moods which, as news from the Polish front kept coming in, turned rather pessimistic. It must be admitted, however, that the indecision of the large political centers and social organizations did not halt the spontaneous and widespread efforts of the Polish American community in various states to gain the right to serve in the Polish armed forces. Numerous, often very emotional, applications in this matter have been preserved in the files of the former Consulate General of the Republic of Poland in New York. This enthusiasm was neither properly utilized nor channeled. Nor was there any success in taking advantage of it for later recruiting efforts connected with the mission of Polish General Bronisław Duch in the United States and Canada.[6]

Financial contributions poured in, as did offers of material help. They were directed to the Polish Embassy in Washington, D.C., and to the Polish consulates in New York, Chicago and Pittsburgh. September 2, 1939, at the New York World's Fair was especially memorable. Festivities were planned for that day under the patronage of the Polish National Alliance, with the participation of New York's governor, and of New York mayor Fiorello La Guardia. The act of war was already common knowledge, and sympathy for Poland was widespread, so it's no wonder that the ceremony metamorphosed into a great manifestation of solidarity with Poland fighting against the German invaders.

At news of the aggression, Polish Americans all over the country organized solidarity meetings. In some sense they raised the issue that was later to be a focal point for the activity of the PAIRC in that they propagated self-taxation on behalf of relief that was being organized, and they emphasized the horrors of war which became the lot of millions of people. Unfortunately, no practical measures followed from those meetings. The president of the Zjednoczenie Polskie Rzymsko Katolickie (Polish Roman Catholic Union of America) in Chicago, Józef Kania, declared: "We are on a misguided path on how to aid Poland. Meetings aren't enough.... Shouting, casting thunderbolts, and lambasting won't help tortured Poland, crying out for help. Today more than ever we need calm and movement as a united front to tax ourselves.... Meetings are good, but only to uplift the spirit, to amplify the rescue efforts, but they are no substitute for action." For the duration of the war, Kania voluntarily taxed himself $25 per month on behalf of the Polish cause.[7]

At this stage, refugees were not an issue. Clearly, war refugees in Poland who ran from the Germans, then ran back again to the German-occupied territories to escape the Bolshevik occupation, and those who escaped through Hungary, Romania, and the Scandinavian countries to the West, did not knock on America's door. This problem would not appear until the close of the war. The Polish cause in America and the scope of activity of Polish American organizations were severely limited by President Franklin Delano Roosevelt's declaration of neutrality on September 5, 1939. It rendered impossible not only fund-raising on behalf of the Polish army, recruitment for the Polish armed forces, or purchase of arms, but also all manner of political propaganda, not to speak of plans to join the Polish army on an individual basis. Immediately after that proclamation, several organizations tried to have the embargo of arms shipments and war materiel lifted. Such an appeal was sent to congressmen and senators by the participants in a Polish American journalists' and publishers' convention in Chicago, which was held on the day of the neutrality proclamation. The initiator of this intervention was Karol Burke, a Polish American journalist well known in the Polish American community. This and other interventions did have a certain effect, namely, that on September 30, 1939, the U.S. Senate and House of Representatives lifted the embargo on arms shipments to Great Britain and France. This expanded indirect means for acting on behalf of Poland.

The Związek Narodowy Polski (Polish National Alliance — PNA) was the largest Polish American organization at this time. Founded in 1880, it had considerable influence, especially in Chicago and the Midwest, and it also had considerable funds. The 28th Convention of the PNA was held September 10–16, 1939. Its deliberations, planned well before, had to take place in a transformed atmosphere. Nonetheless, the delegates gathered at the Book Cadillac Hotel in Detroit did take up the issues of aid for Poland, and of aid for refugees.

With regard to the latter, the convention did not grasp the full scale of the problem — that would only become apparent after the conclusion of the war — but it did draw attention to the importance of the issue. The Budget and Review Committee recommended as follows: "Creation of a fund to help the victims of war in Poland, for which ½ cent monthly is assigned from every 21 cents of the turnover tax. The Central Board will set the payout rules." In the following point, the Committee: "Recommends to establish a Welfare Fund of ⅛ cent from each 21 cents of the revenue tax, which is to be paid out as recommended by the Central Board."[8]

This tax was to supplement the considerable sums that came from other PNA sources. In his address to the convention, PNA President John Romaszkiewicz appealed for support of the Fund for Aid to Poland, which already had $250,000. He even made an appeal to collect "Ten million dollars to help Poland." Conducting the collection for these purposes was weakened, and even suspended, in connection with the United States' neutrality declaration; nonetheless, as a result of Romaszkiewicz's appeals to President Roosevelt and Secretary of State Cordell Hull, the matter was placed on an appropriate track. Respective chapters of the PNA became obliged to fill out specific applications and to submit them to Washington. Such a procedure took time, of course, but it also allowed for a continuation of work in this area.

Individual declarations made by the PNA Convention participants became an excellent opportunity for support of the fund. The $100,000 transferred from the Alliance College Fund was augmented by $7,500 in individual contributions obtained when the delegates enthusiastically declined one per diem payment during the convention's sessions. These considerable sums offered an optimistic prognosis for the effectiveness of relief activity. Aside from the purely PNA track, American organizations were also tapped. In the middle of October 1939 a PNA delegation went to Washington to present a $150,000 check to the Red Cross at its headquarters there for aid to Poland. Numerous members of the House and Senate dignified that ceremony with their presence. It should be noted that efforts in that direction were already being made at the Detroit convention. The arrival of General Aleksander Osiński was awaited. He, as the president of the Polish Red Cross, was visiting the United States at that time. The delegates wanted to seek his opinion. Thus, the sum of almost half a million dollars that was presented by the PNA for Polish causes was a serious shot in the arm which, in some way, also impacted the issue of war refugees.[9]

The PNA donations did not measure up to the contributions of the Rada Polonii Amerykańskiej (American Relief for Poland — ARP), the precursor where charitable activity during World War II was concerned, and to some extent the initiator of efforts to unify Polish American organizations in the United States. The ARP attempted to give a new direction to the work of the entire Polish American community. It wanted to augment the significance of the Polish ethnic group in the United States and to play the role of representative of Polish interests in the United States. The ARP had political objectives — though these, in practice, did not dominate its activity — and also economic and cultural ones. The political elements were jettisoned during the course of World War II. This happened shortly after the establishment of the Polish Government in Exile (first located in Paris and subsequently in London) in which some influence was retained by Ignace Jan Paderewski, who had tremendous rapport with the Polish American community. This influence reached back to World War I and President Woodrow Wilson's declaration on the Polish question, with which Paderewski was linked in a positive way in people's minds. During World War II the American Relief for Poland assumed the burden of organizing relief for Poles — victims of war — which it continued until the founding of the PAIRC in New York.

The ARP had its genesis in 1936. On May 2 of that year representatives of 50 organizations, convening in Chicago, called to life the Polish American Inter-Organizational Council. The members of its executive board included: the Rev. Dr. Franciszek Świetlik as president, and as vice presidents Honorata Wołowska, an outstanding activist and secretary of the Związek Polek w Ameryce (Polish Women's Alliance of America) founded in 1898, and Józef Kania, the president of the Zjednoczenie Polskie Rzymsko Katolickie (Polish Roman Catholic Union of America) founded in 1873. American Relief for Poland was founded at the third convention of the Polish American Inter-Organizational Council, which deliberated in Chicago from April 30 to May 1, 1938. Świetlik was also chosen to head it. The ARP actively participated in fund-raising for the Polish National Defense Fund, which was a very popular campaign. Meanwhile, the above-mentioned declaration of neutrality made it impossible to support the National Defense Fund with its military objectives. The place of the NDF was taken by the Polish American Relief Fund, and American Relief for Poland tried, as an unofficial extension of the Polish government in London, to represent Polish American interests. That is also how it was seen by the government of General Władysław Sikorski, who appreciated its adherence to his political line and its disinclination to conduct independent, or even anti-government, political action. This did not mean that there was no alternative to the ARP. There undoubtedly was, as for instance the Komitet Narodowy Amerykanów Polskiego Pochodzenia (National Committee of Americans of Polish Descent) founded in 1942, or another organizational initiative, the Zjazd "Amerykańsko-Polskich Zrzeszeń na Wschodzie" (the Congress of Polish American Associations on the East Coast), which deliberated in New York on March 11 and 12, 1944. The latter presaged the establishment of the Kongres Polonii Amerykańskiej (Polish American Congress).[10]

However, both these bodies quite strongly criticized General Sikorski's government. Because the ARP unequivocally and uncritically opted for the political line of General Sikorski, it enjoyed the support of the London Government of the Polish Republic and in some sense was in favor with the administration in Washington. The latter had to do with permissions for conducting a fund drive, help in transporting material goods in ships sailing under neutral flags, and the transmittal of funds.

The policy of the American Relief for Poland with regard to the war situation was worked out beginning with the convention that deliberated in the Chicago headquarters of the Związek Polek w Ameryce (Polish Women's Alliance) on August 29, 1939. Several days later, at news of Germany's aggression against the Polish Republic, a special meeting of ARP directors was convened (September 2, 1939). The participants decided that the most important task was to coordinate the efforts of the entire Polish American community to render aid to the fighting nation:

> The American Relief for Poland calls upon Polish American organizations and our entire community to immediately collect even greater, much greater contributions for the Polish Relief Fund, which will be destined for aid to victims of war in Poland that does not contradict the neutrality act. We have to gather at least ten million dollars! Let us give even more than we could have!

Administrative matters, among them permission from the federal authorities to conduct the fund drive, were successfully accomplished thanks to the intercession of Matt Szymczak, the governor of the Federal Reserve Bank in Washington, D.C. On September 11, 1939, the ARP reported that with the consent of the Department of State it could continue to conduct a fund drive even prior to the completion of appropriate administrative procedures. At a special meeting of the Executive Committee of the ARP on September 18, it was decided to call a special convention whose objective was to define policy toward the war in Poland. The convention took place in Chicago on October 19, 1939. One of the resolutions concerned walking away from political goals in favor of strictly charitable ones, which among other things gave access to several forms of aid from the federal government. On this basis, the ARP was able to develop an impressive campaign on behalf of the suffering population of the occupied territories, including help for refugees from Poland. The first litmus test of the ARP's relief activity for refugees was the 1940–1941 period in Lithuania. There were tens of thousands of Poles in that territory who had sought shelter there after the September 1939 campaign. Throughout 1940 and 1941 they found themselves in incredibly difficult material circumstances, not to speak of the danger of arrest by the NKVD. To alleviate the plight of the impoverished population and the refugees, the Komitet Uchodźców (Refugee Committee) and the Towarzystwo Samopomocy Obywatelskiej (Civic Self-Aid Society) began operation in Vilnius. On October 28, 1939, the Lithuanian authorities agreed to the activity of foreign charitable societies, and a mission of the American Relief for Poland, headed by Dr. Redfern, arrived in town. The financial capability of the ARP and the personal attributes of Dr. Redfern placed it at the forefront of charitable activity in Lithuania. Thanks to donations from this source, the Civic Self-Aid Society could monthly serve 50,500 low-cost and free meals to the residents of Vilnius and to the refugees. This assistance mainly concerned refugees from central Poland. Anyone born in Vilnius or Lithuania after 1920 was considered an alien by the Lithuanian authorities, which increased the ARP's scope of activity. Redfern's assistance also encompassed thousands of people deported from the Vilnius area deep into Soviet Russia. Parcels of food and clothing were sent there. Administrative obstacles were surmounted by utilizing market days when peasants from Belarus came. Parcels were transported by peasant cart to Belarus. From there, without any further obstacles, they were sent to specific addresses in the gulags or to the forced settlement areas. The American Relief for Poland paid the cost of transport to Belarus, and also the cost of mail to the final destination. The return mails brought much sincere proof of gratitude from the deportees.[11]

Unfortunately the noble activity of the American Relief for Poland in Vilnius was cut short with the arrest of Dr. Redfern by the NKVD on May 25, 1941, less than a month before the outbreak of hostilities between Nazi Germany and Stalinist Russia. His co-workers most probably left Vilnius at the moment the Nazi–Soviet war broke out on June 22, 1941. Resumption of relief activity became possible after the Sikorski-Majski Pact of July 20, 1941, when, on the basis of an "amnesty," Poles were released from prisons, gulags, and other places of forced settlement. The first transports with aid from the American Relief for Poland arrived in Murmansk (East Siberian Russia) in December 1941. They were immediately passed on to outposts of the Polish Republic's Ministry of Labor and Social Welfare, which were scattered over those parts of Russia that were not occupied by the Germans. This action was carried out in close cooperation with Professor Stanisław Kot, the Polish ambassador, and it could be divided into the following stages:

1. November–December 1941—delegates go out into the field and outposts are organized.
2. January–March 1942—expansion of outposts in southern Russia and a more intense relief activity.
3. April–August 1942—the delegations' most intense period of activity.
4. September 1942–March 1943—gradual winding down of the delegations.

Although the ARP's activity was mainly directed to the feeding and material support of those who did not make it into General Anders's Polish army, it also included all those who had left their camps for southern Russia. It was often the only way by which the former prisoners could reach encampments of the organizing Polish army. The help proved even more important for those who were unable to leave their Kolkhozes, or places of forced settlement. Many lives were saved thanks to the food and clothes distributed by representatives of the ARP. The assistance for Poles in Russia lasted as long as relations between the governments of the Polish Republic and Russia were maintained.

The Katyn graves were discovered in April 1943. The Polish government requested an explanation. In response, the Soviet government severed relations. Later, two other death camps were discovered — at Charkov and Mednoye. More than 15,000 Polish officers and members of the intelligentsia were murdered by the Soviet NKVD in the three death camps.

The Polish population in Russia was then deprived of all help, including from the American Relief for Poland. It should be noted however, that after the Polish army left Russia in March–May 1942 the ARP continued to support soldiers' families in the Near East.

The ARP also had offices in Western Europe, where relief work began in the fall of 1939. In accordance with the limitations imposed by the neutrality act of the United States, the work encompassed Polish refugees in countries that were not engaged in the war. A rather extensive umbrella of aid was stretched over the refugees in Romania, Hungary, and Yugoslavia. In October 1941 a delegation of the ARP for Europe was opened with headquarters in Portugal. The government of this country, with Prime Minister Antonio de Oliveira Salazar, was very partial to the work of the ARP. Many accommodations were allowed which made it possible to circumvent limitations and obstacles resulting from wartime conditions. This also concerned facilitating transportation and expediting the delegation's financial operations.[12]

The delegation, through the intermediary of the Red Cross, sent food parcels to camps where Poles were present. After the occupation of Germany by the Allies, the ARP signed an agreement in Frankfurt am Main on July 10, 1945, with UNRRA (the United Nations Rehabilitation and Resettlement Administration) permitting it to operate in Germany, Austria, Italy, and France. From the point of view of American legislation, the ARP was treated in terms of the so-called "Permit 26" as a Voluntary Agency cooperating with UNRRA. After UNRRA's refugee relief activity wound down, a new agreement was signed with IRO (the International Refugee Organization) on December 3, 1947, in Geneva. On the basis of both agreements, a network of missions was established by the ARP in the aforementioned countries. All told, the ARP assisted 1,539,813 persons in Germany, 16,568 persons in Austria, and 112,866 persons in France, not counting other countries. Up to 1957, that is to the close of business and the closing down of the ARP's offices in Europe in 1958, $10,678,497 had been spent for aid to Polish refugees in Europe and the Near East. That was an enormous sum of money, made available thanks to the provident care of the Polish American community, the receipt of donations from various sources, and the receipt of contracts from U.S. government agencies involved in refugee problems.[13]

The plight of the refugees was not known to the American public. The situation improved after the war when the first press reports arrived in America, as did the letters of refugees to their families, and the reports of witnesses. It should be remembered that during the war there was a mail blockade between the United States and Germany, and between the United States and countries occupied by the Third Reich. All contacts were maintained by circuitous routes through neutral countries or by individual couriers. The reaction to the first reports was in proportion to the perceived enormity of the havoc, including the presence in the territories of the Third Reich of hundreds of thousands of people without means of support. The number of refugees was well above the estimates and calculations made before the Allies entered Germany. Especially large was the number of Poles who had been forcibly removed to Germany, or who had sometimes been recruited to work in Germany during the occupation. By October 1939, about 110,000 civilian workers were recruited for work in the Third Reich from annexed Polish territories. To this should be added about 180,000 members of the Polish armed forces who had been taken prisoner during the September campaign and placed in various POW camps within Germany. In tandem with the escalation of the war and with the growing needs of industry and agriculture, the number of forced laborers increased quickly. By the spring of 1942, 1,080,000 Poles were working in Germany. The estimates vary according to the sources. For instance, the ARP figured that in 1945 in all of Western Europe there were 629,453 Polish refugees, in 1948 there were 332,450, and in 1954 there were 150,626.[14]

According to another source, at the conclusion of the war there were over 800,000 displaced persons and more than 150,000 Polish prisoners of war in Germany and Western Europe.[15]

The lowest of the cited numbers ought to be taken as the lower limit, since in the case of the ARP's estimates only those in need who were registered were taken into consideration, which doubtless only partially reflected the true numbers. The numbers were certainly higher because beginning in the second half of 1945 all of Germany's occupied zones were exposed to an ever wider stream of refugees from behind the Iron Curtain, which had been put in place at the end of 1945.

After the Americans entered Germany, refugees were classified into the following categories: evacuees, political and military refugees, political prisoners, slave laborers, voluntary recruits, soldiers of various formations fighting under the German command, deportees, interned civilians, former prisoners of war, people without a country, workers of the Todt organization, and several other categories. This classification was done under the auspices of the Supreme Headquarters, Allied Expeditionary Force (SHAEF).[16]

UNRRA remained the main body handling refugee matters in Germany, Austria, and Italy. It was replaced in the fall of 1947 by the International Refugee Organization (IRO). Aside from organizations of a general character, a number of national religious and charitable organizations worked in this field. These included the Red Cross, the YMCA, the American Friends Service Committee, the Church World Service, and the National Lutheran Council. To this list should be added a multitude of ethnic organizations in the United States that took care of arrivals from the moment they entered the United States. In addition to usual operations, there were also more spectacular ones, designed to handle specific age and professional groups. Among these was Operation White Cygnets, on the basis of which Great Britain admitted a certain number of refugee women to work in hospitals and hospices. On the other hand, Westward Ho! dealt with 75,000 refugees who were contracted to work in English factories and mines. The enumerated enterprises, though they also dealt with Poles to a certain extent, were undertaken without the participation of Polish American organizations, which undoubtedly reflects the small number of Polish nationals who were encompassed by those programs. Where religious organizations are concerned, some of them helped people of various faiths. Operation Good Samaritan, for example, did not limit itself strictly to Episcopalians. Other organizations, for instance Jewish ones, combined efforts on behalf of persons of a specific religion and nationality.[17]

The analysis of Polish refugee needs pointed to the necessity of establishing a specialized Polish American organization. Conclusions of this sort were drawn both by the ARP and the Polish American Congress. The thesis could be advanced that the real crisis in the situation of the refugees in Germany began with the start of tensions between Stalin, Atlee, and Truman at around the first half of 1946. A factor that additionally complicated the situation was the American and British policy toward demobilized soldiers of the Polish armed forces who fought under British command in the West, and toward the refugees. Particularly noteworthy was the speech of Foreign Minister Ernest Bevin in the House of Commons on March 20, 1946. Bevin at that time reported that the government of Her Royal Majesty had made contacts with the Rząd Jedności Narodowej (Government of National Unity) in Warsaw (later disbanded by the Communists) concerning conditions for the return to Poland of soldiers and officers of the Polish armed forces. The British government found the conditions submitted to it to be satisfactory and in the aforementioned declaration urged the servicemen to return to Poland. Bevin added that this was an exceptional opportunity to engage in the rebuilding of the war-ravaged nation.[18] The conditions presented by the Warsaw government were appended to Bevin's declaration and published together with this document for wider distribution among Polish soldiers and officers. The declaration stated that there would be no negative consequences for the members of the Polish armed forces returning to their homeland, with the exception of those who had served in the German armed forces (even though these people, from annexed Polish territories, had been forcibly drafted) or those who had engaged in criminal activity. The benefits derived from the amnesty of August 21, 1945, were emphasized. This statement of the British government provoked a sharp reaction from the Government of the Polish Republic in London, which was the legal representative of national interests, and which was founded on the April 1935 Constitution of independent Poland. In a statement issued by the Polish Government in London on March 20, 1946, we read:

> It must be stressed, however, that the vast majority of Polish servicemen abroad refuses to return to Poland, not because they fear personal reprisals but because they want to live the life of free people in their own country, to which they have longed to return for many years.[19]

This was followed by a statement from the Polish Press Agency in Edinburgh which questioned the genuineness of the "invitation" from the Soviet puppet Bierut's proxies and which also doubted the premises guiding Bevin. The whole situation made it clear that the British government wanted to get rid of the Polish soldiers, who had so bravely served in the defense of the British Empire, and was willing to achieve this goal not only over the heads of the soldiers, but also over the Polish government in exile in London, from which recognition had been revoked on July 5, 1945, but toward which moral obligations still existed. The whole action did not bring any greater results. Of all the soldiers and refugees, over a span of several years, only a small number decided to return to Poland, and there were cases of repeat escapes to the West from this group of repatriates. The living conditions in Russia were too well known, including from personal experience, and too much information was coming from Poland. The terror of the security services against non–Communist activists, and also against ordinary citizens, alarmed public opinion in the West. As a result, part of the soldiers of the Polish armed forces in the West became, with time, open to emigration to the United States. All the more so as Bevin stated in his declaration that it might become impossible for all the Polish soldiers within the borders of the British Empire to stay there: "What is more the British Government cannot give the members of the Polish Armed Forces any guarantees, that all of them may be able to settle on British territory, be that in Britain or its overseas territories."[20] The Americans had no less an ambivalent position with regard to the refugees. On the one hand, UNRRA and the Red Cross supplied enormous amounts of food and sanitary products; on the other hand, there were quite a few cases of pressure to force the repatriation of persons who came from or just happened to stay temporarily to the east of the line held by the Red Army on June 22, 1941, the date of the commencement of the German-Soviet war. In other words, at issue was the affirmation of the annexation of Polish territories and of the territories of other nations in this region. Certain indications as to the obligations of the Western powers toward Stalin, which could have been made at the Yalta Conference, surfaced in an article in *East Europe*, a periodical published in London. An order of the American authorities in occupied Germany was cited there, dated November 7, 1945 (USFET — AG-387-GEC), in which it was stated that: "Those persons who were physically present in the USSR, who were citizens of the Soviet Union on 17 September 1939, and who were removed from [that part of Poland which was annexed by — *Trans.*] the USSR beginning the 22nd June 1941, are to be considered as Soviet citizens subject to repatriation in accordance with the Yalta agreement.... No Soviet citizen subject to repatriation in accordance with the Yalta agreement will be able to benefit from assistance and support in any D.P. camp after the 8th December 1945, except those camps that are under Soviet administration."[21]

In fact, during the Yalta Conference, commitments were made concerning refugees — Soviet citizens. Official agreements were signed in this matter, one between Soviet Russia and the United States, the other between the Soviets and Great Britain. One of the conditions of the agreement carried the obligation that Soviet and American citizens: "will without delay, after their liberation, be separated from enemy prisoners of war and be maintained separately from them in camps or points of concentration until they have been handed over to the Soviet or United States authorities."[22]

This was troubling in that it also included a large group of Poles who, on the basis of a unilateral Soviet decision, were forcibly gifted with Soviet citizenship after September 17, 1939. Moreover, the apparent principle of reciprocity in this instance acted exclusively to the detriment of refugees from East-Central Europe. During May 22–23, 1945, an agreement was signed in Halle between representatives of the Russian, British, and American military authorities that ordered Soviet prisoners of war and Soviet citizens to be handed over to the Russians.[23]

The transfer of Red Army prisoners to the Soviet authorities began immediately thereafter, to the tune of over 50,000 per day. By September, two million Red Army veterans and Soviet citizens-civilians were forcibly sent over the line controlled by the Western allies.

The American authorities tried to keep their pledge in their relations with the civilian refugees in Germany. They also stepped over the line frequently, as Soviet Special Services officers were brought into contact with the refugees, giving them a wide scope of prerogatives. It was basically these officers who participated in the commissions that conducted the hearings and decided who was a Soviet citizen. The instruction manual of the American Armed Forces for 1945–1946 states: "Individuals identified by the Soviet repatriation representatives as Soviet citizens were subject to repatriation without regard to their personal wishes."[24]

It should be remembered that the obligations in this matter were kept hidden from Western public opinion. Nonetheless, there was no lack of voices affirming the outlined suspicions. R.R. Stoke, the socialist delegate to the House of Commons, said in one of his interviews: "It seems that a most inhuman decision was made in Yalta, which is totally at odds with the stipulations of the Atlantic Charter. In light of this decision a Soviet citizen is anyone who lived behind the Soviet border as of June 22, 1941.... Every such 'Soviet citizen' is to be forcibly repatriated after the conclusion of the war."[25]

The decision or commitment of the Western powers concerning Poles is not known; nonetheless, the way the American authorities acted indicated a strong tendency to persuade Poles, Lithuanians, Latvians, and Estonians, not to speak of Belarussians, to return to the place of their birth or prior domicile. "Operation Carrot" gained a very bad reputation — 60 daily rations were offered to persons who declared their return to the Eastern zone. Fiorello LaGuardia, who had earlier been the mayor of New York City and was popular with the Polish American community there, was the director general of UNRRA in 1946, and was connected with this operation. This initiative did not bring the desired results, simply because the number of repatriates ready to return was cancelled by the number of those who were fleeing from the East to the Western Allied occupation zones.[26]

Regardless of the official actions, the Poles were not spared petty harassments. For example, the Polish camp press was not allowed to develop in the American zone. Instead, the U.S. armed forces periodical *Stars and Stripes* was distributed, in which articles frequently appeared encouraging repatriation. For instance, in the January 3, 1946, issue those Poles and citizens of the Baltic states who refused to repatriate were called reactionaries and fascists. In the periodical *Die Neue Zeitung*, which the Americans published for the Germans, a map was published indicating which nations were hostile to the United States. Poland was included. Despite protests, a correction or apology was never printed. The Americans themselves printed several periodical titles which "smelled strongly of Bierutian propaganda."[27]

Journalists reported that these practices were widespread. On January 30, 1946, the London-based *Dziennik Polski* (the *Polish Daily*) printed an article by Ryszard Kiersnowski, who witnessed the following events:

> The American authorities want at all costs to completely liquidate the Displaced Persons camps, forcing the Poles — by means of moral pressure and other methods that make life miserable — to repatriate.... Things are happening that demand a protest. For instance, at 7 in the morning on December 10, 1945, trucks loaded with soldiers came roaring into the Polish camp at Hohenfels, located within the territory of the American Third Army. As I noted, these were soldiers of the American Fourth Armored Division, under the command of Captain Robert G. Innes. These soldiers rushed into the housing blocks occupied by the Poles and yelling in German "hände hoch" (put your hands up) and also "get up ... Polaki" began chasing the Poles out into the hallways, without even giving the women time to dress.... After chasing the Poles out of their living quarters the Americans began a thorough inspection. They took all the food supplies saved up for the holidays, that had been received from UNRRA and the Red Cross, even the canned milk for babies, which went hungry that day.... In block Nr. 20 block leader F. Malczewski brought it to the attention of the Americans that all the items they were confiscating came from UNRRA and the Red Cross. For that statement he got slapped in the face by one of the American soldiers.... The event described here is not an isolated instance. Searches in Polish camps are ever more frequent. In the Polish camp at Wildflecken a search was conducted on the day after Christmas and all the cigarettes that the Poles had been given by the American authorities, as a reward for cutting down trees in the forest, were confiscated. What is the purpose of all this? It's simple. The Poles must leave Germany."[28]

Of course this sort of treatment had to have its source in official instructions, and it resulted not just from the presumed fulfillment of the Yalta commitments. A large role was played here by an ignorance of or a lack of desire to get informed about the living conditions under Soviet occupation. The increase in the number of refugees since the end of the war seemed a clear indication, but not everyone wanted to notice it. Arguably the most prominent Polish American publicist, Ignacy Matuszewski, asked in one of his articles:

> Why don't the Poles want to return to Poland? Of course fear plays a role here, due to the awareness that everybody who submits to the Soviet authorities faces the threat of a send-off deep inside Russia, where millions of Poles

disappeared without a trace during this war. Of course people desire freedom and know that they won't find it under Soviet rule. It seems that in the phenomenon of mass resistance one other motive plays a role: the instinctive feeling that a return could be damaging not only for the person returning — but what is more important — for Poland.[29]

Matuszewski noted further that a Polish miner returning to his native land was impoverishing his own country by his labor, because Polish coal was being sold to Soviet Russia for 315 zlotys per ton, while the cost of mining it was 1,400 zlotys per ton. It was just one example confirming that the national economies of all the countries occupied by the Soviets were working on behalf of the Stalinist occupier. This was one more reason for the escapes to the West and the resistance to returning behind the Iron Curtain. As Matuszewski said:

> If the masses do not want to return to Poland and other countries under Soviet occupation, if the resistance against pressure to repatriate is so universal and so enduring — then it is not born of fears for personal freedom alone. It is our conviction that the hundreds of thousands of Poles from all social levels who do not want to return, who must be forced to return, have an instinctive sense that one can work more effectively for Poland outside of it than in it.[30]

The refugee camp conditions in Germany also were within the orbit of the Polish American community's interest, and particularly of the Polish American Congress. Members of the New York–based Komitet Narodowy Amerykanów Polskiego Pochodzenia — KNAPP (National Committee of Americans of Polish Descent — NCAPD) tried to alert Senator Arthur Vandenberg, the Republican Senate majority leader, to this problem. Elected from Michigan, Vandenberg had a cordial relationship with Detroit's Frank Januszewski, the publisher of the *Dziennik Polski* (the *Polish Daily*) in Detroit. The senator supported many of the political postulates promoted by the NCAPD, which was under the patronage of a group of the late Marshall Piłsudski's followers who were refugees from Poland and were supported by Januszewski. *Dziennik Polski* published the correspondence between Vandenberg and Walter Cytacki, one of the NCAPD leaders, on the subject of refugees and the Polish question. When, in January 1946, Vandenberg went to London as a member of an American delegation for a meeting of the United Nations, Adam Tarnowski, the Polish Government in Exile's minister of foreign affairs, met with him unofficially regarding the necessity of aid for Polish refugees. Vandenberg was already for some time in favor of giving the Poles "Nansen" passports (a personal ID provided by a special committee formed by the League of Nations in 1920 for Russian escapees, and later a passport issued to persons without national affiliation) because in light of the Polish Government in Exile's loss of international recognition, passports issued before the war, and those issued by the Polish authorities in London, were no longer recognized anywhere in the world after July 1945. The senator also expressed his opposition to attempts at the repatriation of refugees to the East against their will:

> Subsequently Mr. Tarnowski asked Senator Vandenberg to undertake all possible steps with the appropriate American government authorities to ensure the most humanitarian treatment of Polish refugees in Germany and Austria and in particular to guarantee that none of them should be forcibly repatriated against their will. Senator Vandenberg demonstrated complete understanding of this plea and added that his own proposal to provide refugees with passports, of some "special" type, possibly under the authority of the UN, was precisely intended to prevent any possibility of repatriation against the will of the interested persons.[31]

In order to learn more about the situation, a special delegation of the Polish American Congress went to Germany led by Ignacy Nurkiewicz, a PAC vice president and industrialist from New York, and also by Karol Burke, the well-known Chicago journalist and director of the PAC's office in Washington, D.C., and a close collaborator of Karol Rozmarek, the president of the PAC and of the Polish National Alliance (the largest Polish-American fraternal organization, headquartered in Chicago).

The delegates visited DP camps from September 23 to October 4, 1946. The report published after the visit stated that there were 400,000 Poles in the three Allied occupation zones, of whom 195,000 were in the American zone. The living conditions were described as inhuman, degrading, requiring immediate intervention. UNRRA was blamed for the state of affairs, and an immediate response was demanded. Several examples were cited, including that of a 13-member family deprived of even a shade of privacy, stuffed into two tiny rooms. Nurkiewicz and Burke emphasized an essential fact, namely, that during the 18 months prior to their visit a large group of refugees arrived at the camps from Soviet-occupied Poland. According to estimates, in June alone 30,000 people arrived in the American occupation zone. What was worse, 68,000 additional people who wanted to come to the West were halted at the demarcation line. Nurkiewicz and Burke stressed that the conditions existing under the Soviet regime were worse than they had been under the Nazi regime. The PAC delegates also stated that UNRRA policy aimed at forced repatriation to the East. This was supported by the existence of mixed commissions, with the participation of representatives of Communist countries, which conducted screenings trying to get refugees to return.

Official documents were quoted that testified to the discrimination against Poles; and the following recommendations were made which were to improve the situation of Polish refugees:

1. All refugees in the American occupation zone, regardless of religious beliefs, are to be guaranteed humane living conditions through the intermediary of the United States government, acting through military occupation agencies and special missions established by UNRRA.
2. The U.S. immigration laws need to be amended so that unused immigration quotas, which went unfilled during the war years due to war conditions, can be used.
3. Prisoners of war and slave laborers deported to Germany against their will should have the ability to use German immigration quotas that were not used up to this time, as also future German quotas, so as to ease their plight.
4. Polish soldiers who fought and were ready to give their lives for the Allied cause, among them many decorated for valor with American medals, should have a comfortable stay in the U.S. ensured until such time as it is safe for them to return to their homeland.
5. Polish soldiers ought to have permission to serve in the American occupation forces, so they could gain the right to U.S. citizenship.
6. The sparsely populated territory of Alaska ought to be opened to the refugees by the U.S. government, especially for prisoners of war and soldiers, not only as a gesture of friendship, but also as a practical approach to the settlement of those territories.
7. An investigation ought to be conducted by the U.S. Congress to explain why such a small percentage of Christians was included in the current immigration quotas, and to ensure the abolition of preferential treatment in the future, so that the system that is installed in the future will guarantee a proportional treatment of right of entry into the United States for all national groups.
8. That all means at the disposal of the United States and its prestige be engaged to fix existing damages and to ensure normal living conditions in the occupation zones.

In conclusion, the report stated that in connection with the American participation in the Yalta agreement, which deprived refugees of the possibility of return to their homeland, America must take full responsibility for the existing moral and humanitarian crisis. "If there were no Yalta in 1945, there would be no war refugee problem in 1947, the report noted."[32]

On the basis of the aforementioned report, Karol Rozmarek, the president of the PAC, presented to Secretary of State James Byrnes a memorandum about the situation in the DP camps. That occurred during a superpowers conference in Paris. Rozmarek, Nurkiewicz, and Burke conferred with Byrnes on October 11, 1946. They demanded that Byrnes change the highly unsatisfactory conditions existing in the camps; they stressed the difficult living and material conditions, and the deficiencies in the feeding of the refugees. They brought to his attention the baseless, repressive shifting of refugees from one camp to another, especially in places where the Poles were able to develop an effective internal network or cultural work. They protested the closing of Polish schools by UNRRA, repressions against periodicals and Polish journalists, especially those opting to remain in the West or those who opposed Communism. Other problems were the closing of access to the camps for clergy and repressions against the newest refugees, who had left territories occupied by the Red Army. No less touchy was the treatment of prisoners of war, estimated at 23,000, and of the 35,000 veterans of the Warsaw Uprising of 1944. On June 11, 1946, the American military authorities withdrew refugee privileges from the above two military categories. Also, the payment of financial stipends was withheld, as was the right to wear a uniform. Finally, an appeal was made to have the soldiers of the Labor Service Companies of the U.S. Army get the same pay as their American counterparts, and to establish a special congressional committee. A report on the Paris session stated:

> We feel that the refugees, who cannot return to their countries of origin, should be moved over to the western hemisphere by emigration. The United States, inclusive of the territory of Alaska, ought to accept 150,000 refugees. The Polish immigration quotas were not used up during the war. The example America sets will encourage other Western nations to accept the remainder. These people are permeated with the ideals of Democracy and they oppose totalitarianism, which will make them good American citizens.[33]

Even the *New York Times,* in an article dedicated to the attitude toward the refugee problem, stressed that Russia was the cause of the greatest crisis in history, which it wanted to resolve with the hands of the United Nations, and said Russia was accusing of fascism those who don't want to repatriate.[34]

At any rate, although the self-organization of the Poles in the camps was without a doubt among the best, as regards discipline and cultural and self-educational work, there was an evident lack of a stronger organization working from the outside which could effectively act on behalf of their plight, particularly to defend them against bad treatment, be in a position to halt the processes of forced repatriation, and, most importantly, pave the way for emigration to Western nations. In connection with this there arose the need to establish an appropriately prepared and financially equipped institution which would represent the interests of Polish refugees. The anticipation of such an organization coincided with the gradual maturing of a solution to the refugee problem in the Washington administration. One historian states:

> The liquidation of the displaced persons problem in the heart of Europe and elsewhere was essential not only for the economic reconstruction of that part of the continent, but to the tranquility of that region. The elimination of the alien surplus population, unable to adjust itself to foreign surroundings was a political imperative caused by the displacement of several million Poles, Czechoslovakians, Hungarians, Rumanians, Ukrainians, Latvians and Lithuanians by the Nazi regime during the Second World War. In helping to rebuild Europe economically, and in organizing a common defense of Western Europe against Soviet aggression, the United States had first to dispose of the displaced persons and refugee problem. Other members of the United Nations "outside of the Soviet Bloc," would not have taken many displaced persons if the United States did not take her share of victims of totalitarian barbarism and oppression.[35]

Thus, after several months of trying to uphold the spirit of the Yalta agreement, the Americans gradually changed their approach, trying to resolve the refugee issue not so much through repatriation as through emigration to the United States and other nations. This approach obviously had its opponents, who especially pointed out the low educational level of the refugees, the danger of Communist infiltration, and, finally, the weak state of health of the candidates. On the other end of the scale, however, there was pacification of social unrest, budgetary relief, the enabling of the reconstruction of ravaged Europe, the acquisition of sought-after labor, and if necessary, of defense potential for America. Finally, there was the propaganda value of immigration, especially with regard to post–1945 escapees. All these elements weighed in on the opening of the door for emigration to America.

IV

The Committee's Founding and the First Period of Activity

Stories about the living conditions in the camps evoked reactions of sympathy in the Polish American community. There was awareness in New York, as well, of the negatives of UNRRA's policy to repatriate refugees to the East. The picture painted by the press and by witnesses was now augmented by correspondence that could finally reach America, with descriptions of conditions in the camps and with pleas for help in emigrating to the United States.[1]

On the other hand, the American Relief for Poland (ARP) faced a problem that it was unable to resolve alone. Up to this point its activity had often taken place without contact with the recipients of its aid. Apart from this, the scale of the problem was beyond the capabilities of the personnel manning the ARP's offices abroad since up to that moment it concerned various aspects of relief work. Utilizing the newly developed situation, a group of Polish American activists from New York decided to form a Polish American Immigration Committee, whose tasks were to focus on relief for Polish refugees in Western Europe and on helping them to emigrate to the United States and other Western nations. The first steps were taken by the Reverend Monsignor Feliks Burant, who for the next several years — more precisely to the time of his death in 1964 — was the heart and soul of the Polish American Immigration and Relief Committee (PAIRC).

Feliks Burant was born on April 18, 1893, in Custer, Wisconsin. He attended St. Lawrence University, then studied theology at St. Joseph's Seminary in Dunwood, New York. He received holy orders on September 1, 1918, and began service in parishes in the New York metropolitan area. In

1924 he became pastor of St. Stanislaus Bishop and Martyr Church at 101 E. 7th Street in Manhattan. This parish was well known for its enormous influence on the Polish diaspora in the New York metropolitan region. At this time, Burant became known as a shepherd with a social conscience, active both in the parish and in large projects of the Polish American community. These included, for instance, the Pulaski Parade, initiated by the parishioners of St. Stan's in 1937, or stewardship of the Polish Pavilion at the 1939 World's Fair in New York. Burant was a member of the Polish National Alliance, of the Polish Roman Catholic Union of America, of the Polish Legion of American Veterans, and of other social organizations. He was the chaplain of the Polish National Alliance of Brooklyn (founded in 1903) and chaplain of the Association of the Sons of Poland, also founded in 1903. All this gave him a genuinely prominent position in the Polish American community. After the outbreak of World War II and the entrance of America into the war, Burant volunteered for the U.S. Army as a chaplain and joined with the rank of captain. He ended his tour of duty in 1945 as a lieutenant-colonel.²

The Rev. Msgr. Feliks Burant, founder and president of the Polish-American Immigration and Relief Committee 1947–1964.

The plight of the refugees, including veterans of the September 1939 campaign and of the Warsaw Uprising of 1944 who were in Germany, was close to his heart. Recognizing the need to help them, and also aware of the limitations of the American Relief for Poland, Burant in 1945 led several ad hoc committees at East Coast Polish parishes in taking up the cause of the war immigrants.³

In 1946 he came up with the idea of a Polish American Immigration and Relief Committee, which was at first officially known as The American Commission for the Relief of Polish Immigrants. It depended not only on the resources of Polish American parishes, but also appealed to the whole community. In addition to Burant, the founders of the Committee included the Reverend Franciszek Szubiński, the Reverend Mieczysław Mroziński, the Reverend Gerwazy Kubec, the Reverend Józef Studziński, Judge Walter J. Bayer and the widow of Maksymilian Węgrzynek, the publisher of *Nowy Świat*, which ensured the Committee an appropriate promotional forum for the Polish American community. This decision matured by the fall of 1946, when the media circulated more detailed information about the plight of the refugees and the displaced persons in Europe. The two terms were differentiated in the following manner: the DP's were seen as persons who were removed from their homes by force, for instance from Poland, to forced labor in Germany. On the other hand, persons who were forced to flee their own country due to political, religious, or ethnic persecution, or due to the threat of such persecution, were considered refugees. Both categories required assistance, though the second did not appear to be a serious problem until a few months after the war ended, when refugees from Poland and other nations occupied by the Red Army began to arrive in the West. The organizers of the Committee were also interested in using up the emigration quotas assigned to Poles, which had gone unused due to the turmoil of the war. According to Ignacy Morawski, the long-standing editor of *Nowy Świat*, the direct stimulus for the founding of the Committee was the arrival from Gdańsk of the passenger ship *Ernie Pyle* in the port of New York. It brought a group of Poles with American citizenship who were returning to America after having spent the war years in Poland. Some of them had been wounded, and all were without means. The arrivals were greeted in New York by a quickly convened committee composed of clergy and representatives of organizations and the press, with *Nowy Świat* in the forefront. The Reverend Monsignor Burant was also among them. The sight of the miserable condition of the American citizens arriving from Poland prompted the members of the welcoming committee to wonder about the situation of those Poles who did not have American citizenship. Their entry into the United States would be impossible, and there was no doubt that thousands of victims of war, persecution, and mass deportation would be making every effort to gain entry. It was precisely during this get-together, since it could not be called a formal meeting, that the idea surfaced, raised by the Reverend Burant, to establish a Polish American Immigration Committee.[4]

The geographic imperatives of this decision ought to be noted here. Just as now, New York was a communication center where passenger ship and airplane routes crisscrossed. The city itself was known as a conglomerate of nationalities and creeds. It was also the headquarters for numerous religious, ethnic, and charitable organizations to whom the issue of aid for those who had been victimized in Europe was paramount. There was also a large Polish American community here, especially on the Lower East Side of Manhattan, in Brooklyn, in New Jersey, Connecticut, and Pennsylvania, and to some degree in Massachusetts (Boston, Springfield). One could count on a ready response there to an appeal for funds and material help for the arrivals. It was also easiest to find work there in industry and also in agriculture (that served the metropolitan region) to the north of Manhattan and on Long Island, which at that time was still mostly farmland. It is also worth noting that the inhabitants of this area were relatively open to emigration and assimilation. The special role of St. Stanislaus Parish as a protector of emigrants and as the administrator and manager of St. Joseph's Home should be noted here, as should the thus-far unsuccessful efforts to create an all–American organization to help emigrants and Polish refugees.

The first organizational meeting of the Committee, initiated by the Reverend Burant, was held in December 1946. The participants were: Janina Węgrzynek, Piotr Yolles, Tadeusz Sztybel, and Kazimierz Dembski. The latter three persons represented *Nowy Świat*. Burant probably wanted to have a publisher connected with the Committee to promote the work of the new organization. Second, Janina Węgrzynek, as the widow of Maksymilian Węgrzynek, the owner of *Nowy Świat* who died in 1944, guaranteed the possibility of plugging up holes in the budget with her money, since she and her husband were well known for their generosity on behalf of charitable causes. *Nowy Świat* did, in fact, participate financially in the Committee's activities. The Committee's report from the first few months of work shows a donation of $434 from the editorial staff.[5] As a result of the discussion at the above-mentioned meeting, the following objectives were decided upon:

a. to begin work within existing means on helping Polish displaced persons, finding jobs and apartments for them, placing the children of immigrants in schools and summer camps, providing them with clothes. To provide medical care, financial subsidy, English language courses and professional training courses.
b. To obtain from the American Relief for Poland whatever financial aid is necessary to carry out the work.
c. To obtain the patronage and cooperation of the National Catholic Welfare Conference (NCWC).[6]

The objectives as outlined seemed to indicate the absolute independence of the Committee, although even at this stage it became clear that the cooperation of the American Relief for Poland and the NCWC was needed. Also, the genesis of the territorial scope of the Committee's work is not entirely clear, especially since it appears that its activity encompassed several districts of the American Relief for Poland on the East Coast and at least initially relied on its financial support. Based on surviving documents, the thesis can be advanced that the Committee was independent. Its ties with the enumerated organizations and the use of organizational and financial support resulted from the specifics of the given situation. The American Relief for Poland was not prepared to address refugee issues, nor was it involved in helping them immigrate to the United States. Therefore, it easily made the decision to formally hand over three of its East Coast districts, and to financially support the activities of the Polish American Immigration and Relief Committee. The NCWC, on the other hand, did not have Polish-speaking staff who could handle the problems of refugees and immigrants on the new scale. It did have the right to maintain a presence in Germany and the right to process refugee applications. Those were rights which the Polish American Immigration and Relief Committee did not have.

On February 7, 1947, the Committee opened offices in the Polish Home at 25 St. Marks Place and at 112 E. 7th Street, near St. Stanislaus Church. Steps were also taken to officially register the Committee. The charter of incorporation was registered with the First Judicial Circuit of New York on April 26, 1947. On June 3 a group of Committee members went before the Bronx County Clerk, Abraham A. Katz, to confirm the membership of the board of the Committee. It should be noted once more that although it was popularly referred to as the Polish Immigration Committee, its official name was American Commission for Relief of Polish Immigrants Incorporated. It is worthwhile to cite certain fundamental stipulations of the charter of incorporation:

Art. II: The purposes for which it is formed are: without the object of making pecuniary profit, to assist in the relief and the care of the health, education and social welfare, primarily of displaced persons, immigrants and the children of people of Poland by:

a. Studying their needs;

b. Studying the needs of displaced persons, immigrants, and the children of other lands;

c. Helping to develop programs for their adequate aid and the general improvement of their family life;

d. Providing information regarding conditions and needs of displaced persons, immigrants, and children of Poland and other lands, and interpreting this information in all practicable ways;

e. Seeking to correlate social and church forces of America for international work among displaced persons, immigrants and children of Poland and other lands;

f. To send representatives of this organization upon missions to lands and territories outside of the United States in the cause of displaced persons, immigrants and children of Poland and other lands;

g. To inaugurate and carry on campaigns so as to widely disseminate the desperate plight of displaced persons, immigrants and children of Poland and other lands, and the compelling urgency of affording them special and immediate help and ways and means of rescuing them and aiding them;

h. To act as adviser to displaced persons, Polish immigrants and children of Poland and other lands within the limits of the law in connection with their status and aid them in their applications to determine such status;

i. To aid displaced persons, immigrants and children of Poland and other lands in assimilating our political and national life and in conserving their religious faith;

j. To seek and advise relatives of the plight of their kin who are displaced persons, immigrants and children of Poland and other lands and who are detained or who may find difficulty in contacting their relatives;

k. To guide and to give aid to prospective sponsors for people detained or arriving refugees or immigrants who may need guidance to adjust themselves in their new home;

l. To cooperate with authorized child placement agencies;

m. To voluntarily protect and assist immigrants to and in the United States and other persons who are in need of advice, guidance and assistance and to voluntarily aid them in obtaining employment without any fees therefor and to relocate them with a view of promoting their moral welfare;

n. To provide and maintain suitable offices for this organization without profit for conducting the work of this corporation;

o. To secure and administer funds in carrying out the activities of this corporation;

p. To lease, own, take or hold any real or personal property by gift, testament, will, devise, purchase, or otherwise, except in trust, necessary for or incidental to the objects and purposes of this corporation as herein specified or any of them or for the benefit thereof;

q. To do all and everything necessary, suitable and or proper for the accomplishment of any of the purposes or the attainments of any of the purposes or the furtherance of any of the powers and objects herein set forth.

Art. III. The territory in which the operations are to be principally conducted is in the City of New York, State of New York, other States, territories and possessions of the United States and or foreign countries.

Art. IV. The principal office of this corporation is to be located in the Borough of Manhattan, City, County and State of New York.

Art. V. The number of directors of the corporation who shall be known as a Board of Trustees shall be a minimum of three (3) and a maximum of twenty-one (21).[7]

The document was signed by the founders, who also gave their addresses as required by law. They were:

Reverend Monsignor Felix F. Burant, 101 E. 7th Street, N.Y.
Reverend Gerwazy Kubiec, 392 Adelpine Street, Brooklyn
Reverend Mieczysław Mroziński, 119 Eagle Street, Brooklyn,
Reverend Joseph Studziński, 607 Humboldt Street, Brooklyn,
Reverend Francis Szubiński, 420 East 156 Street, Bronx,
Janina Węgrzynek, 380 Second Avenue, N.Y.
Walter J. Bayer, 61 St. Marks Place, N.Y. (near the Church of St. Stanislaus).

The document was prepared by W. Bayer, and its postulates safeguarded an appropriately wide field for the development of the Committee's activities. Characteristic, especially from the perspective of our time, seems to be the care to safeguard religion and the moral health of the charges of the Committee. Moreover, the presence of such a large number of clergy guaranteed at that time an appropriate direction to the work and the credibility of the Committee in relation to the Polish American community and the municipal authorities. On June 9, 1947, the charter of incorporation of the Committee was approved by Judge Edward R. Koch of the State Supreme Court in the First Judicial District of the State of New York. From that moment, the Committee was a legal body, capable of developing official activity to aid refugees.

In the initial period, the major task was to get an adequate number of affidavits of support or sponsorships, in other words, a declaration by the person signing the document, without which, in light of existing legislation, it was impossible to obtain permission to enter the United States as a refugee or immigrant. To this end, Polish radio programs were employed, as was *Nowy Świat*, the largest Polish daily in metropolitan New York and one of the largest Polish dailies in the United States, whose offices were located at 380 Second Avenue in Manhattan. Both the radio stations and the press ran the PAIRC's monthly press releases and spur-of-the-moment appeals. In this way, care was taken to erase and equalize the differences between the old Polish American community and the immigrants. Assuming lack of error in the report of the Committee's secretary, during the first eighteen months his office reviewed 26,723 letters, secured 356 affidavits of support, and obtained over $72,000 for the transportation costs of 530 persons. By the end of October 1948, some 1,212 assurances of employment were secured, thus guaranteeing employment and housing for 3,115 Polish displaced persons.

Very early on, in June 1948, the board approved having representatives at all ports that were to receive immigrants from Europe. The most important sites to have a presence were Boston, New Orleans, Baltimore, and Philadelphia.[8]

Relief activity was extended to seven railroad stations, primarily helping scores of Polish soldiers from England who came to the United States through Canada. The work there consisted of receiving individuals or groups coming off the ships, transporting them to a railroad station (most often Grand Central Station in Manhattan), buying a ticket to the railroad station at the final destination, arranging for the transport of baggage, and finally, bringing the voyagers to the train conductor's attention. Parish committees or sponsors in the destination cities were notified by telegraph to arrive at the train station. Most frequently, the cost of the railroad ticket was covered by the Committee, which frequently also offered a $25 supplement for the trip. As of May 17, 1948, more than 10,400 persons were thus taken care of in the ports and train stations. Jan S. Pargiełło was the supervisor of the volunteer groups and was assistant to the director of the Committee, and to 1950 was also its secretary. Taking into consideration that the work was based on volunteers, the accomplishments and numbers cited are quite impressive. If we add to these numbers that from 1947 to September 1952 the PAIRC received assurances for 17,893 Poles from Germany, Austria, and Italy, for 4,592 Poles temporarily residing in Great Britain, and for 1,065 immigrants from other nations, the so-called out of zone refugees, then the picture of activity is even more complete.[9]

The practical activity of the Committee included several functions. Apart from the Displaced Persons Act of 1948, which is discussed later, the Committee also tried to embrace those who were outside the scope of benefits of the aforementioned act. This primarily concerned members of the Polish armed forces in the West, who in America were called "the soldiers of General Anders' Army" from the name of their most popular commander. They were located in Great Britain and Italy, where the end of the war and partial demobilization found them, and also in other West European countries and in the Near East. Assistance rendered to Americans of Polish descent who, after having endured the war, sought help in returning to the United States, was considered an important function of the Committee. Regarding the arrivals covered by the act, the Committee's help concentrated on finding jobs for individuals and groups, on finding housing, and on practical assistance for persons arriving on American soil which included everything from legal matters to language problems.

The Committee organized a group of 120 volunteers recruited from Polish American organizations, who devoted their time to working as translators, to helping receive immigrants in ports, and as workers in shelters and places of temporary transit for those arriving from Europe. The Committee offered financial assistance to cover the cost of travel by ship, and also to pay expenses from New York to the final destination of the given immigrant. This continued until the legislation changed and these responsibilities were taken over by the federal government. The help of the Committee in this regard was treated as a temporary loan. An important form of assistance was legal and material aid for people detained by the immigration authorities at Ellis Island in New York. This concerned instances when the arrivals did not have the appropriate documentation. The Committee tried to stay deportation, and instead arranged for emigration to other nations, including instances of transfer to South America, and even Australia. The Committee provided the detainees with clothes, underwear, and other items of everyday use, supported them morally with visits by clergy, and by the care of minors, and supplied them with books and periodicals. Nonetheless, the most important aid was legal assistance — intervention with the Immigration Bureau, help in completing documents, and assistance to Polish American families in adopting minors and orphans. Often the Committee paid the bond that allowed the detained to go free. The latter type of assistance was connected with help the Committee gave to other charitable organizations and to the immigration authorities in the form of translators for a quicker and more proper processing of Poles. Some of them worked as volunteers for various agencies, including the Travelers Aid Society.

Just as important was the securing of housing upon arrival in New York. The Committee collaborated with two hotels, and it also rented, at its own expense, two four-room apartments used for this specific purpose. An active file was maintained of available apartments offered by the Polish American community and by Catholic organizations, in the form of permanent as well as temporary rentals — as, for instance, for a vacation period or for the period of the owner's departure for a professional contract away from his or her permanent residence. According to surviving reports, there was not a single case of a person needing assistance who remained without a roof over his or her head.

An active file was also maintained for employment opportunities. It concerned Polish American employers, but also American companies that were searching for qualified workers, or even unqualified labor, without knowledge of English. This procedure protected (though there were negative cases) from abuse, as well as from being taken advantage of due to a lack of knowledge of local conditions and an inability to communicate. The

Committee's good relations with labor unions played an important role here. Up to May 17, 1948, that is, during the first year of operation, the Committee arranged employment for 524 individuals.[10]

Moreover, in 86 cases (in the period 1947–1948) arrivals were given medical attention at the Committee's expense. The Committee also organized various types of relaxation and recreation for children. Every effort was made to choose the kind of venue that helped in the integration with local children and young people. This accelerated the assimilation of the immigrants into the mainstream of American life. In addition to summer camps, children were given presents at Christmas and at Easter. Thus the Committee, from its very beginning, was able to overcome all the problems that cropped up after the conclusion of the war.

Financially, in the period from February 4, 1947, to October 31, 1948, the Committee received $57,600 from the American Relief for Poland, received $3,100 from the Polish American Congress designated for assistance to persons detained at Ellis Island, and received $4,847.87 from other sources. In sum, after deducting petty expenses and fees, the budget for that period was $66,444.84. Of this sum $62,951.45 was used for purposes connected with the refugees.[11]

In the period 1948–1949 the American Relief for Poland paid $4,000 per month into the Committee's account, while the Polish American Congress from 1949 to November 1951 gave $1,000 per month.[12] These were not the only funds designated for the Committee by that latter organization. Up to the third convention of the Polish American Congress in Atlantic City in 1952, the PAC contributed $29,000 to the Polish American Immigration and Relief Committee in New York. This support, after the funds of the Polish American Congress were exhausted, was suspended that year. Nonetheless, considering the buying power of the dollar at the time, this was a considerable sum.[13]

Moreover, funds were solicited from various organizations, associations, and private persons. The Committee's annual ball began playing a considerable role in gaining support and garnering funds. The first ball was held at the Statler Hotel in New York on September 17, 1949. The choice of date was not incidental. It was related to the treacherous attack of Soviet Russia on Poland in 1939. Subsequent balls were also held on or close to September 17.

The first banquet was not a typical affair. Its organizers were Edward Witanowski and Edward Kosowicz, the hosts of the popular *Two Edwards* radio program. The same arrangement occurred in 1950. In both cases the entire profit was designated for the Committee. From 1951 on, the ball was organized directly by the PAIRC. Aside from promotional and recruiting

Debutantes with a U.S. Military Academy at West Point cadet escort, at the Committee's ball in 1964.

functions, the balls were also a fund-raising opportunity for Committee activities. This sort of income made it possible to carry on charitable activities, to send packages to the needy for the holidays, or to support refugee organizations in Europe. The banquet brought in from several hundred dollars during its first years, to $7,000 in the 1960s. One of the notable examples of reallocation of funds from this source was the offering of $1,000 in 1950 by the Reverend Burant to the Holy Father, to assist Polish priests-refugees.[14]

In speaking of the cooperation of the *Two Edwards*, it is worth noting that they did not just advertise the Committee's information and press releases free of charge. The Reverend Burant was also given free air time for the work of the Committee on the *Two Edwards* show on Sunday mornings at seven. In addition, several other radio programs cooperated with the Committee and ought to be mentioned here. One of them was *The Voice of Polonia*, on WLIB 1190 in Long Island City, run by Michael Kęcki. For the "Christmas Eve Fund 1952," Kęcki contributed $1,826.25. For Christmas 1955 he collected $712.50 for the Committee, and for Easter 1958 he gave another several hundred dollars. The next radio program pressed into service on behalf of the Committee was the *Polish Hour* on WHOM — Atlantic Broadcasting Corporation (ABC) — headed by Kazimierz Jarzębowski and his wife, Florence, a frequent organizer of the Committee's balls. For Christmas 1952, Jarzębowski contributed $1,063.50 on December 19; and he held similar fund-raisers over the next several years. Outside New York, the owners of radio programs from other cities acted on behalf of the Committee, such as Przybyła from Philadelphia, Szuberla in Springfield, Mass., and Jaskólski in Boston.[15]

In its ongoing work to receive and resettle immigrants, the Committee — which was, in sum, a new and inexperienced body — availed itself mainly of the help of the NCRC (National Catholic Resettlement Council). First, the organization had conducted activity to help refugees before the Committee was founded; it had a trained cadre of people and had a good knowledge of the issues. Second, this organization's help in Europe made possible a legal anchoring in Germany, which contained the largest number of people who were awaiting assistance and emigration to the United States. It was significant that the Reverend Aloysius Wycisło was the executive director of the NCRC and as such was part of its board. Thanks to this cooperation, the representatives of PAIRC took an active part in the unloading of every passenger ship arriving in the United States, not only in New York, but also in Boston and in New Orleans. At that time those were the three main ports serving the passenger traffic to and from Europe. The first suggestions to more closely cooperate with the National Catholic Welfare Conference (NCWC), which served as an umbrella organization for several other Catholic relief agencies and the NCRC, date from June 1948. It was resolved at the June 24 meeting of the Committee that: "Those present, as a result of a wide-ranging discussion decided to contact the local Diocesan Refugee Committee for the Eastern States." As a result of further efforts, the Committee became a member of the NCRC, while retaining complete autonomy.[16]

In addition to the ones already mentioned, the Committee cooperated with Catholic organizations in other countries, especially in Caracas, Venezuela, where 46 Poles settled after having been detained by the immigration authorities at Ellis Island. The Committee had to maintain contact with military agencies in London, with the Union of Polish War Refugees in Brussels, with resettlement referral agencies in Germany and in Austria, with veterans' organizations in Europe, with the Polish Canadian Congress, with the Polish Information Center in Havana, Cuba, and with U.S. consulates in many nations around the world.

Another forum in the search for allies was, for the Reverend Burant, the convention of the Polish American Congress in Philadelphia at the end of May 1948, a few weeks before the passage of the Displaced Persons Act. Burant prepared an address for the convention, which was a report on the work accomplished up to that point, and a projection of what still had to be done to improve the plight of the Polish homeless wanderers. The monsignor's official function at the PAC's Philadelphia convention was to chair the Immigration Committee. Thus already in Philadelphia in May 1948, the position of the founder of the PAIRC was recognized in the field of relief work on behalf of refugees. In his address, the Reverend Burant focused on a new problem, namely, the flood of refugees from behind the Iron Curtain. He noted that the reason for the exodus was the political situation in the countries occupied by the Red Army and subjected to Stalin's control. The monsignor criticized the position of the Western powers, emphasizing that thanks to their collusion with Soviet Russia, the Polish Republic (the first nation to stand up to Hitler militarily) found itself under successive occupations as a result of the war:

> The Polish Depees [displaced persons] should never be treated as beggars stretching out their hand for support. They realize perfectly well that in refusing to return to their country they have chosen the difficult life of an emigrant — an emigrant who will have to win his daily bread for himself and his family by hard toil. We should avail ourselves of this fact to the fullest extent to make the American public realize that the people who will arrive here — are political refugees, but are also emigrants capable to earn their own living and desirous of contributing by their work to the growing power of the United States, which is the embodiment of their Ideals of Freedom.[17]

The Reverend Burant devoted a lot of time to the Displaced Persons Act that was being prepared for passage in Congress, and criticized several of its aspects. First of all, the originally binding stipulation that gave immigration rights to those escapees who found themselves in Italy, Austria, or the three occupation zones in Germany prior to April 21, 1947, needed to be changed; and later it was changed. That stipulation cut off the constantly growing multitude of current refugees fleeing Communist rule. Another problem was the exclusion of other nations where escapees were to be found. The legislators had recognized only those nations that collaborated with the Third Reich, while the refugee issue had a Pan-European dimension. Burant also criticized the method of qualification for immigration quotas. It was based on place of birth. Thus, the Polish quota might include Germans born in the territory of Poland, which in effect decreased the number of Poles. His next objection concerned the exclusion of persons with university degrees. He opted for a full scope of professions and occupations, which would serve to enrich the national fabric of the United States and of the given ethnic group. He clearly wanted to avoid deepening the disparities between particular groups, obviously including the Polish one, which did not have to be associated just with agricultural occupations, domestic help, or mining. The attempt to bring about the change at this stage was not successful.

The next part of the address concerned immigrants. The Reverend Burant proposed an informational campaign among the refugees who planned to come to the United States, in order to avoid many troublesome situations resulting from unfamiliarity with American living conditions. Equally interesting was the proposal to organize professional courses that would ease the new start in life. In this way, the strength of the Polish ethnic group would also increase in the United States. The Reverend Burant did not forget about the need to organize English language courses which, just like the previously mentioned proposals, would ease the acclimatization and the new start in America.

Continuing down this path of practical considerations, the PAIRC chief tackled the issue of immigrants immediately after their arrival in the United States. He proposed an appropriate geographical distribution of the arrivals. He felt that to concentrate them in one place would have a negative effect on their chances for housing and employment, and said, "It is essential to arrange transitory centers where every Polish newcomer, directly upon landing, will get a bed and a hot meal. They should dwell in such a center the shortest time possible." This last aspect was no doubt meant to avoid a repetition of DP camp conditions — an ad hoc atmosphere, and a lack of permanent employment and perspectives. The sooner the immigrants could be employed and housed permanently, the better for their future, he reasoned. Once more he stood up for the refugees from behind the Iron Curtain, whom the International Refugee Organization (IRO) did not offer any aid, and for the Poles from the Far East (12,000 persons) and the Near East (30,000 persons), who did not have access to the benefits offered by the Displaced Persons Act in the form that was prepared for passage by Congress.[18] The final passage of the Displaced Persons Act occurred on June 25, 1948.[19]

The first transport of immigrants to arrive in the United States under the new law pulled into New York on October 30, 1948. The welcoming committee on the dock consisted of: Francis Cardinal Spellman, archbishop of New York; Sylwin Strakacz, the former consul of the Polish Republic and earlier a collaborator of Ignace Jan Paderewski; editors of *Nowy Świat*; and representatives of the Committee. A second transport docked in Boston, where it was welcomed by the executive director of the NCWC, Monsignor Edward E. Swanstrom. By June 30, 1950, slightly more than 169,000 persons of various nationalities had arrived in the United States under the new law.[20]

Both events increased enthusiasm for the Committee's work, though they did not nullify the negative aspects of the act. The Polish Immigration and Relief Committee actively engaged itself in promoting amendments to the new law, with special consideration for the needs of Polish refugees. The amendment to the Displaced Persons Act that passed on June 16, 1950, served this purpose. The amended law extended the obligations of the D.P. Act of 1948 by one year, from June 30, 1951, to August 31, 1952. On this basis, an increased number of persons were allowed to immigrate to the United States (341,000, including 5,000 orphans). The persons admitted under this law were divisible into two categories. The first was individuals admitted on the basis of a procedure administered by the Displaced Persons Commission, and the second was persons admitted on the basis of State Department procedures. Poles qualifying under the two categories were both displaced persons and refugees as defined by the IRO, and they were the primary group for which the prior termination date for obtaining visas had been determined, i.e., June 30, 1951. To this category belonged all those who found themselves in Germany, Austria, or Italy between September 1, 1939, and January 1, 1949, and simultaneously those who did not permanently settle in those territories and for whom assurances of employment and housing had been obtained in the United States. The assurances could be given by charitable organizations as well as by companies and private citizens of the United States. Persons admitted on this basis could not present a threat to the public. Understood here were both prior conviction in the light of existing law, and a lack of counterindications from the point of view of the national security of the United States. Unfortunately, in many cases criminal histories were treated too strictly. It was known that because they lacked the means for survival, slave laborers occasionally committed petty theft, for which administrative punishment was meted out in Germany. This punishment then figured in the personal documents of many people, making it impossible for them to get through the screen of formal immigration requirements.

The group of refugees administered by the State Department included members of the Polish armed forces who found themselves in Great Britain after the armistice, and also the out of zone refugees, including those who found themselves in nations of Western Europe outside the American, British and French zones of occupied Germany, and outside Austria and Italy. These refugees had to have been in the given countries between September 1, 1939, and January 1, 1949. In order to access immigration processing privileges, they could not be permanent residents of the given countries. Family members of persons fulfilling the above conditions, that is, a spouse and unmarried children below 21 years of age, had the right to get an entry visa if they fulfilled the basic requirements, and did not have to reside in the given country in the aforementioned time period. Certain categories of people were granted easier terms depending on the closeness of the relationship to the citizen or resident of the United States and on the profession. Occupational preferences included farmers, construction workers, domestic help, garment and textile workers, and persons with the highest scientific and technical qualifications. With regard to professional groups and individuals with relatives in the United States, an additional preference was created for members of the armed forces of nations that fought the enemies of the United States, and for members of families such as wives and unmarried children under 21 years of age. Sponsors had to be citizens of the United States or companies whose main business was conducted in the United States. The sponsor made a commitment to provide employment, with remuneration that was close to the market rate in that region, but with the proviso that this would not take work away from local Americans. It was the sponsor's task to provide a safe and clean apartment, to receive the immigrant at the port of entry and to refund the cost of transportation from the port of entry to the final destination in the United States. The sponsor also had to ensure that the immigrant and his family would not constitute a budgetary burden on the government.

According to existing law, several categories of support were recognized. The basic one was an affidavit of support, issued for a specific person. The second kind was an assurance of employment, and the third was an assurance issued by an organization recognized by the federal government or obtained through such an organization. This last type of assurance could concern a specific person or persons, or else could be issued for a specific number of invitations, in the initial stage without specific names, and was called a blank assurance. It should be noted that the PAIRC, as an institution cooperating with the National Catholic Welfare Conference — War Relief Services, was authorized to issue assurances directly as of July 1, 1951. Prior to that, it had to go through the NCWC. On February 6, 1951, a formal agreement was signed between an agency of the National Catholic Welfare Conference, namely, War Relief Services, and the PAIRC, which was officially called the American Commission for the Relief of Polish Immigrants. The agreement defined the procedures for obtaining assurances and the method of processing them.

1. The American Commission for the Relief of Polish Immigrants, Inc. is engaged in obtaining home and job assurances in the United States for displaced persons in Europe, the Polish soldiers in England, and Polish refugees and displaced persons eligible under Section 3c of the Displaced Persons Act.

2. Assurances of homes and jobs obtained by the American Commission for the Relief of Polish Immigrants, Inc., are submitted to War Relief Services — NCWC for processing, and the American personnel of War Relief Services, NCWC in Europe, England and other countries are responsible for selection and process.
3. Here in the United States the Commission assists War Relief Services, NCWC in the pier operation and with many welfare and relief activities involved in the early adjustment period of displaced persons and refugees.[21]

The above-mentioned agreement also confirmed that the NCWC had audited the books of the PAIRC and found them in good order. However, after 1958, when the Committee opened its own offices in Europe, the above regulations were no longer in force. Nonetheless, cooperation with the NCWC (Migration Refugee Services) continued to 1990, in obtaining loans for refugees for passage from Europe to the United States from the funds of the Intergovernmental Committee for Migration (ICM), which later became the IOM (International Organization for Migration) with which the PAIRC did not have an agreement.

The processing procedure for job and housing assurances collected in the United States was handled as it had been prior to the signing of the above-mentioned agreement. After obtaining an assurance, the given organization sent it for verification to the Displaced Persons Commission in Washington, D.C., after which the documents were sent together with an assigned number to the appropriate organization in Western Europe. It should be remembered that the PAIRC did not have authorized representatives in Europe in those years. On the basis of such documentation, the verification process began for the given candidate, as to his or her professional capabilities and health, and also included a security check. The interviews were conducted with the participation of a representative of the International Refugee Organization in Europe and, when necessary, U.S. armed forces counterintelligence personnel. The next step in this procedure was the transmittal of a written report about the given person to the Displaced Persons Commission, which decided whether to admit the candidate to an interview with an official of the U.S. consular corps in Europe. Normally, an official of the U.S. Public Health Service participated in an interview, assessing the candidate's ability to perform in his profession as well as his general state of health. If these consultations were favorable, then a decision was made to grant a visa. Prior to its issue, however, the candidate had to sign a good-faith declaration about fulfilling the conditions of employment and residence guaranteed by the sponsor. This was not the end of the bureaucratic hurdles. After having received the visa, the candidate for emigration met with an official of the U.S. Immigration and Naturalization Service. That official, after a positive interview of the candidate, made an appropriate note on the candidate's visa. The last hurdle was the transmittal of a list of passenger names to the FBI, whose officials analyzed them once more from the point of view of national security. There were instances of immigrants being detained upon landing in the United States and being denied right of entry. Simultaneously, passenger lists were made available to sponsoring agencies and organizations to enable them to pick up the given persons at the port of entry.

The qualification and acceptance procedure had many steps and was steeped in bureaucracy. Nonetheless, it should be remembered that it concerned several hundred thousand people of various cultural, ethnic, and professional backgrounds; and what is more, the level of knowledge about this mosaic was basically minimal. This was particularly dangerous in light of the Cold War that was just beginning. Improperly qualified immigrants could constitute a serious threat to the public order; others were exhausted by the war and by diseases to such a degree that in certain instances they could become a source of danger to the health of the entire society. Many candidates, in addition to suffering malnutrition, exhaustion, wounds, or amputations, were carriers of tuberculosis and other contagious diseases. The successive steps of the emigration recruitment process also tested the determination of the candidates to begin a new life, and brought to the surface those personality traits which helped or disqualified them. The lengthy qualification procedure postponed the moment of departure from the camps for the refugees; on the other hand, it made possible the proper preparation for the reception of the candidate at his place of employment, locality, or social group. The PAIRC influenced the shaping of the atmosphere in which the immigrants were received and the organization of their settlement in the United States. In addition to that work, the Committee found the time to undertake the effort, independently as well as with other organizations, to change the provisions of existing laws that did not fulfill the expectations of Poles in refugee camps and in the Polish American community.

The appeals mentioned before for further changes in the law and for adjusting the law to the needs of Polish refugees did not just occupy Monsignor Burant's mind. The Polish American Congress, on the basis of proposals made by Monsignor Burant, began serious pressure on behalf of federal legislation, and also on behalf of assistance to Polish refugees. This was done in cooperation with, and also parallel to, the efforts of the PAIRC. This signaled that the Committee had no intention of monopolizing immigration matters, especially since it had neither sufficient funds nor staff. It very evidently wanted to get registered on the map of the Polish American community's nationwide political representation and to inspire it, as it had inspired the Congress, to act in a specified direction. In 1948, at the second national convention of the Polish American Congress in Philadelphia, a Polish Displaced Persons Committee was formed, whose task was to:

> ...bring to the United States the largest possible number of Polish displaced persons from Europe and former Polish soldiers from England. The Polish American Congress has devoted a lot of effort to this important seg-

About 20 percent of the refugees living in the camps were children under the age of 14. (UNHCR/M. Benamar)

ment of our work in the last four years. We have added our efforts to ensure that the Displaced Persons Act be passed by the U.S. Congress, that it, further, be amended and extended, and we have organized the American Committee for Resettlement of Polish Displaced Persons whose membership includes representatives from our largest Polish American organizations in the United States.[22]

This committee, headquartered in Chicago, was chaired during the several years of its existence by Wanda Rozmarek, the wife of the president of the Polish American Congress.

The U.S. Congress consulted the Polish American Congress and the PAIRC during the legislative process for the new law, the so-called Displaced Persons Act of 1948. The PAC began sending telegrams and letters to congressmen and senators, both by individual members and also in the form of resolutions by the PAC's state chapters. President Karol Rozmarek was called to testify at hearings before congressional committees, where he lobbied hard for as wide an inclusion of Polish interests as possible. Despite the great success of the 1948 law, Rozmarek, in the name of the Polish American community, continued the pressure to include an additional 18,000 Polish soldiers in Great Britain. The passage of an appropriate amendment on June 6, 1950, should be recognized as the success, in equal degree, of the Polish American Congress and the Committee headed by Monsignor Burant.

The new legislation raised the total number of displaced persons permitted to immigrate to the United States from 205,000 to 341,000, including the aforementioned soldiers in Great Britain. Aside from this, the Polish American Congress, parallel to the efforts of the PAIRC, developed its own action to obtain assurances and opportunities for housing and employment. This was done in the name of the Congress by local committees established by PAC members. In addition, the Displaced Persons Committee (ACRPDP's) in Chicago planned to organize an office in Europe to take care of refugee matters on the spot. The new body, anchored in the Polish American Congress, received its accreditation from the Displaced Persons Commission in Washington in November 1948 and also, on September 17, 1949, from the Department of State through the Advisory Committee for Voluntary Foreign Aid. This allowed for the issuance of assurances and for an official presence in Germany. The accreditation of the ACRPDP's by IRO in Geneva was dated November 28, 1949. Also, appropriate financial backing was secured through a funding promotion campaign in several Polish American organizations, mainly among members of the Polish National Alliance. Thanks to this endeavor, $25,000 was collected. The PNA treated this sum as a loan to the American Committee for Resettlement of Polish DP's. In addition, the PNA gave $10,000 for direct aid, to cover the costs of passage from New York to settlement destinations.

A photograph from a publication series, published on the occasion of the World Year of the Refugee — 1960. A refugee family's room in a DP camp near Salzburg, Austria. (UNHCR/M. Benamar)

Like the PAIRC, Chicago noticed the significance of the problem with the so-called hard-core cases, that is, those people who were sick or old (or both), for whom the possibility of emigration to the United States was very limited. Such cases were treated on a charity basis. Another matter in which Rozmarek intervened in Washington was the proportionally low percentage of Poles allowed to immigrate on the basis of the Displaced Persons Act. The head of the PAC testified in this matter before Ugo Carusi, the chairman of the Displaced Persons Commission in Washington, and three commissioners responsible for immigration as defined by the mentioned act.

The Polish American Congress was able to send Colonel Bolesław Wichrowski and Frances Dymek, the vice president of the Polish National Alliance, as representatives of the Displaced Persons Committee (ACR-PDP's), whose presence on site allowed for a more complete evaluation of the situation. Nonetheless, the possibility of an undisturbed realization of the aforementioned act, amended by the U.S. Congress, sustained yet another blow due to the outbreak of the Korean War in 1950. The war made impossible (if for no reason other than transport) the regular passage, within the indicated time limit, of persons permitted to immigrate to the United States. The Polish American Congress and the PAIRC also took on this issue. It had to do with extending the term limit of the act for at least one more year. Both Monsignor Burant and President Rozmarek engaged themselves in a series of conversations, consultations, and conferences with senators and congressmen. In this matter, Rozmarek sent a widely distributed letter to congressmen, in which he wrote:

> We, the Polish American Congress, Inc., take the liberty of drawing your attention to a situation which is increasingly disturbing the community of six million Americans of Polish descent, desirous to be of help and assistance to their brethren, the Polish displaced persons in Europe, and homeless veterans of the Polish Army, who during the last war fought so valiantly on our side.
> What we have in mind, is the fact that the deadline for the admission of the authorized number of such persons under Public Law 555, 81st U. S. Congress, amending the Displaced Persons Act of 1948, is rapidly approaching, while the actual admission of those deserving and desirable immigrants remains far below the mark set by the Congress.
> As you are certainly aware, the Displaced Persons Commission has just announced the arrival of the 200,000th displaced person. According to the law, over 140,000 more such immigrants are to be granted visas prior to June 30th of this year. Similarly out of the 18,000 veterans of the Polish Army, who may enter the United States until the same date, barely a handful has reached our shores at the time of this writing. There are numerous reasons for this delay, but let us mention only the fact that the thorough and certainly very desirable screening of the immigrants requires up to five or six months in each case. The processing of applicants made eligible under the legislation which took effect on June 16, 1950, could not have begun until after such date and it seems obvious to assume that it could not be concluded in such time as to permit the entire volume of the pending cases to be ready for final action and embarkation of the immigrants before the deadline.
> We do not intend to appeal to you for any increase of the number of persons who may be issued visas under the Displaced Persons Act, as amended. We believe that the truly generous action taken by the Congress under your guidance and leadership in June 1950, will provide for the solution of the displaced person problem, although we are worried about the plight of those refugees from communist oppression who have reached the Western Zones of occupation past the cut-off date of January 1, 1949. We are exploring and investigating this problem at the present time, and we wish respectfully to reserve the right to approach you further in this matter. However, at this time we desire to apply to you with the request to introduce legislation which would extend until June 30, 1952 the time in which the authorized number of displaced persons and veterans of the Polish Army may be issued

immigration visas pursuant to Public Law 555, 81st Congress. It could not be expected that such legislation could encounter difficulties on the floor either of the House or the Senate. Several programs authorized under the Displaced Persons Act, such as the admission of orphans or persons of German ethnic origin are to run until this later date. The Displaced Persons Commission is to remain active until August 1952. The other agencies administrating the program, to-wit, the Foreign Service and Immigration and Naturalization Service are fully equipped to continue their operation. It certainly appears to be a simple, well justified amendment to be submitted to the Congress at an early date, early enough so as not to bring the presently operating machinery of Federal and private agencies to a premature stop.[23]

It turned out that Rozmarek's and Burant's appeals fell on fertile ground. Many congressmen reacted affirmatively to the suggestion of extending the deadline, which had key significance for the Poles who were still in Germany and other countries. In the House of Representatives, an appropriate resolution was presented by Congressman Tadeusz Machrowicz of Michigan, who was very engaged in refugee matters. In the Senate, Senator Brian McMahon of Connecticut sponsored an amendment, and presented it on February 5, 1951. After passing in the House of Representatives, the amendment was approved by the U. S. Senate in June 1951. This rescued thousands who were waiting for departure. The extended law provided that immigration visas were to be issued up to December 31, 1951, and that those who received them had the opportunity to come to the United States until the end of April 1952. Assurances for Polish soldiers in Great Britain were also accepted to the end of 1951. About 11,500 military men took advantage of this opportunity. The remaining 6,500 visas (of the 18,000 provided for) became the object of successive efforts by the PAIRC and the Polish American Congress. In the end, these visas were shifted to the Polish refugees in Germany because interest among the Polish soldiers in Great Britain to emigrate to the United States was somewhat less than anticipated. In addition, pressure was brought to bear to extend the deadline for 7,500 unused visas for displaced persons. Thanks to the efforts of the PAIRC and the Polish American Congress, the Judiciary Committee of the House of Representatives passed HR 411, sponsored by its chairman, Congressman Francis E. Walter, which permitted the utilization of 7,500 immigration visas which could not be issued prior to the December 31, 1951, deadline.[24]

Aside from humanitarian considerations, there were strong behind-the-scenes premises for allowing young people with military training to immigrate. Part of them could work as highly qualified professionals, strengthening the intellectual and industrial potential of America. Also, it was important to effectively raise the state of readiness of the armed forces during a period of strong tensions in the international arena. As Monsignor Burant mentioned in his appeals, many of the immigrants who were allowed to settle in America on the basis of the DP Act of 1948, were drafted for military service and fought in Korea. The utilization of the newest immigrants for military service became a widespread practice. But not all agreed to a change of uniform. In 1950, the case of Józef Wyrwa became widely publicized. He was a lieutenant in the Polish Home Army who, after the defeat of the Warsaw Uprising, ended up in the prisoner of war camp in Wentorf, Germany. From there, on the basis of the DP Act of 1948, he emigrated to Chicago. After getting a notice to appear before the Draft Commission on August 3, 1950, he emphatically refused to serve in the U.S. Army. He maintained that he was bound by his oath to the Government of the Polish Republic in London, which was the only one that could demand a sacrifice of blood from him. A storm erupted in the American, Polish, and even the British press around Wyrwa's refusal. Many bitter accusations were made against Wyrwa as a DP who did not show gratitude for American hospitality. Wyrwa reacted with a carefully worded declaration, which was met with silence in certain newspapers. The Home Army veteran claimed that as recompense for the sacrifice of blood, and for devotion to the Allies and the ideals of the Atlantic Charter, his homeland was shorn of territory, exposed to new slavery, and betrayed into the hands of the Soviet occupier. He maintained that he continued to be faithful to the Government of the Polish Republic in London and would not try to obtain American citizenship. He argued as follows:

> The Allied nations agreed to the ruin of Poland, and together with it, of the remaining peoples of Central Europe, all told 125 million people, just so that in return for this Russia would renounce further aggression. And if Russia had agreed to this, such a state could continue for many years, during which all those nations would become thoroughly communized and ruined. What guarantee do we have, that also after the coming war Poland will not be betrayed and handed over to this or some other invader. What guarantee do we have that the war that erupted in Korea will not develop into a general war against Soviet aggression, into a war that will bring freedom to Central Europe and will free the world from the horror hanging over it like a Damocles Sword — Communism?[25]

Wyrwa's position was supported by a declaration of the Government of the Polish Republic in London on August 14, 1950, which stated unequivocally that: "without the agreement of the legal Polish authorities, no Polish citizen can serve in any foreign army."

This affair continued for some time, and it revealed some of the motivations of the immigration authorities, and of presidents Truman and Eisenhower. The influx of young, healthy, militarily trained men was a serious factor during the period of tension which, it was believed, might lead to another world war. On the other hand, the situation in which Wyrwa found himself attested to what refugees could expect after arriving in the United States. It should be noted here that obligatory military service in the United States was abolished after the Vietnam War, but registration of men to the age of 26 continued.

At this time, legislators were ever more involved in the issue of escapees from Communist countries outside Europe. The problem appeared prior to the outbreak of the Korean War. The mass exodus from China after the Communist victory there in 1949 proved to be a great challenge. It was hard to expect unanimity in such circumstances. On March 12, 1952, Senators Humphrey and Lehman proposed new legislation to replace the DP Act, which was expiring at the end of 1952. A second project was proposed by Franklin D. Roosevelt, Jr. Both proposals assumed a revision of the immigration quota system that included abandonment of the antiquated use of the 1920 census as the basis for the system. It was proposed to use the more up-to-date 1950 census as the base. The mentioned legislators also proposed a merger of unused quotas and an abandonment of the practice of crediting quotas, that is, the additional use of visas from future years (the so-called "mortgages"). The McCarren and Walter proposal, which passed in the U.S. Senate, kept the quotas.

The McCarren-Walter Immigration Act was passed on June 10, 1952, but was vetoed by President Truman on June 25, 1952. The veto was overridden on June 27, 1952. The new law (PL 414), and in particular the retention of the quota system, was severely criticized by President Truman:

> The idea behind this discriminatory quota policy was, to put it boldly, that Americans with English or Irish names were better people and better citizens than Americans with Italian or Greek or Polish names.... It denies the humanitarian creed inscribed beneath the Statue of Liberty proclaiming to all nations, "Give me your tired, your poor, your huddled masses yearning to breathe free." It repudiates our basic religious concepts, our belief in the brotherhood of men, and in the words of St. Peter that "there is neither Jew nor Greek, there is neither bond nor free ... for ye are all one in Christ Jesus."
>
> The basis of this quota system was false and unworthy in 1924. It is even worse now. At the present time this quota system keeps out the very people we want to bring in. It is incredible to me that, in this year of 1952, we should be enacting into law such a slur on the patriotism, the capacity, and the decency of a large part of our citizenry.[26]

From the beginning, the new law was disliked by several ethnic groups, including the Polish American community. The PAIRC therefore continued

THE NANSEN MEDAL

The Committee charged with the award of the Nansen Medal instituted by the United Nations High Commissioner for Refugees for outstanding services given to refugees,

Expressing its deep appreciation for the unremitting efforts of the Voluntary Agencies and dedicated individual voluntary workers in bringing succour to refugees,

Recognizing the devotion and humanitarian spirit displayed by the Agencies and their staff in the accomplishment of this task,

Desiring to pay a tribute to their major contribution to the solution of refugee problems throughout the world and to their indispensable role in fostering international solidarity towards this end,

Hereby awards the Nansen Medal for 1963 to the

INTERNATIONAL COUNCIL OF VOLUNTARY AGENCIES

with a view to honouring all the agencies and their constituencies as well as individual voluntary workers who have shared in the common effort of assistance to refugees.

Geneva
10 October 1963

As a token of appreciation for services rendered to the cause of refugees, this certificate is presented

to the Polish-American Immigration and Relief Committee.

A photographic reproduction of the Nansen Medal.

its pressure to amend certain provisions concerning Poles. And since 1952 was a presidential election year, it was expected that both presidential candidates would take up the issue. General Kazimierz Sosnkowski, released from informal internment by the British government in Arundel, Canada, discussed the political issues with the candidates of both parties. During his consultation on October 30, 1952, he pressed the Republican candidate, General Dwight D. Eisenhower, to reject the Yalta agreement, to restore recognition to the Polish Republic's government in London, and to conclude political agreements with it, including guarantees of the borders that existed as of August 31, 1939, on the East and the border of the Oder and Nyssa rivers on the West. Sosnkowski repeated the same message to the Democratic Party candidate, Governor Adlai E. Stevenson, in a conversation that took place the following day. Eisenhower, who had leaned toward the rejection of Yalta, included the issue of immigration legislation in his campaign.[27]

Eisenhower favored increasing the number of immigrants from Europe, abolishing the quotas, and revising the immigration law. This was pursued by the PAIRC, which disseminated several declarations and testified before the presidential Immigration and Naturalization Committee. On October 1, 1952, Monsignor Burant testified before the committee. In a lengthy appearance, he underscored the need for a broad revision of immigration law, which in his opinion was not current with the changing requirements of the moment. He gave several very provocative examples as evidence. He criticized the existing immigration quota system, under which, out of 153,000 visas issued annually, only 6,524 were earmarked for Poles. Burant drew attention to the fact that many nations, such as Great Britain and Germany, did not completely fill their quotas, which were then lost. The monsignor felt that they could be used for those most in need. He also opposed credits for immigration quotas, the so-called mortgages, which caused the surplus of immigrants of a given nationality from the war period to burden immigration quotas of later years. This caused such paradoxes as 50 percent of the Lithuanian quota to be frozen until the year 2090, and, in the case of Latvia, to the year 2274. In the above-mentioned appearance before the Committee, the Reverend Burant stated:

> The existing quota system does not at all correspond to the present conditions and needs, but it does correspond to the discrimination against the countries of Central and Eastern Europe. Accepting the year 1890 as the basis, it is formed on a tendentious and artificial estimate, because the main wave of immigrants from the countries of Eastern-Central Europe came principally after that date. But leaving aside this historical and statistical consideration no one will deny that precisely those countries are today the greatest producers of refugees, scattered families and homeless people. The conclusion therefore is very simple; either the whole antiquated quota system should be thoroughly revised or the Department of State should be authorized to utilize, depending on the situation and real needs, the unused quotas of Western and North European countries....
>
> Our immigration law should emphatically distinguish between political refugees who have no place to return except to prison, from those who are not victims of war and all its consequences....
>
> Knowing the situation behind the Iron Curtain, we should rather accept a definite rule whereby no one except the communists or fellow travelers be deported to their original countries.[28]

Among the recommendations to the Committee, Burant stressed the need to permit the immigration of 15,000 refugees who were still in Germany. He emphasized that in this number the concern was for those who, for various reasons, did not get their visas before the cutoff date of January 1, 1952, or had not received assurances prior to July 31, 1951. He noted that the health exams of candidates for emigration ought to be more liberal, taking into consideration the conditions in which they had to live during the war and after its conclusion. Monsignor Burant appealed, moreover, for permitting the immigration of about 7,000 former members of the Polish Army who, for various reasons, did not register before June 16, 1950. Finally, he brought up the issue of the 5,000 escapees from behind the Iron Curtain who had fled Poland after May 1945 and were located in various nations of Western Europe.[29]

Eisenhower's declarations did not turn out to be just another broken campaign promise. In his first address to Congress in January 1953, the new president affirmed his support for changing the immigration law. In this address he opted for the need to allow immigration for a broader group of highly qualified specialists, and proposed enlargement of the overall immigration contingent from 154,657 persons to a ceiling of 220,000 annually. He also proposed the creation of a special annual quota of 5,000 visas to be issued regardless of nationality. This was to make it easier to admit persons who had been victimized by war, without stiff limitations or onetime bills. Finally, he postulated that quotas that went unused in a given year be combined and divided up among those who needed them most, regardless of nationality. Generally speaking, this was an unusually promising basis for stretching an umbrella over the continually large group of refugees who remained in Germany. This matter was all the more pressing because after 1949 the refugees were under the wing of the Federal Republic of Germany, from where there were numerous signals about the reluctant treatment of Poles and other escapees from behind the Iron Curtain. That is why this problem found itself on the action list of the PAIRC.[30]

On February 18 and on March 12, 1953, Monsignor Burant sent out individual letters to congressmen and senators in the name of the Committee, with special attention to the currently arriving stream of refugees from the nations of Western Europe. He also put in a word for the former soldiers of the Polish armed forces, repeating the premises from his address of October 1952:

> To the number of displaced persons still remaining in Germany after V-Day, there have been added thousands of refugees who escaped from Soviet persecution seeking freedom in the West. They were rudely disappointed in their hopes because of the fact that due to the curtailment of emigration possibilities they have to wait indefinitely until they are actually able to settle in new permanent homes.... The unfair and inhuman provision calling the quota 'mortgages' incurred from the recent D.P. Law, should be immediately abolished. These mortgages are tantamount to a drastic reduction over many decades, of immigrants from countries, which have suffered most during the last War.[31]

The response to this appeal was impressive. Several dozen replies were received by the Committee from influential senators and congressmen sympathizing with the proposed changes. The correspondence from the offices of congressmen included letters from future U.S. presidents John F. Kennedy and Gerald Ford. Both politicians supported Burant's suggestions.[32]

In that same period, it is difficult to tell whether the Reverend Burant's letter prompted President Eisenhower to speak out once again. In his message of April 22, 1953, Eisenhower recommended accepting 240,000 escapees and persons driven out of their countries over a two-year period, over and above the allotted quota, in order to resolve the problem described as overpopulation in Western Europe.[33]

The April 22, 1953, declaration met with the Committee's favorable reaction. On June 10 of that year, the Rev. Burant presented his comments on this issue at the hearings before the Congressional Subcommittee on Immigration and Naturalization. The subcommittee deliberated over the new law in light of the suggestions presented by Eisenhower. Burant backed the basic premises of the new law. However, he proposed certain modifications to the definition of "refugee" and "escapee," proposing that they refer to persons of European origin who as a result of World War II or its consequences ceased being residents of countries or territories dominated by Communists, and whose deportation could not take place because of the danger of persecution. These people could not be considered as permanently settled. In this last aspect, permanent settlement meant that a person made an application for citizenship in the country in which he or she were currently residing. Burant proposed that with regard to persons who were not able to access the benefits of the 1948 law, a procedure be applied which gave preference to those who had been in Germany the longest. He noted that the allocation of 15,000 visas to escapees from behind the Iron Curtain was decidedly too little. In this category, he also proposed the inclusion of Sweden in the group of NATO countries where Iron Curtain escapees could profit from the new law. At issue were the numerous cases of sailors, pilots, and even private boatmen who used various means to get to Sweden, Denmark, and Norway in search of asylum. The proximity of Russia and the Polish People's Republic made longer stays in those nations questionable. In addition, pressure on the governments of Sweden or Denmark could bring tighter border control, or even outright rejection of potential asylum seekers. Burant also stood up, as he had in previous appearances, for the group of veterans of the Polish armed forces in the West who lived in England, and who had been unable to take advantage of the former law. Finally, he mentioned the persons without proper permanent resident documentation, who found themselves in the United States at the end of World War II and who were unable to return to their native land. The same issue concerned families that had been torn apart by the war, with one or a number of family members residing permanently in America. This matter also had to be taken into consideration.[34]

Representatives of other immigration organizations and of the government also argued on behalf of escapees in other parts of the world. There were 1,250,000 Chinese escapees in Hong Kong. This problem, on a comparable scale, appeared after India gained its independence; finally, it also arose after the first Arab-Israeli War in 1948 and the founding of the nation of Israel. It became evident that every major international crisis is followed by a refugee problem, and that the refugees look for help from wealthy nations and for the opportunity to emigrate. This brought home the urgency of the need to open the doors to immigration, and of appropriate legislation. Thus, in response to the president's April message, Senator Arthur V. Atkins of Utah proposed a bill (S. 1917) which, after being amended, was passed by the Senate on July 23, 1953. The House of Representatives passed the bill on July 28, and the next day the Senate accepted the revised version. It was signed by the president on August 7, 1953. This was the so-called Refugee Act of 1953 (Public Law 203).

Many of the suggestions presented by the Reverend Burant to the congressional committees and to the presidential committee were echoed in the provisions of the new law. It permitted the settlement of 214,000 persons, of whom 205,000 were to be refugees, escapees, or persons thrown out of their countries, or else relatives of U.S. citizens. Four thousand visas were allotted to orphans under the age of 10 (at the moment their visa was issued), 5,000 were for persons who had legally entered the United States prior to July 1, 1953. The latter also included the aforementioned group of the Polish consular-diplomatic corps and soldiers who found themselves in the United States at the conclusion of the war. Their cases fell under the jurisdiction of the Immigration and Naturalization Service, a part of the Justice Department. As to the national allocation of visas, 55,000 were designated for Germans who had been forced out of their homes due to the war, and 35,000 were allotted to escapees in West Germany and Austria. This, clearly, also concerned the Poles. Another 10,000 visas were allocated to escapees who found themselves in other European nation-members of NATO, and also Turkey, Sweden, Iran, and the territory of Trieste. These visas had to be issued in the given countries, exclusively to escapees located there. Also, in this case, there was convergence with the appeals of the Committee. The next 2,000 visas were allocated to members of the Polish armed forces located in Great Britain who had not accepted British citizenship. Another 60,000 visas were allocated to Italians, 17,000 to Greeks, 17,000 to the Dutch, and smaller amounts to several other nationalities. From the Polish point of view, it was important that 2,000 visas had been allocated to escapees not originating in the Far East, but located in far eastern territories within the U.S. consular district. A sizable group of Poles was to be found there, who had arrived during World War II and after its conclusion. A novelty in the legislation was the discontinuation of blank assurances; however, the cost of transportation within the United States was covered by the refugee or his sponsor. What remained in force were the strict health requirements for the candidates and stricter security regulations. The legislation was in force until the end of 1956 and differed from prior legislation by its greater flexibility and scope. It was an attempt at a global approach to the refugee problem, instead of just a European approach.[35]

It is difficult to prove to what degree the attitude, appeals, and efforts of the president of the PAIRC influenced the work of the subcommittee and the final shape of the new law. No doubt the fact that during the war Burant had been an army chaplain with the rank of colonel, and that he was the head of an active organization working effectively to improve the lot of the refugees, lent greater weight to his statements. It ought to be generally noted that the PAIRC, together with the Polish American Congress, played an important role in the passage of the immigration legislation and its amendments. In the first phase of the work, from 1952 to 1953, these issues were at the forefront, because never had such a massive immigration of Poles been admitted in such a short time and under such particular circumstances. The Committee deserves recognition for having come to terms with the situation, for having been able to stimulate both the Polish American community and also to a certain degree the U.S. Congress in the direction of recognizing the interests of Polish refugees. A big argument, often used, was the large size of the Polish American community and the fact that Poland was the first nation to put up armed resistance against Hitler. Also, the presence of several Polish American members of Congress helped. It would not at all be out of turn to recall that the beginning of the Cold War worked in favor of accepting a greater number of refugees, especially since the administration of President Truman, a clear-cut anti–Communist, tried to move away from the Yalta agreement. What also favored the PAIRC was the considerable strength of Catholic organizations at that time and the dominant role that Catholic parishes played in the life of the Polish American community. The strong representation of the clergy on the Committee boosted the credibility of the PAIRC and favored its ability to get funds; that was true all the more so with the passage of time, as the tasks did not diminish. To the contrary, even with a decrease in the absolute number of immigrants, the issues proved more difficult to resolve.

Unfortunately, the enactment of the law of August 7, 1953, did not meet expectations. Many senators, congressmen, and social activists decried the very slow enactment of the new law. More and more voices called for additional amendments. In his January 1954 State of the Union address, President Eisenhower did not mention the indispensable revision of immigration law; but such a necessity was brought to the president's attention by one of the champions of immigrant issues, Senator Herbert H. Lehman (D–NY). According to press reports, he also informed the president about the establishment of the Coordinating Council for Amending the McCarran-Walter Immigration Law. This body consisted of 45 organizations, included 150 activists involved in immigration issues, and was led by Congressman Anfuso. This augured a better-organized pressure for the acceptance of further amendments and changes, despite the gradual toning down of Communist terror after Stalin's death on March 5, 1953.[36]

Pierce J. Gerety, the new deputy administrator of the Refugee Relief Program from the White House side, tried to speed up the enactment of the law. But this proved impossible because the agreement's very premises proved to be the source of the problem. The Germans had little interest in filling the entire quota given them, while the Poles, Latvians, and the residents of the Balkan nations were left with an inadequate number of visas in proportion to the number of people ready to emigrate.

Application review and visa issuance was slow, mainly due to bureaucratic roadblocks and tougher criteria concerning security matters. Even the press and some of the congressmen criticized this failure. The *New York Times* wrote:

> The law did not work quickly or well.... The first person to be admitted under its provisions came from Italy and landed in this country on December 24 of this year. Subsequently immigration under the Refugee Relief Act has continued to be slow and scanty. One reason has been the restrictive requirements in the law itself, such as, for example, the stipulation that the countries from which the refugees immediately came should be willing to take them back if there were any fraud in their passport applications. Another was that each had to have an individual sponsor here. A cause of delay was that a new staff had to be built up to process applicants, and it took time to give this staff the necessary security tests and to train it in its duties.... One hopes that the red tape will be cut and that the State Department, although exercising necessary precautions to keep out the seditious and the conspiratorial, will not insist on limiting the newcomers to saints with halos.[37]

The president himself was aware of the new difficulties. His good will was clearly demonstrated by the appointment of Gerety as the new administrator of the law, and also by putting pressure on the other agencies responsible for executing the program. During a meeting with a group of governors' representatives for issues concerning the Refugee Relief Act, on August 2, 1955, Eisenhower confirmed that changes were necessary. He stated that the law was too restrictive and very difficult to administer. The following was stated in the report of this meeting: "Criticism has been made that the intensive security screening and health requirements put to immigrants, coupled with strict demands of individual sponsorship, have made the act extremely difficult to administer."[38]

For example, regarding the escapees in Germany, barely 9,000 visas were issued up to 1955. In the spring of 1956, Gerety stated that of the planned 214,000 visas, most probably about 60,000 would not be used. According to his assessment, the reason was a lack of interest in emigration on the part of escapees residing in Germany and Austria. He obviously did not mention the formal obstacles. At any rate, the numbers were alarming. With regard to the 10,000 visas set aside for refugees in European NATO countries, only 5,084 had been issued by April 20, 1956. It is not known how many Poles this included. Regarding another category, by April 20, 1956, some 1,813 assurances had been issued for Polish veterans in Great Britain. Counting family members, that amounted to 3,735 persons, or well above the ceiling of 2,000. In general categories, by the law's expiration date (December 31, 1956) 184,306 refugees were permitted to immigrate, of which 170,418 came from Europe, 11,793 came from the Far East and 1,124 came from Israel and Palestine.[39]

Eisenhower's noble plan had been distorted on the road to enactment. In contrast to the DP Act of 1948 the new administration ran out of enthusiasm for enacting the law. On the other side of the coin, there was a calming of the international situation after Stalin's death in March 1953. Slowly, signals started coming in about the gradual receding of the wave of terror. In 1953 death sentences in political cases started being stayed in Poland, and little by little the opportunities for international cooperation and "peaceful coexistence" started opening up. Undoubtedly, this also influenced the attitude toward enacting the Refugee Relief Act. Given these restrictions, one ought to remember that the Polish ethnic group, among the refugees still remaining in Europe, tried to utilize their visa quota in full, as was also the case with Polish World War II veterans living in the British Isles.

Before the onset of 1956 no one was quite aware that the international situation favored an increase in communication, in tourism, and in various forms of exchange, and subsequently would increase the number of escapes to the West. The Polish American Immigration and Relief Committee perceived these circumstances, since much of its activity had already been geared to that sort of emigrant from the beginning of the 1950s.

V

Other Engagements in the Years 1948–1957

The activities already discussed did not exhaust the Committee founders' inventiveness. Among noteworthy initiatives, a novel way of obtaining assurances deserves mention. It concerned the group settlement of candidates possessing the ability to engage in a particular profession. Since one of the most sought-after abilities was agricultural work, the Committee decided to exploit this need, and to apply for a group settlement for a greater number of demobilized Poles from the Labor Service Companies of the U.S. Army (Kompanie Wartownicze) in Germany. The success of such a maneuver depended on the cooperation of individual farmers, and also of labor unions, or farmers' organizations. Fortunately, Steve Dobroski was on the board of trustees of the PAIRC. He was the secretary and later the vice president of the Farmer's Cooperative on Long Island. Thanks to him, a greater number of job openings was obtained. That was the genesis of the Long Island Operation, which became famous in immigration circles. Thanks to it, 705 single men from the Labor Service Companies in Germany were brought to work on farms in Suffolk County. It wasn't only the members of the Committee, or employers who distinguished themselves in helping the Labor Service Company veterans. Pastor Ceslaus S. Biedrzycki of Riverhead, local Police Commissioner John C. Doscinski, and Judge Henry Zaleski, who was a vice president of the PAIRC and was a Long Island resident with a law office in Riverhead, all played important roles in the success of this project.

The success of this enterprise brought in its wake "Long Island Operation Number Two," thanks to which another 597 Labor Service Company veterans were able to come to the United States and find employment. This initiative, being something of a novelty, was observed with interest by the

Former Labor Service Company members who settled on a tobacco farm in Hartford, Connecticut, march in a Pulaski Day Parade in New York City.

immigration authorities. Another plan of this sort was the employment of Poles on tobacco plantations in Connecticut. The name of the endeavor, "Shade Tobacco Operation," referred to the main sponsor, the Shade Tobacco Growers Cultural Association in Hartford, Connecticut, which made possible the arrival and employment of 732 Poles. Yet another group settlement operation was the Rockland County Operation, which helped 90 people. Its employment sponsor was the Rockland County Growers Association in Suffern, New York, whose president was Michael Sheehan. This is important in that it is evidence of help from non–Polish organizations, as well, on behalf of Polish refugees. Also worth mentioning are the Connecticut Tobacco Operation and the Jackson Perkins Operation, which each employed a group of Labor Service Company veterans from Germany. The latter was connected with the firm of Jackson and Perkins of Newark, New Jersey. All the enumerated operations were completed by 1951. They enabled the admission of close to 2,500 Poles who had served in the Labor Service Companies in Germany. It should be noted, however, that some of them went on to serve in the American Army and were deployed to Korea.[1] The success of these operations went beyond their simply human dimension; it indicated that the Polish American Immigration and Relief Committee was able to rise to new challenges and ameliorate the plight of the needy in an unconventional way.[2]

Aside from the situations already mentioned, the PAIRC had to react to many other challenges not foreseen by existing law and requiring intervention. One of the more widely publicized was the issue of widows and Polish women with children, whose immigration to the United States in the light of existing law was impossible. In 1951, the top brass of the National Catholic Welfare Conference turned to the Reverend Burant for help. The problem was, it is true, of wider scope, because it included women of many nationalities, but the PAIRC was not able to help everybody. Father Burant replied to the director of the NCWC that he was ready to help 100 women and their children. He investigated this matter personally while on a visit to Germany. After returning, he developed a successful campaign to settle those women in the Polish American community, and met with complete success.[3]

The PAIRC's unconventional forms of action manifested themselves through an openness to the immediate needs of the escapees. They also concerned children, who received free vacations, help in getting books and school supplies, and even food and material help. A long list of engaging examples of openness to very particular needs could be cited. For example, the day before Holy Communion of a group of Polish children in Germany, the Committee approved 175 DM toward the purchase of clothes for the occasion. The Communion took place on June 2, 1957. The photographs

A group of Polish children in Germany receives Holy Communion. The Polish American Immigration and Relief Committee contributed toward the purchase of the suits and dresses.

from this event made the rounds of the Polish press in Germany and America, gaining the Committee well-deserved accolades.[4]

Bishop Władysław Rubin, residing in Rome, was the spiritual head of the Polish diaspora. He frequently thanked the Committee for organizing various forms of support for the Poles in Italy. For example, he said:

> May merciful God reward this kind gift a hundred fold. It was of great help to us, because the transportation alone of the kids to summer camp costs about $300, not counting other needs, even though we receive food (dry items) from the *Pontificia Opera di Assistenza*. It is getting increasingly difficult to organize these camps, but when one sees the terrific results in terms of health and other benefits which the Polish children get, then we somehow find the strength to undertake even such a difficult assignment.[5]

More and more frequently the Committee dealt with escapees who jumped ships that flew the banner of Soviet-occupied Poland and asked for asylum in Western ports. The Committee began focusing on this problem in 1948. The escapee category also included workers of the Polish diplomatic and consular service who, after the Polish government in London had its recognition revoked, did not have documents permitting them to remain in the United States. Also included here were soldiers and officers of the Polish armed forces who were in the United States at the time of the revocation of recognition. In such instances, private bills were introduced in Congress on their behalf by individual congressmen. Among congressmen of non–Polish descent who sponsored such bills, one ought to mention Mary Norton, Victor Anfuso, Emanuel Celler, Louis Heller, and Francis Walters, and also senators Herbert Lehman and Irving Ives. The first such bills appeared in 1949, after the exceptionally widely publicized escapes of sailors from the ships *Sobieski*, *Batory*, *Vianna*, and *Merta*. In order to protect the sailors from deportation, Congressman A. Sieminski introduced a private bill on behalf of 134 sailors to facilitate their permanent residence.[6]

On May 11, 1953, Congressman Heller made use of a private bill to enable Piotr Wędrogowski to stay in America. Congressman Graham made a similar legislative maneuver on May 18, 1954, and Congressman Anfuso did so on June 20, 1955. Some of the proposed bills had a mixed character, that is, they dealt with a larger group of people of various nationalities who were linked only by their status as political refugees.[7]

Of course, these are just a few examples of this type of action. It should be remembered that the private bills did not automatically grant legal resident status, but they did halt deportation proceedings and allowed for a calmer awaiting of the final decision from the immigration authorities. After the ratification of the Geneva Convention regarding escapees, the procedure of granting political asylum came into wider use, though this did not exclude special treatment on the basis of interventions by congressmen.

All these steps became a necessity due to the frequent escapes from ships. The case of the mutiny on the freighter *Żuraw* became widely publicized. Its organizers imprisoned 32 crew members and made it to Ystad. Their application for political asylum ran into delays, prompting some of the mutineers to make their way to the United States illegally. The Warsaw government demanded that the mutineers be handed over, and the escapees' situation was rendered additionally difficult by Sweden's neutrality and by the proximity of both the USSR and the Polish People's Republic. The PAIRC and the Polish American Congress both intervened in this matter. The Swedish Embassy in Washington, D.C., was approached to give asylum to the above-mentioned individuals. Thanks to this, many sailors in Sweden were finally granted asylum, over the sharp protests of the Polish People's Republic.

Front row, second, third and fourth from right: W. Zachariasiewicz, executive secretary of the Polish American Immigration and Relief Committee; Captain Leonard Wąsowski of the SS *Praca*, and Captain J. Ćwikliński, former commander of the MS *Batory*, with a group of Polish sailors in the capital of Free China on Formosa (Taiwan).

In 1953 and 1954, there was a much publicized case involving two Polish freighters, *Praca* and *Gottwald*. They tried to smuggle their goods into North Korea despite the blockade of that country. Both ships were held in Taiwan (Formosa), and the nationalist Chinese authorities did not know what to do with the sailors. Most of the crew appealed to the Taipei authorities for political asylum. The matter was delayed, threatening serious political consequences. The American embassy in Taiwan also did not know how to resolve the conflict. Finally, a delegation of the PAIRC headed for the island, with Władysław Zachariasiewicz and Captain Jan Ćwikliński, the former captain of the MS *Batory*, who himself left his ship in one of the American ports. The mission of both emissaries was to gauge the atmosphere, to engage in exhaustive talks with members of both crews, and to recommend a way out of the crisis, which was already almost one year old. After the return of the emissaries to the United States, the Committee took the necessary steps to obtain resident status for those who declared readiness to abandon the banner of the Polish People's Republic. Soon, in 1954, about 30 sailors arrived in the United States, and the remaining crew members were evacuated to Poland by the Red Cross.

Even more widely known was the case of two pilots of the Polish People's Army who escaped to the West in modern Mig-15 fighter jets. The first of them, Lieutenant Franciszek Jarecki, decided to escape at the news of Stalin's death on March 5, 1953. Despite being pursued, he was able to land safely on the Danish island of Bornholm. Lieutenant Zdzisław Jaźwiński took a similar path. The Reverend Burant, the president of the Committee, sent a telegram on March 11 to President Dwight D. Eisenhower, appealing for the soonest possible evacuation of Jarecki to the United States. He brought attention to the significance of such an escape in the propaganda war with the Communists, and the benefits that his emigration to America would bring. Such an act, he argued, would increase faith in the ideals of democracy and the West.[8]

The reaction was swift. Both officers arrived in the United States without any obstacles and participated in an enormous number of gatherings and town hall meetings both in the Polish American community and in the American community at large. In addition, high-ranking speakers noted the achievements of the PAIRC. New York Mayor V.R. Impellitteri said on the occasion of one such meeting with the participation of Jarecki:

> The Statue of Liberty in our harbor is a symbol of the promise made long ago, that our country would always offer a refuge to those who sought it. You, Monsignor Burant, the Polish Immigration Committee, and all New Yorkers of Polish descent have performed a great service in seeing to it that we live up to that promise.[9]

No less a sensation was caused by the escape by kayak of two Poles, Zenon Resiak and Witold Jarzyna, who in August 1954 succeeded in making it to Bornholm. The Committee also took up their case, facilitating their immigration to the United States.[10]

There were further cases of kayak and even hang glider escapes. The very fact of endangering life to gain asylum outside the Polish People's Republic was a great propaganda success for the West. There were other types of escapes, as well. Even more embarrassing for the Communists was the case of the soldiers from General Berling's army who fled to western occupation zones after the war. The verification procedure then in force treated such cases as bad security risks, depriving the persons of the possibility of emigration. Meanwhile, it was clear to those who knew the conditions of recruitment for the Polish armed forces in Russia under the control of the PKWN (Polski Komitet Wyzwolenia Narodowego — The Polish

Polish Immigration Committee volunteers help in the shipment of packages with clothing to Germany and Austria. In the center is the Reverend Ludwik Makulec. The chairlady of the collection drive, Mrs. Florence Jarzębowski, is to the right of the Reverend Makulec.

National Liberation Committee, organized by Polish Communist Wanda Wasilewska) that many soldiers joined up exclusively to get out of the work camps and places of compulsory settlement, or to have the opportunity to go back to Poland to be with their families and relatives. Recruitment in the former Kresy Wschodnie (Eastern Borderlands) was compulsory and did not necessarily signify the choice of a political option. The above-mentioned Colonel Wichrowski and Polish American Congress President Karol Rozmarek intervened in Germany on behalf of the soldiers. As a result of these efforts, 35 "Berling" soldiers received permission to come to America.

CARE packages were an important form of assistance. This sort of action most frequently targeted the physically challenged, war invalids, the blind, persons unable to undertake employment, persons over 65 years of age, and those on social welfare.

In general, these were the so-called hard-core cases which did not qualify for emigration under existing law, and were doomed to vegetate in Germany and Austria. The PAIRC had quite early on recognized the importance of assistance for these people. A very large percentage of ad hoc collection efforts, banquets, and occasional fund drives were organized to gather money, food, or basic items needed for the survival of these people. The Committee also cooperated in this regard with other Polish American organizations which, in their own right, organized collection drives and passed the results on to the Committee for disbursement. The Committee transported them

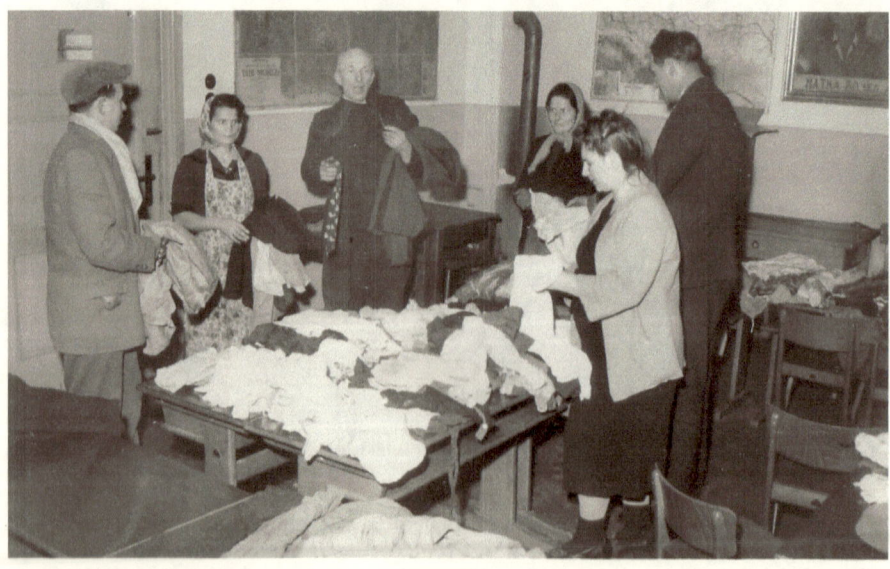

On the other side of the ocean.

to Europe and distributed them through a network of associates. After landing in Europe, the parcels were taken to distribution points that were run by the Association of Polish Refugees (APR) in Germany together with the local office of the PAIRC. For example, in 1955 there were eleven distribution points in Germany where those who were entitled could pick up CARE packages. These centers were located in Hamburg, Oldenburg, Hanover, Goettingen, Augustdorf, Lintorf, Kornwestheim, Wuerzburg, Munich, Amberg, and Landshut.

This specific procedure concerned people who were paid-up members of the APR. Nonetheless, exceptions were allowed based on a review by the field manager. The recipient was obliged to pay a transportation fee of 1 DM, to sign a receipt, and to send a thank you note to the PAIRC in New York. Such expressions of gratitude were also sent directly to the donor; for instance, in 1955 that happened to be the Legion of Young Polish Women. Close attention was paid to the fulfillment of these formalities, which in the opinion of the workers of the APR guaranteed receiving aid in subsequent years. The opportunity, of course, also existed to pass on parcels from individual donors both for a designated recipient and without any special addressee in mind. For example, the New York–based Polsko Amerykańska Robotnicza Kasa Pomocy (Polish American Aid Fund), which cooperated with the PAIRC, donated 20 parcels in 1958 for former colleagues in Germany. In the same period, the Liga Kobiet w Nowym Jorku (The League of Women of Polish Descent), also based in New York, sent 50 parcels to the DP camp in Landshut, 50 parcels to the sole discretion of the Reverend Monsignor Edward Lubowiecki, 46 parcels to the board of the Ognisko (Hearth) in Deggendorf, and three parcels for individually named persons.[11]

The above-mentioned attention to confirmation of receipt from the recipient was also necessary for the New York office. It allowed for an exact accounting of the aid given, a definition of future needs, and, most importantly, it gave transparency to the whole process in terms of accountability to the individual and group donors in the United States and to the board of the NCWC. This sort of activity was given a lot of space in the PAIRC's promotional efforts, especially in radio programs and the press. Several years' experience proved that the Polish American community's generosity could best be aroused by highlighting hardship cases, the needs of handicapped people, and those condemned to stagnation.

Monsignor Burant tried to keep the refugee issues constantly present in the media. Aside from the radio and constant mentions in the press, the Committee's president made use of the Easter and Christmas holidays to make appeals for support. That is how the hearts of the Polish American community were approached. It was not the only method used. The "Appeals to the Heart," as they were called at times, were also sent to a select group of citizens and community leaders. With regard to the latter, in addition to appealing to their pocketbooks, requests were made to have them take up collections in their own locality. This most frequently concerned sympathizers in Buffalo, Detroit, Cleveland, Chicago, and other larger cities, especially those with heavier concentrations of Polish Americans, and also where regional committees of the PAIRC were organized at the beginning of the 1960s. Another opportunity for appeals was the annual Pulaski Day Parade in New York. Usually several days before the event, the monsignor placed an "appeal to the heart" in the media for financial support. Several dozen volunteers would then get cans at the Committee's office or at St. Stanislaus Parish and collect money along the parade route. The cans were numbered, and the permit for conducting the fund drive in specified neighborhoods and over a specified period of time — usually three days — was granted by the city authorities. Every volunteer who took up a collection had to have a tag, a copy of the permit, and some form of personal identification. The point was

The Pulaski Parade in New York. Ladies in folk costumes carry the banner of the Polish Immigration Committee with the slogan: "The Polish American Immigration and Relief Committee needs your support — donate generously!"

to maintain the trust of the Polish American community and the city. A typical collection of this sort would bring in, on average, about $2,000 to $3,000.

This kind of appeal summed up the accomplishments to date and indicated current needs. The time of publication usually coincided with an increased interest in public affairs, and also a traditional time of generosity toward fellow men. The results of each appeal were usually presented during a special meeting in the Committee's offices, which was connected with the issue of an appropriate press release and personal thanks by Monsignor Burant to the volunteers. Representatives of the PAIRC marching in the parade as a separate unit also drew attention to the Committee. Refugees often marched at the head with banners thanking America for its hospitality and expressing the willingness to defend their new country: "We Will Defend America Against Any Foe." Many slogans dealt with the need for opening the borders to the needy and to the oppressed. The East-West rivalry found its reflection here. The presence of so many refugees demonstrating the superiority of democratic ideals and of the United States over the Soviet Union was especially visible in the 1950s and the early 1960s, when the parade also included anti–Communist organizations and all sorts of institutions and federations uniting former citizens of the nations of East-Central Europe.

Volunteers at a meeting to report on collections made during the 1957 Pulaski Parade. They are at St. Stanislaus Bishop and Martyr Parish hall. *Far left, seated*: W. Zachariasiewicz; two rows behind him editor J. Dubicki; *seated, center:* the Reverend Monsignor F. Burant; lady volunteers.

In the second half of the 1950s, there usually were several groups in the parade thanking the Committee for its work, and thanking America for the opportunity to start a new life; they included farmers, sailors, and former Labor Service Company members from Germany who, after settling in the United States, were employed in groups. One should also remember that the major veterans' organizations, including Stowarzyszenie Polskich Kombatantów (SPK; i.e., The Polish Veterans of World War II) and Stowarzyszenie Weteranów Armii Polskiej (SWAP; i.e., the Polish Army Veterans Association of America) had former refugees in their ranks at the parade.[12]

Generally speaking, it should be noted that the Reverend Burant capably utilized public demonstrations such as the parade to promote the work and needs of the Committee.

VI

A Who's Who in the Initial Years

The successful work of the Committee would not have been possible without a devoted team of people. As has already been noted, the active spirit and energy of the Reverend Monsignor Burant pervaded the entirety of the work. He bore the responsibilities of the founder and of the Committee's representative to the outside. Nonetheless, the multiplicity of endeavors required a professional and dedicated group of co-workers. Part of them sat on the board of trustees, others were satisfied to be rank-and-file volunteers. The initial structure of the Committee was as follows. At the head were the president, vice president, secretary, and treasurer. The oversight functions were in the hands of the board of trustees. Advisory functions were performed by the Advisory Council, and the day-to-day management was in the hands of an office manager and a public relations officer. The first board was convened on February 24, 1947. The Reverend Monsignor Feliks Burant was its president until 1964. Adam B. Łyczak, an industrialist and well-known civic volunteer who was also one of the founders of the New York branch of the Skarb Narodowy (Polish National Fund), headquartered in London, was elected vice president. Tadeusz Sztybel of *Nowy Świat* became the secretary and Feliks Popławski, a volunteer in cultural organizations in New York, became the treasurer. Popławski was the president of the Rada Oświatowa Złączonych Towarzystw (Educational Council of the United Polish Societies) and of the Polska Robotnicza Kasa Pomocy (Polish American Aid Fund), founded in 1910.

Aside from Burant, Łyczak, Popławski and Sztybel, the following were also members of the board of trustees: Rev. Gerwazy Kubiec, the pastor of St. Casimir Parish in Brooklyn; Edward Liszka, a community activist and president of the Złączone Towarzystwa (United Polish Societies) in Hartford, Connecticut; Rev. M. Mroziński, pastor of Sts. Cyril and Methodius Parish in Greenpoint, Brooklyn; Attorney S. Obremski, a member of the Polish American Congress in Syracuse, New York; Rev. J. Studziński, pastor of St. Stanislaus Parish in Greenpoint, Brooklyn; Piotr Yolles, another journalist from the *Nowy Świat* daily and simultaneously the president of the Polish Language Press Association (Stowarzyszenie Prasy Polskojęzycznej); and Edward Witanowski, one of the "two Edwards" who hosted the program of that name on radio station WHOM in New York.

The Advisory Council consisted of: W. Bayer, a judge of the New York State Supreme Court; J. Borawski; K. Jarzębowski; Wojciech Klemp, the censor of the Stowarzyszenie Synów Polski (Association of the Sons of Poland); E. Kosowicz (the other Edward of the *Two Edwards*); Rev. L. Makulec; William Stachurski; Rev. F. Szubiński; J. Węgrzynek; and Ignacy Nurkiewicz, the owner of Stop Fire Company, who was also a vice president of the Polish American Congress. Up to 1950, the Committee's office manager was Jan Pargiełło, and the public relations officer was Władysław Zachariasiewicz.[1]

The following year the board membership was augmented by another vice president, Edward Koźmor, president of the Polish American Congress for the State of New Jersey. J. Pargiełło and W. Zachariasiewicz were also added to the board. In 1951 Zachariasiewicz advanced to the post of executive secretary of the board. The board next added the following vice presidents: L.V. Malinowski, the vice-censor of the Polish National Alliance of Brooklyn; and J. Pawłoski from the Association of the Sons of Poland. Other new names were also added to the board. On the other hand, one of the Committee's earliest workers, Jan Pargiełło, left.[2]

In any event, the changes on the board were evidence of the full use of the intellectual potential of people willing to place their energies at the Committee's disposal. From 1951, the executive secretary was, as already mentioned, Władysław Zachariasiewicz, who became the executive vice president in 1959 and remained in that role until 1963. Zachariasiewicz completed his university studies before the war. During World War II he was interned in a Soviet labor camp, and he later worked in London in the Ministry of Labor and Social Welfare — first in the government of Tomasz Arciszewski and subsequently in the government of General Tadeusz Bór-Komorowski. Monsignor Burant wrote of him that: "in his work for the Committee he showed a great knowledge of the issues, great tact and a big heart, he gained great and wide-spread respect and trust. I would not be able to find a more highly qualified person to do the responsible work of our Committee."[3]

In 1952, the founder and president of the Kościuszko Foundation, Stephen P. Mizwa, was elected to the Advisory Council, though his influence

Władysław Zachariasiewicz, secretary general and executive vice president 1950-1963.

on the Committee's work was minimal. As of 1953, the vice presidential group was enlarged by Wanda Pilch, the head of the Committee's volunteer team, who was also a director of the Zjednoczenie Polskie Rzymsko Katolickie (Polish Roman Catholic Union of America — PRCUA). Henryk Korab-Janiewicz was an important addition to the Committee's Advisory Council. He owned Pasco, a meat processing plant in Newark, New Jersey, was a former Polish cavalryman with the First Uhlan Regiment, and in New York he served as the president of the Józef Piłsudski Institute. Janiewicz was well known as a supporter of charitable causes in metropolitan New York. In 1955 he was elected vice president of the PAIRC. In 1953, a new office was created within the Board of Trustees: a financial committee headed by Janina Węgrzynek. The financial committee replaced the financial secretary.

Stanisław Gierat was connected with the PAIRC early on. He was one of its organizers and also for many years served as the president of the Stowarzyszenie Polskich Kombatantów (Polish Veterans of World War II — SPK). Before World War II, he was active with the rural youth movement in Poland, and was a leader of "Siew" (The Sowing) and of the "Grupa Techniczna" (The Technical Group). During the Second World War, he served in the Signal Corps of the Polish II Corps, participated in the Italian campaign, and ended the war with the rank of major.[4]

Finally, the volunteer team is also worth mentioning. It is not possible to list all the names, but the women's group cannot be passed over. It included: K. Chomicka, A. Dziergowska, M. Jasinowska, S. Kasprzak, Z. Kotowska, Z. Laskowska, M. Maryańska, M. Piekutowska, M. Piskor, M. Rynca, J. Siniewicz, H. Strzępek, I. Cieślak, and E. Lubicz. This group was coordinated by Wanda Pilch. Many in the group of about 120 volunteers worked sporadically, some only seasonally. Leopold Babirecki stood out among the regular workers who helped to receive immigrants arriving in ports and saw them off on their further journeys. He was a commissioner of District #3 of the Związek Narodowy Polski (Polish National Alliance — PNA) in New York. Also, Adolf Zakrzewski always helped out as a volunteer in various matters.

An analysis of the people making up the executive body of the Committee indicates common sense and the ability to bring together opposing tendencies that ran through the Polish American community. The Committee included representatives of both the old and the new Polish American community. The Reverend Burant succeeded in bringing together in the PAIRC the most active members of a wide gamut of clubs, aid societies, professional organizations, journalists, and lawyers, which also helped ensure a mediation umbrella for the Committee. The presence of representatives from various parishes raised the trustworthiness of the Committee in the eyes of the Polish American community. There is one other element worthy of note, namely the openness of Monsignor Burant to the new emigration. The best example was the significance and advancement of W. Zachariasiewicz in the organizational structure, and the confidence that his superior had in him. From 1953 on, many important consultations in Washington, D.C., engaged in by The Rev. Burant occurred in the presence of and with the participation of Zachariasiewicz.[5]

The wide scope of activity would not have been possible without publicizing the accomplishments of the Committee throughout many nations of the world, as well as cooperation with many organizations. The already mentioned Zjednoczenie Polskich Uchodźców w Niemczech (Union of Polish Refugees in Germany) had its equivalent in the form of the Związek Polaków (Association of Poles) in Austria. The Polish press appearing in Germany, Austria, and other countries was also a focus of support for refugee aid. An equally useful role was played by the posts of the Stowarzyszenie Polskich Kombatantów (Polish Veterans of World War II — SPK) whose members in many instances worked both in their veterans' organization and in the PAIRC's field offices in Europe. Many of those activists played a leading role in the history of the PAIRC and its field offices. It should be remembered that almost from the beginning of its existence, more precisely from 1954, SPK President Stanisław Gierat was active in the Committee, and after him the next president of the SPK, Janusz Krzyżanowski, held important positions, all the way up to leadership of the Committee from 1981 on. In Rome, correspondence regarding refugees was directed to Witold Zahorski; in Belgium, to S. Merło; in Paris, to Stanisław Domański; and in London, to several officials of the SPK. Organizations in the United States that worked with the Committee and maintained closer contact with it also ought to be mentioned. These included the New Jersey–based Stowarzyszenie Synów Polski (Association of the Sons of Poland), whose active members lent financial support to the PAIRC both individually and as an organization, and were also active in the Committee itself. For instance, in 1960 the Convention of the Association approved $500 toward the work of the PAIRC. The Association continues its close contact with the Committee to this day. One of the most active members of both organizations is Franciszka Szczygielska of Brooklyn who for many years, to the very end of the Committee's activity, served as its secretary.[6]

Another organization of the so-called old emigration which maintained close contact with the PAIRC was the Unia Polska w Stanach Zjednoczonych Ameryki Północnej (Polish Union of the U.S. of North America) founded in 1890, and based in Wilkes-Barre, Pennsylvania. Its most active members in the 1950s were: President Zygmunt Grabowski and Secretary General Piotr Fabian. The Sokolstwo Polskie w Ameryce (Polish Falcons of America), founded in 1895, was equally helpful, especially in promoting the activity of the PAIRC and in ad hoc fund-raisers and donations. Its headquarters continued to be located in Pittsburgh, and there were very active centers in New Jersey. The Committee could always count on the Zjednoczenie Polsko Narodowe (PNA of Brooklyn) especially since Józef Głowacki, the secretary general of that organization, was a member of the Committee's Board of Trustees. Contacts were also established with the officers of the Zjednoczenie Polskie Rzymsko Katolickie (Polish Roman Catholic Union of America — PRCUA) in Chicago. In his letter of June 30, 1966, the Reverend Monsignor Franciszek Kowalczyk wrote in the name of the Committee that the PAIRC was handling 15,000 so-called hard-core cases in Germany, who needed continual aid. He appealed for support from the next convention of the PRCUA. He also asked for support from the Polskie Stowarzyszenie Kasy p.o. św. Jana Kantego (Polish Beneficial Association of St. John Kanty) which, like the Association of the Sons of Poland, was founded in the 19th century. From 1939 on, the association regularly lent its financial support to the local relief committee; but later, in recognition of the PAIRC's accomplishments, the XXIVth convention of the association, deliberating from September 9 to 12, 1962, sent a donation in the sum of $100. This was not the only help rendered to the PAIRC.[7]

Contact with the Liga Morska (Sea League of America) in New York City was also important. Its members were present in the executive ranks of the PAIRC and assisted in special events, in fund-raisers and in immigration help at ports of entry where the refugees arrived.[8]

Organizations of the Polish American community's older generation were especially willing to work on holiday events, in clothes and food drives, and in collecting small donations for specific purposes, for instance for CARE packages which during the holiday season were sent to Germany and other European nations. Organizations, clubs, and groups established by the new wave of immigrants had commitments of an entirely different sort, as many newly minted immigrants were able to set foot on American soil thanks to the Committee's efforts. To these belonged the Samopomoc Nowej Emigracji (New Immigrants' Self-Aid), headquartered at 96 E. 7th Street, near St. Stanislaus Church on Manhattan's Lower East Side; the Polskie Stowarzyszenie Byłych Więźniów Politycznych Niemieckich i Sowieckich Obozów Koncentracyjnych w Ameryce (Polish Association of Former Political Prisoners of Nazi and Soviet Concentration Camps) and the Związek Oficerów Marynarki Handlowej w Ameryce (Alliance of Officers of the Merchant Marine in America), who expressed their gratitude at many public functions for care rendered to the Polish sailor. Organizations were also established exclusively by immigrants who had come to the United States through the intervention of the PAIRC. The Samopomoc Byłych Żołnierzy PSZ Emigrujących do USA (Self-Aid of Former Soldiers of the Polish Armed Forces Emigrating to the U.S.A.) was founded in England in November of 1949. It established contact with the PAIRC in New York.[9]

The clergy was a very special group that existed within the circle of the Committee's interests. The important position of Monsignor Burant and the mission he headed would lead one to believe that the reaction of Church dignitaries in America would also be significant. To this end, the PAIRC prepared a full list of Polish parishes in the United States and an individual list of monsignors and bishops, both Polish and American, who received the Rev. Burant's appeals every year. The response was large, and the amount of donations received by this route constituted an important financial boost. The Committee was highly respected by Philadelphia Archbishop, and later Cardinal, John Krol, who sent a number of checks over time to the PAIRC.[10] Also, after the Rev. Burant's death on August 25, 1964, the Archbishop sent a check for $100 to the Committee.[11]

It should be remembered that the success of this sort of fund drive was connected with the presence of a substantial number of Polish priests in prominent posts in the hierarchy of the Catholic Church in America. Addressees of the Committee included Bishop S.V. Bona of Wisconsin, Bishop Stephen Woźnicki of Detroit, Bishop Stanisław Brzana of Buffalo, Bishop Aloysius Wycisło of Chicago, known for his work in the NCWC, Bishop (later Cardinal) John Krol of Philadelphia, Auxiliary Bishop R.R. Atkielski of Milwaukee, Auxiliary Bishop Henry T. Klonowski of Scranton, and several others.[12]

Appeals of this sort had an additional positive effect in that they acquainted the church leaders with the Committee's activity and opened the door to future collections where Polish parishioners did not have a Polish shepherd.

From the mid–1950s the Committee tried to directly acquaint itself with the situation of Poles in Western Europe and to more closely assist them. In the summer of 1955, Zachariasiewicz went on an extended tour of refugee centers in Western Europe, which resulted in the first comprehensive scrutiny of the situation by a Committee employee. This allowed the establishment of work priorities in that area, preparation for the possibility of a broader participation in, or even takeover of, the American Relief for Poland's role in Western Europe, and, finally, introduced the Committee onto the list of organizations consulted by various agencies of the U.S. government. The problem of filling the void after the American Relief for Poland shifted operations to Poland, was as pressing as rendering aid to the hardcore cases in Europe, who were most frequently victims of war. The worries of veterans' circles, first of all the Polish Veterans of World War II — SPK, were at the fore on this issue. This was the source of the initiative to replace the American Relief for Poland with the PAIRC on the European continent, as the most frequent recipients of aid were war veterans, concentration camp victims, forced laborers and Poles forcibly resettled to Germany during World War II. Of the many public statements on this issue, one most notably comes to mind; that is, the address that National Polish Veterans of World War II — SPK President Janusz Krzyżanowski made during Soldiers' Day ceremonies on August 18, 1957, at the Falcons' picnic area (Polanka Sokoła) in Sommerville, New Jersey. He challenged the Committee to undertake the care of the victims of war in Europe.[13]

Without a doubt, Zachariasiewicz's inspection tour was connected with the activation of President Eisenhower's immigration policy. It was most probably a matter of another on-site opinion as to the state of and the progress in the enactment of the legislation that the President had recently signed. Zachariasiewicz left New York on May 9 and returned on July 5, 1955. He visited Great Britain, Sweden, Norway, Denmark, Belgium, Germany (where he stayed for 18 days), Austria, Italy, and France. In 1955, the following concentrations of Polish refugees were to be found in the various countries: 150,000 in Great Britain, 52,000 in Germany, 30,000 in France, 15,000 in Belgium, 2,500 in Sweden, 2,000 in Holland, 1,500 in Austria, 1,000 in both Italy and Norway. In several other countries, such as Greece, Switzerland, Denmark, Spain, Portugal, and Ireland, there was on average less than 1,000 Poles.

Zachariasiewicz's report consisted of two sections. In the first section, the author analyzed the political aspect of the problem. He drew attention to the political propaganda attributes of refugees from behind the Iron Curtain, especially of the Poles, as dyed-in-the-wool anti–Communists. The report reiterated this point by stressing the positive influence of the new immigrants on America's social fabric. These people, after coming to America, remain uncompromising opponents of totalitarian ideology; they therefore strengthen the political spine of the American people, and quickly adjust to their new conditions. Their presence on the new continent is also beneficial because, both directly and indirectly, for instance by means of the radio, or by correspondence, these refugees influence the thinking of people behind the Iron Curtain. The potential risk of the "Fifth Red Column" did not destroy the benefits flowing from admitting a wide stream of refugees to America. Therefore, Zachariasiewicz concluded, it is necessary to render aid to the refugee centers quickly, to prevent the deepening frustration, and to counteract the pressure of Communist propaganda on the refugees to return to their native countries. Free transportation, cultural and educational programs, free vacations for children, and several other propaganda maneuvers were being used by the Communists. The report's author also drew attention to the fact that assistance for tried and true allies of democracy should be rendered immediately, especially since, in the light of a progressive relaxation of tensions on the Washington–Moscow line, the importance of the political refugee problem might diminish. Zachariasiewicz spoke five times on Radio Free Europe, which indicates the importance of his European visit for propaganda purposes.

He began the analysis of refugee centers with Great Britain. Of a total of 150,000, mostly former soldiers, only about 10 percent accepted British citizenship. The organizational network was very well developed, with the SPK at the forefront. The report's author noted that all 2,000 visas granted in 1953 on the basis of the Refugee Relief Act would be used. Regarding the situation in Sweden, the main organizational body there was the Polska Rada Uchodźcza (Polish Refugee Council) and, of course, the SPK. Despite its neutrality, the Swedish government had a favorable attitude toward the refugees. Nonetheless, the main goal of the Poles there was further emigration. According to the report, the Polish American community in Sweden had better conditions than in any of the other Scandinavian countries. The two main organizations in Norway were the Zjednoczenie Polskie (Polish Union) and the SPK. Unfortunately, a by-the-book adherence to the procedures with regard to escapees made it impossible to extend widespread care over the refugees. This was exacerbated by the indifference of the Norwegian people. In Denmark, which hosted 500 Poles, agents of the Warsaw Communist regime succeeded in destroying the Związek Polaków (Alliance of Poles). This deprived the Poles there, scattered all over that country anyhow, of organizational support, and rendered relief work or legal protection even more difficult. It can be cited as evidence that up to 1948 the Danish government sent escapees back to Soviet-occupied Poland. Only after 1948 was a uniform procedure applied to the escapees. The procedure consisted of sending them out to work on farms until they received their visas to the countries of their final destination. Where emigration to the United States was concerned, the waiting period was two years. Zachariasiewicz proposed a shortening of this period. In Belgium, where 40,000 Poles were located, organizational life was richer. Aside from the Związek Polaków w Belgii (Alliance of Poles in Belgium), there was another organization run by the church, and there were also the Scouts and several other professional organizations, not to mention the SPK. But there was a greater danger than in the previously mentioned countries from the activities of the Communist regime in Warsaw, which, among other forms of persuasion, invited children to the "old country" for vacations, and distributed publications and the Communist government-backed press.

The worst conditions existed in Germany, where about 52,000 Poles were to be found. The standard of living of many of them was well below acceptable norms; moreover, the total included 16,000 women and 10,000 children. An alarming 25 percent of those 52,000 were hard-core cases. The legal status of escapees who had entered Germany prior to 1950 was formalized under 1951 legislation concerning the "legal status of stateless foreigners," and with regard to those who arrived after that date, their status was defined by the Geneva Convention concerning post–1953 refugees. Nonetheless, the situation of the Poles was difficult because, ten years after the end of the war, the standard of living of the German population was much higher than that of the victims of the Nazi regime. It was paradoxical that huge financial resources were invested in the reconstruction of Germany, while the people who had remained loyal to the Allies since the very beginning of the war continued to live in refugee camps. The conditions of camp life brought on a higher rate of disease and subsequently made emigration impossible. Children, less resistant to disease than adults, were especially affected. Direct financial and material assistance in the form of parcels, medicines, clothes, paid vacations for children, and similar items could have played an enormous role in ameliorating the situation. On the basis of these observations, Zachariasiewicz concluded that a specialized organization for this territory would be useful. The presence of the Związek Polaków w Niemczech (Alliance of Poles in Germany) was a good thing, but due to a lack of funds it was unable to handle the problems. The cooperation of an external agency was needed. Additional relief could be rendered through a less rigorous application of health requirements, a speedier visa process, and an individual approach to each case. In other words, the report proposed to abandon the practice of condemning an entire family to further stagnation in the camps because of the illness of one member or due to a misdemeanor charge against another. The situation in Austria was similar in that its camps still held about 2,500 Polish refugees. There were 10 camps there in 1955. The Związek

Polaków w Austrii (Association of Poles in Austria), to which a representative was delegated from every camp with resident Poles, looked after the interests of the Polish refugees. The sanitary and material situation was better because first-class work was carried on in this region by the YMCA in cooperation with USEP Projects. The flip side of the coin was Austria's continuing sensitivity to pressures from Moscow, as the USSR did not remove its armed forces from that country until May 1955. That is the date from which the postwar independence of Austria began. Another problem was the departure of international organizations in order to preserve Austria's neutrality, which gave the refugee population further reason for anxiety.

In Italy, where the problem was small numerically, the SPK played a large role because most of the Polish refugees there were soldiers. A big plus for the Poles was the presence of a Polish Embassy of the Polish Government in Exile to the Holy See and the presence of a seminary with a large percentage of Poles. Rome also had its SPK branch. Further, a group of intellectuals there influenced the life of the refugees through such means as lectures unmasking the essence of the Communist system based on the example of living conditions behind the Iron Curtain.

France differed, among other ways, in that the majority of Poles had emigrated to that country prior to World War II. Another characteristic of that community was that a significant portion of it looked for ways to assimilate. For this reason, many fewer Poles there were open to further emigration. On the other hand, infiltration by the Warsaw regime was strongest in France. The report informed that "Although France is the place where NATO has its headquarters, it would seem that in the field of psychological warfare the adverse side has its headquarters here."[14]

Further on in the report, Zachariasiewicz noted that Warsaw was spending $8,500 per day on subversive activity among the Polish community in France! Contributing to this situation was the fact that Polish organizations were particularly underfunded, including the Centralny Związek Polaków we Francji (Central Alliance of Poles in France), and that the periodical *Narodowiec*, with a circulation of 32,000 was engaged in subversive activity. Low wages even caused several hundred agricultural laborers to return to Poland in the spring of 1955. Each of them was promised 10 hectares (about 25 acres) and several domestic animals.

The conclusions of the report's author focused on the need to facilitate political asylum or other legalization of status for escapees from the Soviet bloc, including, of course, the Poles. A second proposal was to raise the health standards and to disregard minor offenses. Zachariasiewicz called for further work to support refugee communities morally, politically, and financially. This might be done by creating closer contacts with the Polish American community; by better financial support of the press, organizations, and cultural institutions; and by the cooperation of the Committee for a Free Europe and other bodies to strengthen an exchange of ideas and mutual contacts.

A salient aspect of this report was its scope. It touched equally on the refugee situation and on the general picture of émigré community life in several European nations. This was an expansive approach, suggesting the larger scope of the mission, and also the preparation of ground for an organizational presence of the PAIRC in Western Europe. The report's conclusions had considerable impact on the direction of the Committee's efforts with regard to Poles in Germany, where the situation was the most difficult. This bore fruit with a larger portion of charitable work going to the refugees in Germany within the general framework of the Committee's activities. Finally, it enabled an independent assessment of the phenomena occurring there. One of the report's recommendations was more frequent visits to refugee centers. The report was, in fact, a signal of the approaching new phase in the work of the New York Committee.[15]

VII

The Conclusion of the First Phase of Activity: A Summation of the Years 1947–1958

The year 1957 marked the tenth anniversary of the founding of the PAIRC. A ceremonial annual meeting took place on this occasion at the Kosciuszko Foundation in Manhattan. This gathering gave the opportunity for a more general summation of achievements, expressions of gratitude to the board, the staff, and the volunteers for 29,000 entry visas, which changed the lives of Poles handicapped by war, persecution, and poverty. Recognition for the Committee came in the form of congratulatory telegrams from senators, congressmen, New York Governor Averell Harriman, New York City Mayor Robert Wagner, and Polish and American clergy, as well as from several organizations engaged in improving the fate of the Committee's wards. Appreciation also came from the headquarters of the Polish Veterans of World War II — SPK in London, the Union of Poles in Germany, the Council of Polish Refugees in Sweden, Archbishop Józef Gawlina in Rome, and the Polish American Congress in Chicago. A new board was elected. The Rev. Burant once again became the president, and the vice presidents were: Zofia Dattner, Henryk Korab-Janiewicz, Antoni Gordon (an industrialist), S. Obremski, and Florentyna Jarzębowska (cohost with her husband of a Polish-language radio program). W. Zachariasiewicz became the executive secretary, Feliks Popławski was elected treasurer, Edward Witanowski became the financial secretary, and Tadeusz Sztybel became the secretary. Janina Węgrzynek retained her post as head of the finance committee. Franciszek Proch, a former inmate of the Dachau concentration camp, who later became the executive director of the Committee, joined the Advisory Council. Stanisław Gierat continued as a member of the council.[1]

In the period up to 1957, the Committee had obtained assurances for 20,889 refugees in Germany and Italy, for 5,874 veterans of the Polish armed forces in Great Britain, and for 2,150 Polish refugees in other NATO countries and Sweden. In addition, the Committee was able to secure affidavits for 1,109 Poles scattered across other nations.[2]

The tenth anniversary also became an opportunity for The Rev. Burant to prepare a retrospective report, titled "In Search of Milestones," in which he summarized the achievements and highlighted the needs for continuing the mission. The value of this document was all the greater as it came from the founder of the Committee and the main guide of its work, who decided all the key moves. The report, in various, often shortened, forms, was reprinted in the press and in the Committee's publications. Burant began with a quotation from an appeal by New York's Francis Cardinal Spellman of May 6, 1957, in order to drive home the need for continuing the work:

> My voice comes to you this day as an echo of the prayers and pleas of anguished millions throughout the world. Greater in number than ever before, the afflicted of the earth—the homeless, sick, starving and destitute of Europe, Asia, the Near, and Far East—beg our help in their unbounded misery.... We cannot resurrect the dead, but we can resurrect hope in the despairing hearts of enslaved millions.

In the next part, the Committee's president analyzed the passing decade from the point of view of accomplishments in the area of humanitarian and moral aid, and also from the political perspective. He noted that the Committee was founded on and guided by the principles of Christian charity, which enjoins help for the needy. Another principle was action arising from national pride as understood in the American tradition of an open-door policy for the needy of the whole world. This attitude is best reflected in the inscription at the entrance to the Statue of Liberty, which speaks of taking in the hungry and the homeless. For many Poles, as victims of war, the Committee became that kind of hope. In a subsequent part, The Rev. Burant noted the organization's goals and its work conditions, emphasizing the great dedication of the staff, the volunteers and the entire Polish American community: "To me, one affidavit, one assurance and what it meant to a Polish family, what it meant in moral terms in the life of our communities and families here, is the criterion for evaluating these ten years of our efforts...."[3]

In a further section he stated that not all of the effort could be measured with numbers. One of the Committee's most noble tasks was to protect or restore the human dignity of the victims of persecution or war. Only sensitivity born of the Articles of Faith could fulfill this sort of assignment. Still another part of the Committee's mission was to represent Poland:

> The homeless Pole arriving here knows that he has no government and no country of his own to protect him. Washington and the United Nations recognize representatives of Poland who are his enemies, whose enemy he is. He is not only homeless — he is also stateless. We are his Poland, we are his representative and protector, who speaks for him.[4]

Nothing better illustrates The Rev. Burant's thesis than the fate of Marian Sykurski, the heroic 14-year-old fighter in the 1944 Warsaw Uprising against the Nazis. At the beginning of the uprising, Sykurski volunteered for courier duty in the Polish Home Army. He penetrated into various parts of the city with dispatches while under constant enemy fire. He had to overcome not only natural obstacles, but also the whole crosshatch of battle stations occupied either by the Polish fighters or the Germans. It was an extraordinarily dangerous job, which made him a permanent invalid. Both his hands had to be amputated as a result of his wounds, and of gangrene that spread before first aid was able to reach him. But Sykurski did not become despondent. He survived the war, completed a university degree in foreign trade, and learned four foreign languages. He wanted to serve society. Unfortunately, the society was not free, which was enough for a young man with his load of experience to decide to flee Poland. He made his decision in June 1956 without any guarantee that he would be able to find employment. The American authorities in Germany, especially the United States Escapee Program (USEP) took care of him very cordially. He was placed in a hospital, received medical attention, and also orthopedic care and moral support. But his chances for further emigration were next to zero. Sykurski qualified as a hardcore case, condemned to years of stagnation on scant social services as the only form of support to cover his daily needs. There is no doubt that even with the highest professional qualifications, Sykurski's eventual employment depended on the employer's good will. At this very moment PAIRC arrived on the scene, and through its representative in Germany began efforts to secure Sykurski's emigration to the United States. The Committee devoted two years of work to his case. First, admission was obtained for him to the Institute of Physical Medicine and Rehabilitation of New York University at Bellevue Medical Center in New York City, where he came under the direct care of world-famous specialist Dr. Howard Rusk. The general cost of the treatment was estimated at $3,000, a sizable sum in those days. One of the results of the treatment was new, more effective prosthesis. The Committee assumed the responsibility of providing the necessary guarantees, and presented the State Department with a specific rehabilitation plan. On this basis, the INS waived the high bond requirement, which allowed him to come quickly to the United States. The airplane with the Polish freedom fighter on board landed at New York's Idlewild (now Kennedy) Airport on April 22, 1958. Representatives of the Committee were waiting for the refugee, as was his plan of treatment. Thanks to an appropriate promotional campaign the Polish American community was able to prepare itself for the arrival of this exceptional immigrant.

No doubt Monsignor Burant had this kind of case in mind when he spoke of the great value of rendering aid to the individual refugee in need, and of how essential the Committee's role was in standing in for agencies of the Polish state with regard to those who had escaped from Communist Poland, or to those who were stateless because they had been living in DP camps since the conclusion of the war.[5]

Aside from spectacular work of the kind described above, the Committee performed a series of routine tasks, especially with regard to those who had relatives outside the Iron Curtain. Searching for families, relatives, and acquaintances scattered by war or separated by political borders was a time-consuming and thankless job. It required voluminous correspondence with international or private agencies, beginning with the Red Cross, and ending with Polish parishes in various corners of the world. This work brought tangible results.

Another, less well-known aspect of the Committee's efforts was help for Poles in Poland, who, as a result of the Twentieth Congress of the Union of Polish Workers' Parties in 1956 and of the progressing thaw, were freed from gulags and places of forced settlement, and subsequently sent back from Russia to Communist Poland. That especially hard-hit group required immediate material assistance. Monsignor Burant made fund appeals through the radio and the press on behalf of these people. In four weeks $9,000 was collected. All told, the primate of Poland, Stefan Cardinal Wyszyński, who himself had been released from prison somewhat earlier, received $81,757 for this purpose. The distribution of these funds was to take place through the primate's secretariat in Warsaw. Cardinal Wyszyński acknowledged the receipt of this sum with a telegram on April 17, 1957, addressed to the Committee.[6]

Outside observers noted the metamorphosis of the Polish American Immigration and Relief Committee from an emergency squad to an organization rendering organized social assistance. This resulted from excellent internal organization and the ability to adjust to the changing work conditions, both in the United States and in the world. These factors were not reflected in the statistics. The crowning point of the ample report presented by the Rev. Burant was the belief that the Committee's mission was not over, that it ought to be continued so long as there are escapees, homeless, and seekers in the world, and so long as political conditions force people to escape to freedom.[7]

The Rev. Burant's appeal regarding the latter point was in reply to the voices that appeared here and there, saying that after October 1956 the Committee's role ought to gradually diminish. The extent of political changes in East Europe in the years 1956–1958 altered the Committee's perspective and work conditions. The subsiding of political terror and the abandonment of the worst practices of the Stalinist period brought, among other things, the removal of a series of restrictions in the obtaining of passports, in the tourist trade, and with regard to trips to western nations. This resulted in numerous applications for political asylum after a tourist trip to the United States, or as a result of scientific or sports exchanges. This was, in fact, an entirely new category of people. They differed from the war refugees not only in age and experience, but also in their attitude toward emigration. For the war emigrants, departure from the DP camps to Western nations was an absolute necessity. For the post-1956 escapees, it was a conscious and premeditated decision to forsake property, family, and small material comforts in Poland, in favor of an unknown future in the West. Another factor characterizing this period was the expiration on December 31, 1956, of legislation signed into law by President Eisenhower in August of 1953 that included war emigrants. In September 1957, Public Law 85-136, a new immigration law, went into effect. It concerned escapees from behind the Iron Curtain. Their entry into the United States took place outside of the immigration quota. By the end of 1958, 1,000 such persons arrived in the United States as permanent residents, and another 14,000 applications were waiting to be processed. This was a response to the new challenges of that time, to which the Committee had to adjust. The Committee significantly enlarged the range of its activity. Between June 1, 1957, and the end of December 1958 the PAIRC arranged for affidavits for Polish refugees from the following countries: Argentina — 48, Australia — 5, Austria — 33, Belgium — 110, Brazil — 36, Canada — 21, Denmark — 59, Ecuador — 5, France — 91, Germany — 76, Great Britain — 191, Guatemala — 4, Holland — 25, Italy — 5, Kenya — 3, Lebanon — 4, Morocco — 18, Spain — 5, Sweden — 12, Turkey — 5, Venezuela — 5, Poland — 3 (for family unification), Ireland — 1, Norway — 1, for a total of 764 persons.

In that same period, thanks to the Committee's efforts, these totals of Polish refugees arrived from the following countries: Argentina — 27, Australia — 8, Belgium — 57, Brazil — 3, Ecuador — 3, Canada — 6, Denmark — 27, France — 23, Germany — 3, Great Britain — 73, Holland — 28, Italy — 1, Morocco — 7, Portugal — 1, Sweden — 4, Switzerland — 4, Turkey — 5, Uruguay — 1, and Venezuela — 4.[8]

However, even these figures and their geographical spread did not fully express the scope of the work, because not all efforts were successful and, secondly, the Committee was in the throes of correspondence or of attempts to help in matters that were not within the scope of its basic interests. In many instances, the long waiting period in the country of temporary residence for an INS decision eluded reports and statistics. There was a sizable category of Poles who had come through other channels, who turned to the Committee with job and housing questions when they were already in the United States. Finally, some had come to join families, and, in these cases, the Committee only assisted with the paperwork. Generally speaking, the work in the second half of the 1950s was much more varied and required meeting ever new challenges.

Preserved correspondence excellently expresses the ever-changing horizons of the Committee's work. The following example of gratitude to the Committee from a Pole is very characteristic. A member of the Foreign Legion, he was drawn by fate to Algeria:

> Thank you for such polite and exhaustive advice regarding my emigration.... In my youth destiny dragged me into this exile, which began in Germany and continues, but soon, after completing my 5 year tour of duty, I believe that with your help I will be able to get out of this hell. If you knew my life, you'd be crying, seeing me in this plight. Not having a Father, I take you as my adopted parents.[9]

This confirms that the Committee's work was not limited to Europe. More and more frequently, help was given to Poles who were driven to South America by the winds of war. A larger wave of emigrants, consisting of soldiers from the Polish II Corps (which operated in Italy and the Near East during the war), went to Argentina at the invitation of President Peron in the years immediately after the war. But living conditions in South America did not live up to expectations. The high inflation rate, frequent political revolutions, and a general lack of stability turned the gaze of many freshly minted immigrants toward the United States. The situation of these people was more difficult because many of them tried for a second emigration. This category was not covered by existing American law. The Argentine chapters of writer Witold Gombrowicz's life and the problems connected with them are well known, as are those of the author Florian Czarnyszewicz. The law offices of Dr. Wieniawa-Ślesiński in Buenos Aires served as an informal contact point for immigration matters, and the intermediary was the local chapter of the SPK (Polish Veterans of World War II). Ślesiński was in constant touch with the New York PAIRC, and mediated in the arrangement of work assurances and immigration formalities. In most instances, the only way to leave Argentina was to wait for the immigration quota, which took several years. Finally, in the 1960s, there was a large wave of Poles departing Argentina. Most of them settled in the United States on the basis of the quota. Many of them ended up in Chicago and in the areas surrounding New York City. One of those who made it to New York was the well-known journalist Zdzisław Bau, a correspondent of the Spanish press assigned to the United Nations and also of the Parisian *Kultura* monthly.[10]

There was a similar trend among the Poles in Brazil, some of whom wanted to emigrate to the United States. The best-known representatives here were the poets Jan Lechoń and Kazimierz Wierzyński, the graphic artist Zdzisław Czermański, the miniaturist Zygmunt Sowa-Sowiński, and Tad Szulc, the journalist and author of books on Pope John Paul II and on Chopin. Most of them emigrated to the United States without recourse to refugee legislation. There were even cases of returns to Poland, an example of which was the well-known sculptor August Zamoyski. At any rate, the Polish Brazilian community also knew that it could count on the help of the Committee. Let one of the letters which arrived from Sao Paulo serve as proof:

> On September 3, 1958, the American Consul in Sao Paulo personally informed my husband and me that we have clearance for emigration to the USA. The only missing document to the final resolution of our case is the so-called affidavit of support. He advised me to turn to the Polish American Immigration and Relief Committee with a request to supply the document, and he emphasized that speed is of the essence.[11]

Help for the needy also concerned cases of joining families, as described in the following letter of thanks:

> I want to cordially thank you for the help offered in bringing my son and his family from Germany. Please understand me. I am up in years and my son's arrival in the United States is a support for me in my old age, because I have no family here. Thanks to the Committee's help I firmly believe that I will soon be able to greet my son in the free land of Washington. Though my earnings are modest, I will never forget the PAIRC.[12]

As in the cases described above, with the passage of years more and more appeals coming to the PAIRC were on an individual basis. Simply put, the Committee had become well enough known in refugee communities that many people sought the possibility of obtaining affidavits individually. Typical of this category of emigrants was the letter of C.A. Konopacki of London to W. Zachariasiewicz in New York, requesting an employment assurance. The applicant had received his diploma from the Graduate School of Economics in Warsaw in 1935. After the 1939 campaign, he found himself in Lithuania, and after the Sikorski-Majski Pact he joined the army that Polish General Anders was organizing in Russia. After demobilization, he settled in London, finished a professional course and worked in synthetic jewelry. He even opened his own workshop. Unfortunately, the seasonal nature of the work and the lack of better prospects persuaded Konopacki to start fresh, as he put it, in America.[13]

New assignments appeared before the Committee in the period under discussion, including efforts to obtain refugee status from the INS for those who after 1956 jumped ship and demanded political asylum. The INS and its commissioner, General Swing, who was a close friend of President Eisenhower, made obtaining such status difficult, arguing in favor of political change in Central Europe. Among widely publicized cases was that of Ryszard Eibel, a Polish sailor. On July 24, 1958, he disembarked from his ship in New York Harbor, went to the offices of *Nowy Świat*, and requested political asylum. From there, he was directed to the PAIRC. There, without warning, while he was talking with W. Zachariasiewicz, two officials of the INS walked in, arrested Eibel, and sent him back to his ship against his will. In response to this raid, the Committee called a press conference, to which correspondents of the biggest papers were invited, including the *New York Times*. The next day an article sympathetic to the case appeared in the *New York Times*, criticizing the methods of the Immigration and Naturalization Service agents. In addition, the Committee alerted congressmen and senators via telegram, and also directed a sharp memo to General Swing, the INS commissioner. It demanded that Eibel be released and interviewed in the presence of a PAIRC representative. The matter created even more of a stir when 60 congressmen joined the fray, sending protests to the INS, and also after the popular radio personality Fulton Lewis, Jr., weighed in on the issue during his daily radio program. As a result of this crusade, the well-known American attorney Tenze arrived in the Committee's offices and offered his services *gratis* in the Eibel case. The many-sided pressure forced the crew of his ship to release Eibel, after which he was interviewed. In time, he received permission for permanent residence. Soon thereafter Eibel began studying at one of the local universities.[14]

This case was important because, on the one hand, it illustrated the continuing refugee problem so long as the Communists remained in power in Poland, and, on the other hand, it pointed up the presence in American politics, especially after 1956, of a clear tendency to normalize relations with Warsaw. For these reasons the Committee's role remained important, especially in its stewardship of political refugee matters, and also for the "old country," whose citizens saw in this institution a pledge of help that could be counted on.

The Committee's work was never devoid of political accents, and not only for the above-detailed reasons. As the wave of escapees from behind the Iron Curtain grew, the Committee became a spokesman and protector of the opponents of the Polish Communist government. And that is how it was perceived. With regard to the American authorities, it served as a transmission belt in matters of defense of human rights, and as an essential element in relief work on behalf of escapees from Communist Poland. One might conclude that as normalization progressed after 1956, the Committee's political task kept growing, especially since the amount of assistance available for war refugees kept diminishing in favor of the newer — political — refugees. The Committee was widely recognized as an opponent of the Communist system.

VIII
Enlarging the Scope of Operations: The Field Offices

Field offices of the Committee became necessary beginning in the initial phase, when the resettlement of arriving refugees and the gathering of affidavits of support proved to be impossible without help from the resettlement destination points. At first, Polish parishes extended a helping hand. However, many tasks were time-consuming and could not be properly performed without the construction of a field organization. The report of the Committee's executive secretary for the period June 1, 1957, to December 1, 1958, referred to such a need. First, the fact that the Committee was accredited by the State Department gave it the right to coordinate refugee activities. Second, the issues piloted by the Committee concerned the entire Polish American community, and, therefore, also larger and smaller concentrations of the community beyond the East Coast, which up to that time had borne the brunt of the responsibility. The Committee's board felt that all possible groupings of Polish Americans ought to be activated. Some of them had hastened to help already. Aside from organizations mentioned before, many others developed efforts on behalf of the Committee, becoming *de facto* surrogates for local branch offices of the PAIRC. For example, Stowarzyszenie Uchodźców z Albany (The Association of Refugees from Albany in the State of New York), Stowarzyszenie Polskich Kombatantów (The Polish Veterans of World War II — SPK — sometimes referred to in this text simply as SPK) chapters in Elizabeth, Newark, and Plainfield, New Jersey, and the Klub Weteranów im. Józefa Piłsudskiego (the Józef Piłsudski Veterans' Club) in Elizabeth held a picnic on September 7, 1958, in Avenel, New Jersey, from which the entire revenue of about $500 was forwarded to the Committee.[1]

Sometimes events organized for a completely different purpose generated revenue on behalf of the PAIRC. For instance the Reduta Choir, which was an activity of Nest 281 of the Polish Falcons in Plainfield, New Jersey, organized a charity ball on January 10, 1959, and 50 percent of the profit was sent to the Committee in New York.[2]

PAIRC headquarters made it plain that one of the main premises for organizing field offices was the organization of financial support in the field. In connection with this, Msgr. Burant personally got in touch with potential organizers of the Committee's field offices. To this end, he visited several centers and carried on a vigorous correspondence. One of the first to get established was the PAIRC's field office in Buffalo. An orientation meeting of 13 persons took place at the Polanie Club on March 8, 1958. Several well-known figures arrived for the meeting. They included Wanda Kogut, the wife of one of the most prominent activists in the Komitet Narodowy Amerykanów Polskiego Pochodzenia (National Committee of Americans of Polish Descent); the Reverend Peter Adamski of St. Stanislaus Parish; Zbigniew Piątek, the director of the Polish Scouts; Władysław Sułkowski, the president of the local chapter of the SPK; Władysław Chrzanowski, the president of the Koło Lotników (Polish Airmen's Association); and Kazimierz Jankowski, the president of the Polanie Club. Aside from Kogut and Piątek, the other individuals did not participate actively. Most of the work fell on the shoulders of the long-standing president, the Reverend Max T. Bogacki of St. Adalbertus Basilica Church, who was assisted by John Umiński (whose day job was with the Niagara Frontier Port Authority), and by Barbara Wysocka and Wanda Kogut. The PAIRC Buffalo Chapter, as it was called after 1958, tried to obtain affidavits of support and funds. The offices of the chapter were located at 1210 Broadway. On January 9, 1961, at the conclusion of the World Year of the Refugee proclaimed by the United Nations, the New York Committee acknowledged receipt of $150 collected in Buffalo. This donation was the result of a radio fund drive and the proceeds of a dance at the Polanie Club. These were typical fund collection methods used outside the New York metropolitan area. Unfortunately, the declaration of the Buffalo region as a federal economic disaster zone in 1960 did not make it possible to get work assurances for Poles arriving from Europe. The chapter's activity was also undermined by internal squabbles and an inability to get the support of the local Polish American community. Attempts to hold an annual ball for the benefit of the Committee were unsuccessful, as were collections outside churches, which had worked well in other areas. The one and only banquet to benefit the Committee took place on May 9, 1959, at the Statler Hilton Hotel in Buffalo. The Buffalo Chapter closed shop in 1967.[3]

Another chapter was established in Ohio. On May 5, 1958, Monsignor Burant wrote to Polish American activist J. Bogdanowicz of Cleveland:

VIII — *Enlarging the Scope: The Field Offices* 105

In connection with the total withdrawal of American Relief for Poland from refugee work and our Committee's assumption of all responsibility for immigration and relief work in line, anyhow, with the Committee's resolution, we have to gradually organize cells of the Committee in all the states. Over the last 10 years the ARP had 20 chapters, which supported the work to a greater or lesser extent. It would be both unwarranted and would diminish all possibilities of action, if the responsibility for this work were to rest exclusively with the New York metropolitan region. We are taking our first steps in Buffalo, where the organizing meeting of the PAIRC Chapter will take place on the 12th. A similar meeting will take place in Detroit on May 14th. The foundation has been well laid in both cities. We have decided on Cleveland as the subsequent site."[4]

The Cleveland chapter was established on May 15, 1958. Those who took part in establishing it and in its further work included: Zygmunt Zakrzewski, the president of Związek Polaków w Ameryce (Alliance of Poles of America); B. Jaroszewski, the president of Zjednoczenie Polskie w Ameryce (Union of Poles in America); Zygmunt Dybowski, owner of *Wiadomości Codzienne* (*Daily News*); and Franciszka Tesny, who was the head of Stowarzyszenie Polek w Stanach Zjednoczonych (Association of Polish Women of the U.S.). In the end, it was Tesny who became the head of the PAIRC chapter in Cleveland. Its offices were located at 75–32 Broadway. The last letter is dated April 24, 1968.[5] The chapter's main assignment was to raise funds for the Committee's work. This was done through fund drives.

The Detroit chapter was active from May 1958 under the leadership of Judge Benjamin C. Stańczyk. The first vice president was Julia Rooks, president of the Hamtramck Common Council, the second vice president was Assistant Wayne County Prosecutor Carl Ziemba. Bogdan Bereźnicki, a World War II veteran, was the secretary, Jerry Brzeźnicki held the treasurer's post, and John Pela, the district commandant of the SWAP (Polish Army Veterans Association of America) in Michigan was the director.[6]

In those days Detroit was a dynamic center, which kept in close touch with the PAIRC even before a chapter was officially established there. A moving example of care for fellow sufferers was a letter from the Stowarzyszenie Byłych Więźniów Politycznych Niemieckich i Sowieckich Obozów Koncentracyjnych (Polish Association of Former Political Prisoners in Soviet and Nazi Concentration Camps). In its letter to the PAIRC of September 3, 1957, the association inquired about the possibility of financing a certain number of CARE packages through the PAIRC for the sick and for those unable to work in Germany. The relationship was the result of direct contact of former prisoners with President Franciszek Proch, who was active in that group and was also a member of the PAIRC in New York since 1949. Several other organizations were active in the Michigan chapter. Of donations, so crucial to the overall work of the Committee, one ought to mention $1,000 which was sent to New York by the Detroit chapter in 1964.[7]

The largest field chapter of the PAIRC was, assuredly, in Chicago. As noted earlier, the Polish American Congress at its Philadelphia convention in 1948 had established a Refugee Committee, with offices in Chicago run by Wanda Rozmarek, the wife of the PAC's president. Its work paralleled that of the committee in New York. Almost simultaneously, there appeared the need to widen the scope of care for the new generation of refugees, this time from Communist Poland. In the meantime, that is, from 1948 on, the stature and significance of the PAIRC grew enough so that the idea matured in Chicago to establish a chapter of this organization in place of the existing committee. In 1958, Msgr. Burant had probed the possibility of organizing a Chicago chapter in a letter to Judge Thaddeus Adesko, a well-known activist of the Polish American community there. The letter said:

"Even though you haven't heard from us for some time, nonetheless the fact that we do not have an official presence in the largest Polish American community does not give us any peace. Organizational satisfaction or prestige is not at issue here, rather, it is a necessity. After the American Relief

A group of new immigrants, recently arrived in Chicago, with representatives of the PAIRC on June 29, 1961. *Seated, from the left*: Vice President Edward Matuga (an attorney and a delegate of the Central Board of Polish Supplementary Schools), Vice President Edward Pankowiak (president of the Clubs of Little Poland), Anna Migoń, Władysław Zachariasiewicz, Vice President Jadwiga Bielański (president of the Second District of the Falcons), Kazimierz Łukomski (president of the New Emigration Self-Help Society). *Standing, fourth from the left* is Gertruda Drozdowicz (treasurer of the Second District of the Falcons). Behind her is Kazimierz Lenard, the chairman of the Benefit Ball in 1961.

First meeting of the PAIRC chapter in Chicago. *Standing, from the left*: Czester Rzepecki, Edmund Nowak, Maria Kocjan, Edward Pankowiak, Henry Skrzypczynski, Antoni Tyme, Władysława Chałko, Helen Kepa, J. Tyma, Feliks Basista. *Seated, from the left*: Attorney Edward Matuga, vice president; Attorney Marilyn Rozmarek-Komosa, vice president; Jerzy Zaleski, vice president; Anna Migoń, executive vice president; Judge Thaddeus V. Adesko, president; Edward Palewicz, treasurer; Rev. Jan Malinowski, secretary.

for Poland backed out of immigration and relief work with refugees, the whole burden of continuing this very important work fell on our shoulders. At the present — out of necessity — we are the only Polish American organization doing this work. Also, our Committee is the only organization accredited by the State Department to carry on these kinds of assignments.... In fulfilling our mission, of helping refugees in the name of the entire Polish American community, we have to count on the cooperation of all the larger Polish agglomerations. Just because New York has a port and airports through which almost all the immigrants pass who come to this country, placing the heaviest burden on New York, does not mean that other Polish American communities should not participate proportionately in this assignment."

In a later part of the letter, Msgr. Burant announced the arrival in Chicago of Committee representative W. Zachariasiewicz.[8]

More than a year passed from the letter to the establishment of the chapter. After several months of consultations and preparations, the first meeting was called for January 22, 1960, in the office of Judge Thaddeus V. Adesko. He was elected president of the PAIRC chapter in Chicago, and Anna Migoń became the executive vice president.

The first meeting of the board was held on March 20 of that year. A multitude of organizations, a huge concentration of Polish Americans, the presence of the Polish American media, and, finally, the support of congressmen of Polish descent indicated a favorable future for the new initiative in

Chicago. Many organizations, either through their individual members or as a whole, participated in the work and supported the chapter financially. On the day of that first board meeting, the Legion Młodych Polek (Legion of Young Polish Women), which had been chaired by Anna Migoń, gave a check for $2,000 for aid in Europe. The whole amount was forwarded to the head office in New York.

The first fund drive was held in May and June of that year and resulted in a collection of close to $1,000. A banquet was held on December 4, 1960, at the Sherman Hotel, from which the profit of over $700 was earmarked for the Annual Christmas Program for Poles in Western Europe. Among individual donations, T. Adesko's initiative is worthy of mention. He established a permanent refugee fund and gave the first $100. The PNA, the PRCUA and their many groups and districts, the Liga Morska (Polish Sea League of America), and several other smaller organizations donated to the refugee cause. The Chicago chapter tried to forward at least $1,000 annually to the headquarters. That was true for 1963 and also for subsequent years.[9]

The residents of Chicago offered enormous, often incalculable help by giving job assurances, apartments for the immigrants, and space for organizational needs. The chapter tried to advertise its presence broadly on Chicago's Polish American map. Just a few weeks after its founding, the chapter took advantage of the annual May 3rd Parade. The presence of Robert Lewandowski, the popular host of Polish radio and television shows, opened the door to both radio and television. *Dziennik Związkowy* (The Alliance Daily) and other papers regularly printed information, appeals, and reports from the Chicago chapter and the New York headquarters. There was also significant support from congressmen, including Dan Rostenkowski, Roman Puciński, Edward J. Derwiński, and John Kluczyński. Many of the veterans' groups also lent a helping hand, including chapters of the First Armored Division of General Maczek, and the Fifth Kresowa (Eastern Borderlands) Division, as well as chapters of the SWAP (Polish Army Veterans Association of America) and SPK (Polish Veterans of World War II). Among the most active members of the PAIRC's Chicago chapter were Dr. Edward Różański, Wanda Harcaj (the wife of Colonel Harcaj of the Polish Army, an activist connected with the "Zamek" political group in London), Krystyna Litwińska, Zbigniew Radoniewicz, Piotr Inglot, Lt. Col. Jan Jurewicz, Dr. Feliks Krzan, Maria Kowalska, Mr. and Mrs. S. and J. Chęciński, attorney Stanley Kusper, Walter Kozioł, Karol Poprzęcki, Helena Szymanowicz, Julian Piech, Czesław Żyro, Chester Sawko, Wacław and Zbigniew Skonieczny, Jerzy Frąckowiak, Chester Maziarz, Aleksandra Rygiel, John Cielak, Stanisław Dzwoniarek, Edward Chwastek, Bohdan

Grzybowski and many others. It would be virtually impossible to mention all those who helped with housing and job guarantees for the new arrivals.

The Chicago chapter held an annual ball and organized fund drives, and it stepped up its activity even more during the 20th anniversary year of the PAIRC.[10] In 1967, a kickoff party and a Christmas Appeal were organized. It was characteristic of this chapter that it tried to budget at least half of its funds for local needs. The chapter became considerably more active after the declaration of martial law in Poland in 1981, and it lasted until 1992. In this period the expense of resettling the newcomers was almost completely covered by the PAIRC's New York office.

The New Jersey chapter was important because of its geographical proximity to the head office in New York and because of its ability to closely coordinate a number of activities. It was founded in 1962, but the groundwork was laid well before then. The report of the PAIRC's executive secretary for the period from June 1, 1957, to December 1, 1958, informed that a Polish Day of the Polish American Immigration and Relief Committee had been organized in Jersey City by Tadeusz Giergielewicz.[11]

Marian Święcicki, who lived in Dunellen, New Jersey, was the major force in the chapter after 1962. The chapter took advantage of the many events, and even of the vacation time of the residents of its own state, and of the Polish American community in New York, to fundraise on behalf of the PAIRC. One of Zachariasiewicz's letters to Święcicki gives an excellent idea of the atmosphere, using Yonkers in the state of New York as an example:

> Last Saturday I attended a meeting of our Yonkers Chapter which, I might note, I nursed from the cradle and that is why I did not want to say "no" to their invitation.... That small group of simple people in the last three years has collected at least $2,000 for the Committee (which included a Church collection of $700). The meeting was connected with the conclusion of a lottery which they had been conducting for the last two months. They printed 500 booklets at $1 each and, believe it or not, they sold 438 of them!! Aside from the cost of printing the booklets they had no other expense! They got all the prizes for free from various people in Yonkers.[12]

The letter illustrates how much depended on the creativity and commitment of the people doing the field work. In 1962, the New Jersey chapter was able to organize a banquet in Newark (with a profit of $607.86) and to engage itself in the events of other organizations that took place at the Falcons' picnic area in Sommerville or in other areas. For instance, the Polish Immigration Committee Day in Budd Lake, New Jersey, in 1963 netted $479.26, and a year later took in $512.80. In 1963, the sum of $1,052.21 was collected at the Falcons' picnic area in Sommerville, and $840.51 was gathered in 1964.[13]

Collections were also frequently taken up in front of churches, with especially good results in Elizabeth, where Rev. Smoleń was the pastor. The activity of the Polish American communities in this state was big enough to warrant the formation of several additional outposts in the bigger urban Polish American communities. The Jersey City chapter, founded in 1968, held dances, film showings, and even organized an advice and employment service. Another chapter was organized in Middlesex County, New Jersey, and was responsible for the annual carnival and the spring ball (called the "Green Ball") with part of the proceeds going to the headquarters in New York. Easter appeals were also held, as well as various other onetime events. According to the report for 1967–1968, there were also chapters in the making in Newark-Irvington, Trenton, and Paterson, New Jersey.[14]

Several events were held simultaneously on the Committee's 20th anniversary. During a Committee Day on July 30, 1967, $1,167.75 was collected in Rahway, and on September 1 $371.33 was gathered in Sommerville. On September 21, 1967, there was another anniversary event, a banquet, in Paterson, which was repeated a year later in the Alexander Hamilton Hotel. A banquet and a Polish Immigration Committee Day (July 28, 1968) were also held in Rahway that same year. From the incomplete list of events that can be reconstructed from archival documents, the following also ought to be mentioned: Polish Immigration Committee Day in Perth Amboy on July 19, 1970; PAIRC Day and a September Ball in the same town on August 27, and September 28, 1972, respectively; and a Carnival Ball of the Zjednoczenie Polaków w Ameryce (United Poles in America — UPA) in Perth Amboy to benefit the Committee on January 27, 1973. Moreover, there was a PAIRC Day on July 30, 1972, at the Falcons' picnic area in Sommerville, which was organized regularly with the United Poles in America.

The picnic area of the Związek Narodowy Polski (Polish National Alliance) at Budd Lake, New Jersey was the regular site of PAIRC Days and other events to benefit the Committee. There was a PAIRC Day on June 21, 1969. Another Sunday meeting place was the Morskie Oko (Mountain Lake) picnic area, where one of the events benefiting the Committee was held in 1972. Another one at the same location was planned for September 9, 1973; other events were held in Sommerville on July 29, 1973, and at Perth Amboy on July 1 of the same year. The United Poles in America did a lot to assist in organizing the above-mentioned events:

> The UPA, as it is known for short, is of significant help to the Committee both financially (it organizes income-producing events) and in resettling refugees in this region. It often assumes the Committee's financial commit-

ments, paying for the apartment, granting loans and finding jobs. The Union's loan office has helped quite a few of our refugees in their initial difficulties.[15]

Hieronim Wyszyński played an important role there. The activity of the sympathizers and co-workers of the Committee in New Jersey was undoubtedly without parallel in all of America.

The Yonkers chapter, Komitet Niesienia Pomocy Uchodźcom Polskim w Yonkers (The Committee to Aid Polish Refugees in Yonkers), was founded in 1960, and began vigorous activity almost immediately. Fortunately for this chapter, Msgr. Vincent Raith became its great promoter from the start. He not only permitted frequent collections in front of St. Casimir's Parish, but also mobilized organizations concentrated around the church, as well as the wealthier parishioners, to help the refugees. One of the first collections in 1960 brought $630.82, another one netted $765.82, and they were designated for financing special Refugees' Year projects, especially for the so-called hard-core cases. The Refugees' Year lasted from July 1, 1959, to June 30, 1960, and helped inform a broad spectrum of American society about the importance of the issue. It also made fund-raising easier.

Alongside Honorary President Monsignor Vincent Raith, others who were active in the Yonkers chapter included: Polish National Alliance activist Franciszek Dombek (who was the chapter president from 1960 to 1962); Kazimierz Polak, secretary and then president from 1963 on; and W. Dziuban, treasurer. Jan Klamka, an active member of the Society of St. Adalbert (which counted many postwar emigrants in its ranks) became chapter president in 1962. In addition to the Society, the following organizations were helpful to the Yonkers chapter: the local post of the SWAP (Polish Army Veterans Association of America) and the Towarzystwo Dobroczynne Pań Polskich (Charitable Society of Polish Women). The Polish Community Center on Waverly Street was the site of the chapter's home office.[16]

The Connecticut chapter, headquartered in Hartford, developed its work much later than the others; nonetheless, it carried on exceptionally dynamic and successful work to improve the Committee's financial situation. The chapter's members personally distributed subscription letters, which they then collected together with donation commitments. The total amount collected was sent to New York. The following fragment was found in the PAIRC's report for the year 1964–1965:

> The annual Polish American Ball organized by friends of our Committee at the exclusive Hartford Club in Hartford, Connecticut was an exceptionally successful affair, both socially and financially. The Ball netted more money on behalf of the Committee than in the prior year. Assistance for

our Committee in Connecticut is not diminishing. We continue to get funds from there twice a year, during the summer from the Polish Immigration Committee Day event, and in the winter from the annual ball. Both events are organized by friends of our Committee who belong to the Polonia Society, with members from the new emigration who are cooperating with the Polish American community that had settled here some time before. As is well known the Reverend Marian Karwacki is the President of our Chapter in Connecticut, and he is currently the Pastor of the Polish parish in Waterbury.[17]

The Hartford ball netted $490.12 in 1963 and $608.30 in 1964. In 1967 the proceeds brought $1,263.51. There also were other Polish American communities active in Connecticut. In 1963 the Polish Immigration Committee Day in New Britain collected $2,200, and in 1964, $2,000. Also, $2,500 was collected in 1967 for the central office in New York at the Polish Falcons' picnic area in New Britain.

The Committee had the cooperation of several companies in that state, which employed immigrants, provided assurances, and individually donated funds to the Committee. The most committed was the Budny family factory.[18] According to people employed there, its owner provided several thousand job assurances.[19] Not all of them were connected with the Committee, however.

The above-mentioned types of fund-raising proved to be long-lived. The Polish Immigration Committee Day became a permanent annual event in various Polish American communities in Connecticut. A successive event of this type took place in New Britain on July 30, 1967. On August 25, 1969, and on August 16, 1970, a Committee Day was organized at the Falcons' picnic area in Middletown, Connecticut. The same was true of the Polish American Ball, which regularly netted about $1,000 for the Committee's needs. The ball held on February 10, 1968, brought in a similar amount; and on February 23, 1974, during the ball at the Polish National Home at Pulaski Plaza in Hartford, $972 was collected for the Committee. On May 11 of the same year, a Spring Ball was held that netted $506.50. That money was also forwarded to the headquarters in New York. In 1973 there was yet another PAIRC Day in Connecticut, which was also profitable. There was a change in the political situation in Poland in those years, and there were greater difficulties in getting people to donate for immigration purposes in the 1970s. Nonetheless, the example of Connecticut indicates that despite resistance, the efforts did pay off. The most important activists next to Rev. Karwacki in that region were Wincenty Kiejna and his wife, and also Lucjan Daum and Feliks Urbaniak.[20]

A chapter of the PAIRC was also organized in Springfield, Massachusetts, on March 16, 1969. The officers were Piotr Cimmer, president; Stanisław Kwiatkowski, first vice president; Julian Grabowski, second vice president; Jerzy Bayor, treasurer; and Katarzyna Masalska, secretary. B. Węgiel also participated in the Committee's efforts in that state. Wincenty Kiejna of Connecticut played a major role in founding the chapter.[21]

There were active PAIRC chapters in Houston, Texas, headed by Barbara Tomaszewska, and in Milwaukee, Wisconsin, where the most active were Professor F. Świetlik and Emil Pankiewicz, an active member of the SPK (Polish Veterans of World War II — SPK). Chapters also sprang up in Philadelphia, Pennsylvania, where the Polish community was energized by the Reverend Peter J. Klekotka together with Wacław Gawrysiak, and in Los Angeles, California, where the most active member was Hanna Górska.[22]

A few communities active in Canada need to be mentioned as informal Committee outposts. They were unable to establish a PAIRC chapter; nonetheless, they tried to work with the Committee, promoting it and trying to activate the local Polonia (Polish Canadian community) on its behalf. Efforts in Canada on behalf of refugees were favored by large Polonian organizations, including the Canadian branch of the SPK and the Polish Canadian Congress, which in its promotional activity published appeals calling for help for immigrants and for indicated regional parishes, its own chapters, as well as for other organizations that could render aid. In 1960 at the Canadian SPK convention in Montreal, the veterans passed a resolution on the need to help 1,000 Poles from Germany to emigrate. A resolution of this sort was also approved at a Polish Canadian Congress convention that same year. Unfortunately, it was not acted on. The Millennium of Poland's Christianity observations became another opportunity that could have become a good occasion for financial support and for helping a group of Poles from Germany to emigrate to Canada. This project also did not bear fruit.

In 1963, Zachariasiewicz tried to interest Polonian activists in Canada in an idea to organize a local Immigration Committee similar to the one that was functioning in New York. But he found no takers. Over the next several years, the PAIRC maintained contact with successive presidents of the Polish Canadian Congress — T.A. Kołodziejski and then Z. Jarmicki. Ludwik Łubieński, the Committee's delegate for Europe, also appealed to the latter, calling for the establishment of a separate division of the Congress to help the refugees. It was a well-thought-out proposal, prepared by Łubieński on the basis of his personal visits to Polish centers in Canada in 1967. He proposed the founding of an independent organization, connected with the New York Committee only by the identity of the mission. In this matter, both Łubieński and Ignacy Morawski, the PAIRC executive director, wrote to a number of Polonian activists in Canada.[23]

The independence of the new organization was meant to protect the Committee from accusations of draining the Canadian Polonia. Morawski wrote to Colonel Stefan Sznuk in Toronto:

"As to the possibility of organizing an Immigration Committee in Canada, we are aware that it would have to be an independent unit in Canada. We of course are not thinking of stripping the Canadian Polonia of its money on behalf of our Committee. Zachariasiewicz, who continues to be our Vice-President, sees this the same way as you do."[24]

In Toronto, the Committee could count on the support of Tadeusz Krychowski, editor of the SPK's quarterly; on Benedykt Heydenkorn, the editor of *Związkowiec* (*The Alliancer*); and on J. Rusinek, the publisher of *Głos Polski* (*The Polish Voice*), to whom Ignacy Morawski turned for support in establishing a "Komitet Opieki nad Uchodźcami Polskimi" (Relief Committee for Polish Refugees). Contact was also maintained with Colonel M. Sadowski in Toronto. In Ottawa, the Committee could count on Colonel Sznuk to be favorably disposed toward refugee matters. Various forms of relief for the Polish refugees were discussed with him by correspondence. The Committee also found T.Z. Michalski and Adam Synowiecki of Winnipeg, the publisher of *Czas* (*Time*), to be favorably inclined. Representatives of the Polish clergy in Canada also supported the proposal for a new organization. Later on in New York, Janusz Krzyżanowski became the advocate of closer ties with the Canadian Polonia. But he also did not succeed in establishing formal cooperation. The main obstacle was the Canadian Polonians' fear of losing subsidies for local social assistance from the government of the province of Ontario (where the Polish Canadian Congress had its headquarters) if they were to have ties with a foreign institution. According to Krzyżanowski, those fears were unfounded. It was more a matter of the personal ambitions of the Polish Canadian leaders.

Nevertheless, the European branches of the PAIRC helped Polish refugees take care of formalities connected with emigration to Canada. Later on, during a period of intense activity, the Polish Canadian Congress helped through its chapters to obtain the needed documents and to resettle the newcomers within the guidelines set by the Canadian government.

IX

The Branches Abroad

The gradual political changes taking place in Europe after Stalin's death, and simultaneously the numerical decline of the basic group of war refugees whom the three main laws of 1948, 1952, and 1953 applied to, changed the attitude of certain organizations toward their efforts in Western Europe. Not all of them were prepared or interested in taking on the new challenge in the form of relief work on behalf of political refugees, which demanded greater preparation, elasticity, and knowledge of the situation in the countries behind the Iron Curtain. The American Relief for Poland was one of them. Beginning in 1955, it systematically wound down its activity with regard to Polish refugees in Europe. On October 25, 1957, the ARP's office in Salzburg, Austria, was closed; on February 15, 1958, the Paris office met the same fate. In Germany, its offices closed down as follows: Hamburg on August 31, 1957, Munich on February 28, 1958, Frankfurt am Main on July 31, 1958, and Zirndorf-Valka on December 28 of that year. In Italy, the Rome office was closed on March 31, 1958. In Geneva, Switzerland, where the ARP's Western Europe headquarters was located, the door of that office officially closed in June 1958, though operations held on for a while longer. The liquidation of the so-called liaison officers happened almost simultaneously in all of Europe. The officers in Brussels, Copenhagen, Amsterdam, Oslo, and Stockholm were pink-slipped on January 31, 1958, and in Barcelona on April 30, 1958.[1]

Not all organizations shared the ARP's approach to the problem (which in fact did not stop work, it just shifted operations to Poland). The PAIRC was of the opinion that although a certain phase of the issue was coming to a close, the war refugees were being replaced by escapees from nations overrun by the Communists, to whom a helping hand ought to be extended. The government in Washington also maintained the view that activity in this sector must continue. The following fragment was found in the

Committee's report for the years 1957 and 1958, written by W. Zachariasiewicz:

> Already in the prior reporting period, within the framework of our frequent contacts with the Department of State, we were asked discretely several times if we intend to enlarge our activity and get involved more with Polish refugees in Europe. Our answer to all such allusions was very simple. We said very clearly that so long as the ARP exists and is active in Europe — even if not all that successfully — we would in no case want to create a second parallel track. When the State Department again approached us with its proposal in September of last year (i.e. in 1957), when the ARP decided to completely abandon its refugee-immigrant work, we had to give it serious consideration. Authorized by the Committee's President and Board of Directors, I began negotiations in Washington and as their continuation, at the invitation and expense of the State Department, I did a short survey of the major concentrations of the newest refugees in Europe, and in conclusion I signed a contract in Frankfurt between the United States Escapee Program (USEP) and the Polish Immigration and Relief Committee.[2]

Zachariasewicz's tour took him to Frankfurt, where USEP's head offices for Europe were located, and to Geneva, where the ARP's main offices for Europe were situated and were directed by Florian Piskorski, and also where the office of the National Catholic Welfare Conference was located, headed at that time by J. Noris. In addition to those two cities, Zachariasiewicz visited Rome, Munich, Salzburg, Linz, Vienna, Nürnberg, Copenhagen, Brussels, and Paris, where he conferred with representatives of numerous organizations, institutions, and offices, and also with the refugees themselves. Among those the executive director of the PAIRC contacted were: the representative of the United Nations High Commissioner for Refugees, representatives of the Free Europe Citizens' Service, and representatives of the NCWC in each country he visited. The tour gave a comprehensive acquaintance with local conditions and permitted a definition of the scope of needs. Thanks to this, the PAIRC temporarily abandoned the idea of opening offices in Rome and Paris, where there were relatively few refugees, but instead strengthened its presence in Germany and Austria, where the problem was most pressing. The contract between the PAIRC and USEP was good for one year. First, however, the Committee needed to obtain accreditation with the Advisory Committee on Voluntary Foreign Aid in Washington, which placed the Committee in a privileged position with regard to other Polish organizations.

The agreement with USEP allowed for the opening of eight Committee branches in Germany, Austria, and Belgium. The Americans also assumed the financing of these European offices, while the Committee obligated itself to expend $10,000 per year on direct aid. In 1958, the Committee was able to forward $15,200 for direct aid, of which $7,300 went to Germany, $4,350 to Austria, $650 each to Denmark and Belgium, and $750 to France (in support of students). Most of those funds were spent on hard-core cases: seniors, sick people, and children. Of the 50,000 Polish refugees in Germany in 1958, 15,000 were children and another 10,000 were people who either were unable to work or did not qualify for emigration. The measure of the need is well illustrated by a very expressive letter that reached the Committee from Germany in July 1958:

> I recently received a grant, for which I thank you with all my heart, which is of great help to me in my current situation. Because here in this invalid shelter, if you don't have any money, then you have to go hungry, and that has happened to me frequently ... I am a 100 percent invalid and I cannot do any physical work.[3]

An ever-growing percentage of the escapees were young people. They were better educated and conscious of their goals. Many of them had personally experienced Communist terror. Polish students in Vienna also received help from the PAIRC. Their past and their motivation to study are best described by a letter of March 5, 1958, sent to New York with thanks for support. It also illustrates the changing social cross section and the sit-

Left: Czesław Rawski, director of the PAIRC office in Munich in the years 1959–1963, executive director of the PAIRC in New York 1963–1964. *Right:* Ludwik Łubieński, director of the PAIRC for Europe in the years 1961–1968, with headquarters in Munich, Germany.

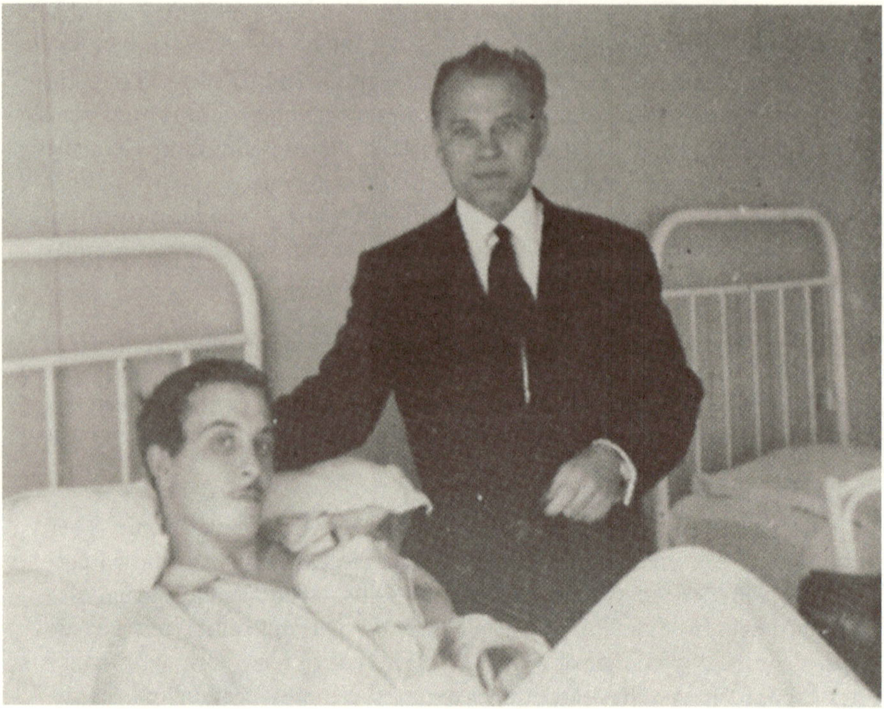

Top: Stanisław Merło, representative of the PAIRC in Belgium in the years 1961–1981. He is visiting a sick refugee in a hospital. *Right:* Witold Zachorski collaborated with the PAIRC in Italy from 1960, and was director of the PAIRC's Rome bureau 1981–1988.

uation of the refugees after the October 1956 breakthrough:

> We were overjoyed and deeply moved at the news of the help provided us by our countrymen in the United States.... Several of us are "alumni" of the Siberian gulags and left our closest relatives behind there, others experienced the hell of Stalinist terror in Poland for personal participation, or for

their parents' participation in the Polish Home Army or other underground organizations fighting for a free Poland, or for the participation of their brothers and fathers in the activity of the Polish Armed Forces in the West.

There are also those among us who, for trying to escape to the Free World, spent several years in prisons or lost their youthful energies and health in the mines — as victims of the Red terror. The others here are Polish university students, who for refusing to spy on their fellow classmates, for participation in anti-Soviet demonstrations, or for membership in the Sodality of the Blessed Virgin Mary even in high school, paid the price by being thrown out of their university under the slightest pretext, and never finished their studies ... and here we received an announcement of steady support to the end of the academic year in the sum of $300 per month. We have already received the February stipend.[4]

In order to deal with student needs, the Committee held a separate fund drive, which netted $3,135.50. In addition to the students in Austria, Polish students in Germany and France also benefited.

Not all the arrivals planned, or even were able to study. The vast majority sought a better life and escape from the terror of the Communist secret services. Part of them escaped under conditions described by a 28-year-old Pole:

At the Munich airport (1962), *from right*: Jan Nowak (Director, the Polish Desk, Radio Free Europe), Archbishop Józef Gawlina — Spiritual Shepherd of the Polish Diaspora, Ludwik Łubieński, Czesław Rawski, and the archbishop's secretary.

After having done a year in jail for political activity, I decided to cross the border on foot through Czechoslovakia into Austria. Without any money, with just a map and a compass, on July 15, 1958, I crossed the Polish border and kept walking, day and night, avoiding villages and towns, for 15 days under difficult conditions, in rain and hunger ... I came to the Czech-Austrian border at night and upon crossing through the barbed wire I tripped an alarm wire, which set off signal lights. I was barely able to hide in a small hay stack, and to sprinkle my footprints with paprika and pepper so the dogs would not get my scent. I lay there for 24 hours, afraid that I might be discovered any minute. The following night I was able to cross the barbed wire, the mine field and two rivers, which separated me from danger and communism, and I became a free man. In Austria, after a few days, I obtained political asylum and immediately began efforts to get to America, having connected with the Polish Immigration Committee in Vienna.[5] (The author clearly meant the PAIRC's field office in Vienna.)

The Committee took over the functions of the ARP in Europe on February 1, 1958. From that date on, one can speak of the permanent, regular work of the Committee in Europe. The main offices for Europe were located in Munich. Naturalized citizens of the United States became the PAIRC's delegates: T. H. Chyliński of Washington went to Munich, and attorney Stefan K. Jankowski (president of the SPK chapter in Chicago) went to Vienna. The latter worked in Europe to November 15, 1961, after which his assignment was taken over by Krzysztof Wize. Ludwik Łubieński of London became the senior counselor for Germany. On June 1, 1959, Chyliński was replaced by attorney Czesław Rawski (an active SPK member, also from Chicago), who later became the executive director of the PAIRC in New York (1963–1964). After the first 10 months of operation, by the end of 1958, there were 14 people in the European branches, mostly new talent recruited from the local Polish communities and from freedom fighter circles. Z. Jędrzejowski was in charge of the Committee's office in Nürnberg. Other staff members were: M. Dachan in Hamburg, W. Jarzębowski in Frankfurt am Main, S. Merło in Brussels (he was replaced by M. Dulak in 1981), D. Suzin in Munich, B. Palski in Salzburg, and Antoni Kokot in Munich. Over time there were various personnel changes, and new offices were established, for instance in Paris (Stanisław Domański) and in Rome (W. Zahorski). The presence of World War II veterans and members of the SPK was characteristic of the Committee's European branches. Of these veterans, the better known were Witold Zahorski in Rome, Stanisław Merło in Belgium, Domański in Paris, and Łubieński in Germany. Łubieński had been General Anders' adjutant for many years. This assured an appropriate political assessment of the situation and an adequate resistance level to possible provocations by agents of Communist Poland.

In each of the aforementioned countries, the organizational structure was somewhat different. In addition to the agreement with USEP, there was the agreement with the Catholic NCWC. The USEP agreement made possible lower transportation costs for the emigrants and a shorter processing time in U.S. consulates, and even in Canadian and Australian consulates. By the end of 1958, there were about 280 Poles in Germany, 352 in Austria and 217 in Belgium who were under the direct or indirect care of the Committee. In Belgium, 90 percent of the refugees were tourists who had come from Poland for the World's Fair. To this number should be added almost 20 refugees in Denmark and Sweden. These numbers indicated the continuing need for help.[6]

In order to get a better idea of the principles of cooperation and funding for the PAIRC's work in Europe, it is worthwhile to analyze the contents of the agreements between the Committee and the Department of State. The contract, similar in content to many others, was signed by both sides in 1969. The agreement called for $40,000 from federal sources for the needs of refugees in Europe who were entitled to assistance under the United States Refugee Program. The Department of State and the comptroller general of the United States, or their authorized representatives, retained the right to audit the expenses from this pool. The Committee was obligated to keep a separate set of books for the sums forwarded by the State Department. Moreover, there were certain restrictions. One of them was the need to get the agreement of the department for any change in how the money was to be spent, and services and expenses connected with program performance had to be in strict accord with the prevailing standards. With regard to those employed in carrying out the program, everyone had equal rights regardless of race or creed. The contractor, that is, the Committee, took full responsibility if legal suits were brought by third parties resulting from the realization of the given program, or due to accidents or other unusual situations. The State Department reserved the right to halt the program on 30 days' advance notice.

The funds could be used for paying staff, for their transportation and per diem, and for other administrative expenditures such as office maintenance, insurance and similar costs. The agreement provided that personal, administrative, and office expenses could not be more than 10 percent of funds designated for a particular category. In other words, the Committee could charge expenses within each of those categories up to 10 percent of the awarded budget. The Department of State transferred funds to the Committee's account every three months, on the basis of periodically submitted reports.

Other expenses provided for in the contract were earmarked for the preparation of documents connected with resettlement, for so-called reception and placement assistance. This cost category included professional training and initial health insurance coverage. The care and maintenance category provided for payment of expenses for the refugee's basic needs, such as food, clothing, and temporary housing for the first several days, if the situation demanded it. Vocational and Language Training was a separate category in the agreement.

Where the actual distribution of funds is concerned, in 1969 $2,300 went for PAIRC employee salaries in Austria, $2,500 for office rental and maintenance and related costs, and $1,700 for resettlement documentation. In Germany, employee salaries amounted to $5,600, travel and per diem was $500, administrative support came to $1,100, resettlement documentation was $1,400, care and maintenance was $2,000, and purchase and shipment of welcome kits was $15,000. The entire operational budget in Germany was $25,600, while in Austria it was $7,150 and in Italy it was $650. In all the remaining countries of Western Europe taken together (France and the Benelux nations), salaries amounted to $1,650, care and maintenance was $3,500 and the total expenses were $6,600.[7] The contract also contained a section on hard-core cases:

> For those difficult-to-resettle refugees, who, because of ill health, old age, uneconomic family composition or other disability or economic problem, cannot be resettled through normal programs: special projects for assistance, approved by the Supervising Officer, or his designated representative, which assistance may include required medical aid, hospitalization, rehabilitative or psychiatric treatment, prosthesis, special counseling and training, temporary or permanent institutional placement, emergency or supplementary welfare assistance or maintenance, tools or equipment, housing and furniture.
>
> Integration into the country of temporary settlement was also supported, and the expenditure of certain sums was provided for: For those refugees situated in the countries covered by this contract, or such other areas as may be designated by the Supervising Officer: projects designated to reestablish such refugees through integration in the local economy, covering material services and supplies. These Project Proposals will be drawn up and submitted in accordance with procedures and specifications established by the Supervising Officer, and will be supported by an explanation of the need for such assistance, together with an itemized list of the goods and services proposed will assist toward the firm establishment of the refugee concerned. The implementation of a project shall begin within 30 days after approval by the Supervising Officer. If for some reason a project has not been implemented within 90 days, it is subject to reappraisal and/or cancellation.[8]

The contract placed serious responsibilities on the Committee, both in terms of expenditure and accountability. The sum of several tens of thousands of dollars per year, with its buying power in those days, was of great help. It allowed the Committee to maintain its operations in Europe. Without the aid of the State Department that would have been impossible. The best proof of this is the fact that, in practice, the Committee's general budget was divided into two parts in the 1960s and in later years. The first part was for office maintenance and operations in America, and the second part was for relief work on behalf of refugees in Europe.

The work of the Committee's European offices was based on set procedures. Since refugee assistance remained the fundamental assignment, defined rules of procedure were established that streamlined the process of receiving and processing applications. Let us first take a look at the procedures applied by the PAIRC with regard to those who were in its care. They looked something like this. Refugees arriving in Western nations registered with the police, with the camp administration, and with appropriate agencies. We will further develop this motif later. In the camp or at the PAIRC office, refugees filled out an evidence sheet, on the basis of which the Committee analyzed the person's emigration possibilities. This was the first mandatory function that initiated the process. Because the United States exclusively accepted political refugees, it had to be proven to the U.S. immigration official that there had been persecutions which became the reason for the escape. The Committee's employees prepared that documentation in English, after which the Committee forwarded it to the INS office. If a review of the documentation merited initiation of the visa procedure, the INS, which most often was located in the U.S. Consulate, assigned an interview date to the refugee in question. During the interview conducted by INS staff, Committee employees sometimes served as translators (in later years the INS designated the translators) or served as assistants. The costs of translation, verification, health exams, and also transportation from the camp (the place of domicile) to the consulate were covered by the PAIRC from funds previously allocated in the contract budget. After the candidate was approved, the next step was to secure funds for the flight to the United States. If there were no other options, usually the Committee, through the intermediary of the International Catholic Migration Committee (ICMC) applied to the Intergovernmental Committee for Migration (ICM) for a loan. After receiving the application, the ICM reserved a ticket and informed the local PAIRC office of the departure date. The office then informed headquarters in New York of the arrival date. This made it possible to pick the given persons up at the airport and to arrange for transportation to the final destination for those people who had sponsors. Obviously, almost none of the candidates had any money to cover even part of the costs. Thus, the Committee had to credit the expense as an ICM loan, which was to be repaid after the person became gainfully employed in America.

Official matters did not totally fill the work time of the Committee's delegates in Europe. They were also interested in personal problems, especially of persons who had left families behind. Spiritual welfare was also a concern of the Committee. At one point, the Committee even debated the possibility of a paid position for a clergyman who could look after the refugees.

The procedures outlined here concerned Poles only after they had taken care of the initial formalities with the German, Austrian, or other national authorities. In Germany, specifically, every alien who sought refuge from persecution had the right to seek asylum there. The legal foundation for the asylum process consisted of: the International Refugee Agreement of July 28, 1951, generally called the Geneva Convention, which went into effect in Germany on September 1, 1953; the union law on aliens of April 28, 1965 (BGBI S. 353) and the executive addenda to this law of July 7, 1967. They were characterized by a broad liberalism, both in regard to rights resulting from that legislation and the Constitution, and in the way they were put into practice by the authorities. For example, a foreigner who crossed the German border illegally with the intention of applying for asylum, had to report without delay to the nearest border control point or agency for foreigners (Auslanderamt). There, after giving pertinent explanations, he was usually directed to the camp for foreigners in Zirndorf or Nürnberg. The case was then forwarded to the Federal Agency for Alien Matters. On the other hand, persons who entered the country legally could remain in their place of temporary residence while their case or application was being considered. After preliminary interviews, the asylum applicant went before the Adjudication Commission of the Bundesamt, where he presented the reasons that forced him to leave his country. On that basis, the Commission made a decision to either grant or deny asylum status. In the latter case, the applicant was given the right to appeal the decision. The appeal had to be made within one month's time. If the request was not accepted there either, there was the right to file a complaint or to nullify the decision in the Administrative Court in Ansbach. If the applicant had no luck there either, and in the meantime other factors worthy of consideration had surfaced, he could try for a renewal of the process. In practice, the need for appeals was rather rare.

One of the significant privileges was that persons who received asylum could travel to other countries on the temporary documents issued by the German authorities. Refugees could seek the aid of several organizations, beginning with the UN High Commissioner for Refugees in Germany, whose offices were located in Bad Godesberg and in Zirndorf. Every escapee and refugee had access to the High Commissioner's offices in Zirndorf. Moreover, the agencies of several organizations, beginning with PAIRC and including the Tolstoy Foundation, the American Fund for Czechoslovak Refugees, and in the initial years also the United Ukrainian Canadian Relief Committee, were present in the camp. Also, organizations of a universal character, such as ICM (Intergovernmental Committee for Migration) and Caritas, offered the refugees legal advice, assistance in agencies, translations, and similar services.

Nonetheless, individual countries differed in their procedures with regard to refugees. A similar role to Germany's Zirndorf was played by Treiskirchen in Austria and by Latina in Italy. Germany's example is given here as the most universal and the one concerning the greatest number of refugees.

Ethnic organizations had enormous significance, first of all, in efforts for further emigration. But they also solidly supported efforts to stay in the given location, as for instance in Germany, to render legal advice, document translation, and help in government agencies. Success in obtaining asylum, and in caring for a given refugee group in a camp, depended first of all on the presence in the camp of specialized assistance in the form of an emigration sponsoring organization, such as PAIRC. Equally important factors were the ability to guarantee housing in the country of final destination and the effectiveness of efforts to ensure appropriate immigration laws in that country.[9]

X

The Committee Fights to Amend Immigration Laws

Up to the expiration of the August 1953 law, that is, to the end of 1956, 184,306 persons had entered the United States under that law, of which 170,418 had come from Europe, 11,793 were from the Far East, and 1,124 had arrived from Israel and Palestine. Despite these impressive statistics, the ceiling set at the moment of the law's enactment had not been reached. What is more, it was clear that changes were necessary, and that was an opinion shared by Democrats and Republicans alike. It can be seen as a breakthrough that both parties had made the immigration issue part of their campaign platforms prior to the 1956 presidential elections. The Democratic platform, announced on August 16, 1956, called for broad changes:

> The Democratic Party favors broad revision of the immigration and nationality laws to eliminate unfair provisions under which admissions to this country depend upon quotas based upon the accident of national origin. Proper safeguards against subversive elements should be provided. Our procedures must reflect the principles of our Bill of Rights.[1]

The Republicans did not want to be left behind, or to lose the votes of a growing segment of society. For this reason, and also out of respect for the long-standing efforts of President Eisenhower, they addressed the immigration problem, emphasizing its political aspect:

> The Republican Party supports an immigration policy which is in keeping with the traditions of America in providing a haven for oppressed people, and which is based on equality of treatment, freedom from implications of discrimination between racial, nationality and religious groups, and flexible enough to conform to changing needs and conditions.[2]

The main criticism from the moment the McCarren-Walter Act was passed, was the issue of abolishing the immigration quotas. Even before the elections were officially under way, the PAIRC and 38 other organizations signed a petition to President Eisenhower requesting changes. An appeal was made to abolish the quotas and the mortgages that stunted immigration from countries most exposed to Communist persecution. It was also proposed to admit a larger number of refugees from Soviet-dominated countries. The signatories also repeated the postulate of accumulating and shifting unused quotas on behalf of those who needed them more. In addition to the president, the petition was forwarded to the secretary of state, to the attorney general, and to all senators and congressmen. Aside from the general, joint appeal, the Committee sent individual letters to members of the House of Representatives and the Senate, emphasizing the Polish point of view. The Polish American Congress joined in the pressure on Congress. Its board of directors passed a resolution in February 1957 demanding the abolition of the quotas and the admission of a greater number of refugees from Poland and East-Central Europe.[3]

The pressure had some influence on the shape of the compromise Walter-Kennedy proposal. Thanks to the passage of the bill before the end of the congressional session, those who had entered the United States with false personal documents (most frequently out of fear of reprisals against their loved ones behind the Iron Curtain) were granted amnesty. The immigration mortgages were suspended and health requirements were loosened with regard to those who had TB, which in most cases was the result of life in the DP camps. The restrictive exams administered up to that time were seen as additional punishment for those who had been most victimized. Kennedy and Walter both noticed the impracticality of strict adherence to non-criminal offender requirements that considered even black market trade a felony, even though it took place because of a painful lack of basic articles during the period right after the war.[4]

With regard to the Poles, several points in the new law deserved accolades. First, the door opened for an additional 14,556 escapees beyond the national quota. This was a move that favored Poles from behind the Iron Curtain, because they escaped in the greatest numbers and were the most effective at it. Second, the executive regulations gave a more clear-cut definition of an escapee in the sense that it now also included persons who left on the basis of legal passports, and who had at first been denied the right of applying for political asylum. They were viewed, as in the case of a group of Czech escapees, as economic refugees. Soon, on the basis of explanations tendered by the PAIRC and others, the authorities accepted the view that it is difficult to demand of those who can legally leave their country, that they endanger their lives by escaping from it. The repressiveness of the system, it was explained, no longer impinged as strongly as before on the right to travel abroad.

The attitude of the lawmakers and the shape of immigration law was put to successive, difficult tests by the consequences of the Polish revolt in Poznań in June 1956, and even more by the Hungarian Uprising in the fall of that year. For several weeks, and to a lesser extent up to March 1957, the Hungarian-Austrian border and the border with Yugoslavia were open. In that period, over 200,000 Hungarians crossed it (180,262 to Austria, 19,857 to Yugoslavia). In the initial period, at the very beginning of November, the United States decided to accept 5,000 to 6,000 Hungarians from Austria. The PAIRC, though of limited means, responded to an appeal from Monsignor Swanstrom of the Refugee and Migration Committee and from the State Department, and decided to help 15 young Hungarian freedom fighters. They arrived in the United States on the deck of *Free Poland*. In the meantime, on December 1, 1956, President Eisenhower authorized the entry of 1,500 Hungarians as parolees. On December 12, Eisenhower convoked a 15 member President's Committee for Hungarian Refugee Relief, which was to coordinate the assistance. And on February 12, 1957, the president sent an appeal to the governors of all the states to help with the situation. These were unheard-of moves at that time. A president had never engaged himself so closely in refugee matters in general, and particularly on behalf of a particular ethnic group. Also, the word "parole" was used for the first time ever. It allowed temporary immigration under exceptional circumstances, by decision of the attorney general without the requisite screening, which in this specific instance took place on board a ship. This was also the first case of refugees coming directly to America. Previously this had always occurred through the intermediary of third countries, where DP camps were located, and where time barriers were erected in the form of several bureaucratic procedures. In other words, with regard to the Hungarians, an emergency immigration was made possible under extraordinary circumstances. In the end, 38,000 Hungarians entered the United States on this basis, of whom over 30,000 came under the parole principle. Most of them, with time, gained the right to permanent residence.

The example of the immigration authorities' action on the cusp of 1956 and 1957 served as an instructive lesson. Given the situation in which the Communist camp found itself in 1956, happenings like the one in Hungary could become more frequent. And though the immigration authorities treated the Hungarian events as unique, not subject to repetition, it soon became evident that similar circumstances would force America to the same treatment of refugees several more times. Chronologically, the closest was the mass Chinese exodus to Hong Kong from Communist-controlled continental China.

At any rate, the Hungarian experience did not bring about any precipitous change in the law. On September 11, 1957, Senator John F. Kennedy's proposal was approved and was enacted as PL 85-316, an Act to Amend the Immigration and Nationality Act of 1952. The new law abolished the mortgaging of immigration quotas, which freed up at least 8,200 visas for the nations most burdened by this procedure. It allowed for the immigration of specified trades and professions sought by employers in the United States, and authorized the utilization of 18,656 visas which had been left unused in Eisenhower's 1953 immigration law, which expired in 1956. Of issues of lesser interest to the Polish group, the new law permitted an unlimited number of visas over and above the quota for adopted orphans, or those to be adopted by United States citizens, as well as for the children of unwed citizens of the United States. Kennedy's law, though still imperfect, nonetheless moved the issue in the right direction. From the Polish point of view, the most important was the abolition of the mortgages and the permission to issue visas which were still unused after December 31, 1956.

As a result of the new law, the Migration and Refugee Committee established an advisory group to develop a proposal on ways to utilize the visas that had been forfeited as of December 31, 1956, and on ways to implement Senator Kennedy's new law. Monsignor Swanstrom chaired the group, and representatives of several organizations involved in that issue constituted its membership. At a special State Department–sponsored conference in Washington on October 16 and 17, 1958, the United States Committee for Refugees was created, chaired by Dr. William Bernard. This organization was established to address the problem of political refugees and escapees in the changed political situation. Almost simultaneously, the problem surfaced of 3,000 refugees chased out of Indonesia by President Sukarno, and the problem of victims of an earthquake in the Azores. These were sudden events, akin to the Hungarian Revolt, and required a quick reaction. They were evidence of the global character of the refugee problem. That is why, several weeks later, on December 5, 1958, the U.N. General Assembly passed a resolution establishing the Year of the Refugee, which was to last from July 1, 1959, to the middle of 1960.

Its task was to bring the dimensions of this phenomenon to world attention and to open the borders of the wealthier nations for those requiring help. In the United States this bore fruit in the form of a resolution of both houses of Congress which passed on July 14, 1960. It permitted the granting of parole by the attorney general for 25 percent of the visas issued by other nations. This was the Refugee Fair Share Law, which was extended without an expiration date on June 28, 1962. After two years of residence, a person admit-

A group of refugees newly arrived from Germany at the airport in New York is greeted by representatives of the PAIRC. *At left*: Władysław Zachariasiewicz, *from the right, back row*: an unidentified person, Matthew Widlicki, and Editor Józef Dubicki. October 24, 1961.

ted under parole was interviewed by an INS official and could obtain permanent residence. This law was applied to the Cuban refugees after Castro's takeover, in particular after the unsuccessful bid to topple him from power, and after the Cuban Missile Crisis (October 23, 1962). Up to that year, 150,000 Cubans had settled in Miami and other parts of Florida, about 55,000 of whom were resettled with the help of various organizations and agencies. Just as with the Hungarians, a special team was organized to resolve the Cuban refugee problem. On February 3, 1961, President John F. Kennedy announced a nine-point plan of action for the Cuban Refugee Program, which was to work together with several other agencies. The situation on this issue changed once again on September 28, 1965, when Castro announced that he would permit the departure of any Cuban who wanted to leave. In reply, President Lyndon B. Johnson stated (October 3, 1965) that the United States would accept anyone who would apply for asylum. This opened the path to a mass migration of approximately 4,000 Cubans per month for the next eight years, until all air communication was suspended on April 6, 1973.

This was not the only refugee crisis the government had to deal with. On May 23, 1962, President Kennedy admitted several thousand Chinese from Hong Kong on the basis of parole. To the expiration date of that program, that is, to December 31, 1964, about 15,000 Chinese were admitted to the United States. In the same period, the problem of economic refugees from the Communist nations surfaced for the first time in postwar history. The "economic refugee" classification was applied to Yugoslavs and Czechs who entered Austria on tourist visas. There was the danger that in the changed political landscape, the Poles would also have a harder time obtaining political asylum in the Western nations and in the United States. For this reason, the representatives of organizations representing Slavic minorities tried to combat this sort of interpretation. The Polish American Immigration and Relief Committee protested, as did Dr. Papanek, the head of the American Fund for Czechoslovak Refugees.

Protests on this subject, and also the experiences of the first several years of the new decade, were a drain on the administration in Washington, which had been surprised several times by the size of the refugee problems that arose in consequence of political coups, wars, and uprisings in various parts of the world. It was becoming ever more evident that the existing immigration law did not live up to the needs of the new era and needed to be changed. President Lyndon B. Johnson took a decisive step in this direction. On October 3, 1965, the president signed a new bill into law at the foot of the Statue of Liberty. The law — amending the Immigration and Nationality Act and for Other Purposes, known as PL 89-236 — abolished the national quota system, which the prior four presidents had not been able to do. In one provision, the new law set a percentage ceiling for escapees from Communist-run countries and for Middle Eastern nations on the basis of conditional entries, which to a certain extent replaced parole. For the first time, a ceiling was set on immigration from nations in the Western Hemisphere. According to the new law, 170,000 persons could be admitted from the Eastern Hemisphere, including 6 percent as conditional entries. Beginning July 1, 1968, 120,000 persons from the Western Hemisphere were admitted to the United States. On the other hand, more stringent requirements went into effect protecting the American labor market. From then on, the Department of Labor had to issue labor certification for non-preference candidates from Western nations.

The new law addressed many complaints of the Polish ethnic group, but was not tailored exclusively to its needs. After October 1956 Poland was no longer the generator of an ever-growing wave of refugees. That role was assumed by Cuba, Near- and Far-Eastern countries, and countries of Latin America. Because of this, the Committee's situation was progressively more difficult. On one hand, the removal of the problem of Polish refugees from center stage made the Committee's struggle for typically Polish needs more difficult. The cause was the hardening of the post–Yalta divisions, which became evident from the example of the 1956 Hungarian Revolution. The lack of help from the West firmed up the belief that the current division of influence zones was irreversible, at least for the foreseeable future. On the other hand, the Committee was facing a decidedly diminishing stream of refugees. There were several reasons. The first was the securing of the borders, and the fact that Poland did not share a border with any Western nation. The second was that after several years of thaw, the passport policy of the Polish Communist government had become more strict. Finally, the small economic stabilization in the Communist countries also played a significant role. The redirecting of budgets after 1956 toward the consumption side, and a greater supply of consumable goods on the market, changed the map of social needs. An ever-increasing segment of the Polish population had no direct experience of independence, and began to come to terms with the existing state of affairs. Only the most determined citizens, aware of the obstacles, made the decision to emigrate. The changes described above allowed the Committee to pay more attention to the care of the hard-core cases in Western Europe.

XI

Swimming with the Tide: Scaling Down, and Transformations

The symptoms of the coming changes were evident enough that in 1962 Committee Vice President W. Zachariasiewicz went on another tour of Polish settlement areas on the Continent. His sojourn in Europe lasted from June 3 to July 5, 1962, and included visits in Brussels, Geneva, Rome, Vienna, Salzburg, Munich, Nürnberg-Zirndorf, Frankfurt, Düsseldorf, Cologne, and Paris. Zachariasiewicz spoke not only with the refugees themselves, but also with the representatives of Polish organizations, and with representatives of American, Austrian, and German government institutions involved in refugee affairs. Zachariasiewicz presented his remarks and conclusions in a report that was a Polish commentary on the changes proposed in American legislation. His most important observation can be summarized in the statement that the problem of refugees continued to exist, and the issue of the Poles, who were the largest ethnic group in this category, represented an exceptional tangle of problems. Escapees from behind the Iron Curtain would have to be treated as a long-term problem which, if used effectively from the political point of view, could bring a plethora of benefits. An escape from a workers' paradise is itself a propaganda success that unmasks the truth about living conditions under Communist rule The other problem that demanded quick resolution was the fate of that group of refugees which, due to health reasons, was not qualified to emigrate and lived on the edge of poverty, only supported by aid from Germany and Austria. The passage of time and the attitude the refugees developed because of their awareness that the Germans were responsible for their suffering, made assimilation in the territory dominated by the German language unusually difficult.

The problem of assimilation was further complicated by disease and by the progressive loss of health by a growing number of refugees in Germany. Immediately after the war they often took jobs in hard, physically demanding professions, only to find themselves, after several years, in a condition that ruled out employment. This sort of situation became painfully obvious toward the end of the 1950s and the beginning of the 1960s. The Committee tried to help these people under the aegis of the WRY (World Refugee Year) campaign, which had set itself the task of resettling these kinds of families. The campaign encompassed applications from 4,730 persons (3,000 from Germany, 1,200 from other West European nations, 130 from Austria, and 400 from Italy). In the end, 278 people were helped. A lack of funds did not permit a broader scope for the project.

According to the report's author, aside from a lack of funds, an overly rigorous way of crediting funds by U.S. government agencies was also an impediment. Zachariasiewicz maintained that institutions and organizations such as the Committee should enjoy greater freedom. The funds granted ought to pay for a broader range of activity, and should not depend on an individual project, or a project currently under way.

In another section, Zachariasiewicz analyzed the situation in the most important refugee camps. There were 8,000 Poles in Germany who had not been resettled permanently, of whom half were interested in further emigration. Another 2,000 were ready to emigrate under the guaranteed sponsorship of the country of destination. In terms of preference, the destination countries for Poles in Germany were, in descending order of preference: the United States of America, Canada, Australia, New Zealand, the Scandinavian countries, and Switzerland. Obstructing the possibility of departure from Germany were the already mentioned health criteria, refusal to accept people who had settled permanently (whereas, in fact, these were families that had never, psychologically, settled down in Germany), and the high costs of emigration, including medical bills, transportation, and burdensome and expensive documentation. Other obstacles were "criminality" in the sense of participation in the black market, etc., and also the refusal to accept (in the case of the United States) broken families. Without special schemes, the resolution of this problem seemed impossible.

Despite the difficulties, the PAIRC succeeded, during the year preceding Zachariasiewicz's visit, to present the U.S consulates in Europe with 537 documented applications for emigration that included 2,425 persons. The situation in France was somewhat different. There, 78,000 prewar and 18,000 postwar emigrants refused to accept Polish passports. For the most part, they were World War II veterans, and a group of political escapees. Only 300 people from this group expressed interest in further emigration. There were

10,000 Poles in Belgium who had immigrated there prior to the war, and who did not accept Polish passports, and 16,000 former members of the Polish armed forces, former DPs and concentration camp inmates. The DPs in this group were a serious problem. They had arrived in Belgium immediately after the war to work in the mines and in the mining industry, and they did not have documents allowing them to have political refugee status. After well over a dozen years of labor, a sizable group of miners was seriously ill. Zachariasiewicz demanded financial assistance for this group, in the amount of $143,250. The situation of the Poles in Italy was less of a problem, mostly because they were a small group of fewer than 600. Some of them were on social welfare. Also, a small group of refugees (according to the classification of the United Nations High Commissioner for Refugees — UNHCR) was to be found in Austria, but no more than 60 persons. Most of these people were able to earn enough for their living expenses. In Sweden, on the other hand, there were 1,400 escapees having a UNHCR mandate and 400 who were escapees but held on to their Polish passports. In the remaining countries of Europe that were included in the report, there were minimal numbers of escapees and refugees — from 144 in Spain down to 87 in Greece. The group of firmly resettled individuals included 140,000 Poles in Great Britain, mainly veterans. The biggest problem for people in this category was that they had, in fact, settled permanently, and some of them had applied for British citizenship, and therefore, in the light of American law, they could not be potential immigrants to the United States. Among them, many persons were mentally ill due to the horrors of the war, which made emigration an even more remote possibility.

Another group analyzed in the report consisted of escapees from Communist Poland. It was believed that 300 to 350 persons per year escaped from the Polish People's Republic to the West. They were members of various professions, who had found the political situation in Communist Poland intolerable. Unfortunately, the long bureaucratic procedure and waiting list for obtaining an emigrant visa often led to frustration and disillusionment. Zachariasiewicz proposed that this problem be paid closer attention to, in cooperation with ethnic organizations such as the PAIRC, which had a better grasp of the issue. He demanded greater flexibility in this matter. He also complained about the high application costs, which were close to $500 per person.

In the report's conclusion, the author remarked on the continuing Communist infiltration of refugee groups, carried on under the guise of various educational circles, of easily accessible literature, of trips to Poland and of cultural promotion in the form of film screenings, folklore dance groups, etc. Zachariasiewicz noted that the enormous trust the refugees had in the PAIRC representatives in Western Europe helped counteract the subversive activity of the Communist agents. The author also stated in his conclusion that of the overall number of about 100,000 Poles in Western Europe, approximately 10,000 required material assistance to emigrate or assimilate. In order to take care of this, he proposed that the U.S. government give the Committee a $150,000 grant for 1963 and two subsequent annual grants of $100,000 each. It was necessary, according to him, to loosen the procedures allowing for emigration and to include the Scandinavian countries, especially Sweden and Denmark, in the group of countries that permitted emigration on the basis of parole. A $70,000 grant was essential for the most recent political refugees.[1]

The report's value went well beyond the immediate circumstances. Its conclusions could be condensed into the statement that although the absolute number of refugees and escapees from Communist Poland had decreased, the problem itself remained topical. The top priority was the sensitive issue of persons who had not previously qualified for emigration, but who as victims of the war required material assistance. Second, the attitude toward the escapees from Communist Poland was important; they should not meet an indifferent fate due to political factors. An equally vital conclusion of the report was the emphasis on the importance of the PAIRC's refugee relief work, and its readiness to cooperate with international agencies and the U.S. government in addressing this problem. The decreased number of refugees did not diminish the Committee's assignments; it even made them somewhat more difficult.

The qualitative change in the situation of the Polish refugees was reflected in the work of the Committee. The big campaigns, such as the one on behalf of the DP Act of 1948, were replaced by ad hoc assistance that reacted to existing cases or to escapes from the Polish People's Republic, with an ever larger role for charity assistance for those who were temporarily settled in Germany or Austria. In large measure, these were special actions — aimed toward children and the sick.

It could be said that as early as 1957 the Committee was aware of the changing work horizon, based on the political transformations that had taken place in Poland. Proof of this was the change in the Committee's name from American Commission for Relief of Polish Immigrants, Inc. to Polish American Immigration and Relief Committee, Inc. Monsignor Burant and T. Sztybel had presented appropriate documents on December 19, 1957. The actual date for the change of name is accepted as December 23, 1957.[2]

In practice, the old name was used for quite some time yet, though in official correspondence the abbreviation of the new name — PAIRC — was used. Almost a year later, on November 17, 1958, the confirmation came that PAIRC was a charitable organization.[3]

The Committee's reports reflect the gradual changes. During the twelve months preceding the summer of 1957, 1,109 refugees came to the United States on assurances the Committee had provided. Of these 729 came from Germany, 190 from England, 79 from France, 68 from Belgium, 13 from Austria, 12 from Sweden, 7 from Denmark, 6 from Italy, 4 from Holland, and 1 from Luxembourg. In that same period, 116 persons came to the United States on affidavits issued by the Committee, of whom 45 were from England, 17 from Argentina, 13 from Holland, 9 from France, 7 from Canada, 6 each from Italy and Belgium, and 1 each from Sweden, Brazil, India, and Uruguay.

In that same year another branch of work developed, which had not been known before. Namely, since the summer of 1956 tourists started arriving from Poland, mostly to visit family members. Part of them planned to stay in America. In such instances, the Committee gave advice and legal assistance. In general, the advisory function of the Committee was enlarged. The counseling also spread to other countries, especially in South America. Above all else, the Committee increasingly intervened with the Congress of the United States on behalf of sailors and refugees who had illegally entered the United States. The help of favorably disposed congressmen and senators was sought here.

Material aid was a growing portion of the Committee's work. In 1957, goods valued at $6,790 were sent to children and the sick in Germany, Austria, and Italy. This sum included 2,500 one-dollar parcels weighing 22 pounds each, and $1,200 in cash forwarded to Germany, $600 to Austria, 200 parcels and $150 to a Polish orphanage in Italy, and a smaller number of parcels to several other European countries.[4]

For the following Easter holidays, the Committee forwarded, on April 3, 1958, $1,600 for Poles in Germany, Austria, and Italy. In 1959, the Committee gave direct assistance to 86 refugees. Simultaneously, 426 refugees were brought to the United States, of whom 300 were of the most recent generation, who had escaped from Communist Poland. In the same period, assistance was given to 650 new immigrants who were under the care of other international and charitable organizations. In 1959/1960, $10,400 was designated for direct aid, of which 80 percent went to Germany, and half of it was received during the Christmas holidays.

Of the more interesting and new initiatives, organizing vacations for Polish children in Germany ought to be mentioned; 86 refugee children, and also orphans, were able to take advantage of a two- to three-week respite.[5] In a truly endearing gesture, the children who went on vacation prepared detailed reports with a chronicle of events, newspaper clips, and photographs. One that survived is the report of the Mariental-Horst DP camp school from the trip to Travemunde-Priwall of August 20–28, 1960.[6]

"Our Trip to the Ostsee."

XI — Swimming with the Tide: Scaling Down

W mieście oglądaliśmy port, gdzie było parę okrętów.

Pan Król kupił nam lody i wróciliśmy do obozu, gdzie zjedliśmy z wielkim apetytem obiad. Po obiedzie chłopcy grali w piłkę nożną i wygrali 3:0. Przeciwnikami byli chłopcy z Hannover.

"Mr. Król, our teacher, bought us ice-cream."

Po dobrej kawie z ciastkami przygoto= wywaliśmy się do pierwszego naszego wieczornego występu.

Nasamprzód pan Król zarządził, że każdy namiot będzie udekorowany chorągiewkami a przed namiotem zrobimy dekoracje z muszli. Najpiękniej udekorowane namioty otrzymają nagrody. Całe bractwo zabrało się do ro= boty, chcąc otrzymać pierwszą nagrodę i pokazać całemu obozowi, co polskie dzieci umieją. Nasze wszystkie namioty udekorowane chorągiewkami,

"After a good coffee with cookies, we prepared for our first evening performance."

XI—Swimming with the Tide: Scaling Down

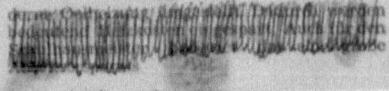

Polish children won over German hearts with the Krakowiak dance.

The figures were not lying: more and more of the aid from the end of the 1950s was charitable in nature; the refugee numbers were dropping; but new problems arose, such as the unfavorable attitude of the INS toward Poles after October 1956. The PAIRC leadership spoke out on this issue. In 1959, Msgr. Burant prepared a memorandum in which he included several observations about the new refugee situation. The main part of the document was dedicated to a discussion of efforts to overturn deportation orders for Poles who had come to the United States during several prior years either as sailors or as stowaways on ships with American port destinations. The point was that the persons responsible for immigration issues in the United States tended to treat the post–1956 changes in Communist Poland as favorable and irreversible. So, efforts were made to decrease the basis on which political asylum was granted; this was opposed not only by the Committee, but also by other Polish organizations. For instance, the Polish American Congress at its September 27, 1958, board of directors' meeting in Williamsburg passed a resolution in which we read:

> And it be finally resolved that the Polish American Congress communicate to the proper authorities a censure of recent harsh and merciless methods employed by our Immigration and Naturalization Service in trying to deliver into the hands of the Warsaw regime deserving anti-communist Poles — regardless how they reach our shores — seeking asylum in our country. This change of policy seems to be based on the false theory that some relaxation of the notorious Stalinist methods of terror signifies a genuine change in the situation in Poland.[7]

The Conference of Americans of Central and East European Descent, which took place on February 28, 1959, in New York, voiced similar concerns. Several other statements were made on the subject, including those of independent European observers. The Committee believed that deportations were not serving American interests. The purpose of the memorandum was to shed light on the real situation in Communist Poland based on what was related by refugees, as well as by independent journalists and other sources. The memo was also an attempt to get the issue of Poles back on the agenda after the Hungarian Revolution of 1956, which dominated the attention of INS officials and the U.S. government.

The Committee tried to find its niche on a scale adjusted to the prevailing conditions. Projects were undertaken on the basis of observations made by the Committee's executive vice president on his trip to European refugee camps. Zachariasiewicz drew attention to the need for further aid to refugees in Germany, with the proviso that in a growing number of cases an individual approach was necessary. This had to do with the increasing percentage of hard-core cases, that is, people who were sick, old, or previously rejected in their attempts to emigrate. The author pointed out USEP's very narrow criteria, which eliminated an enormous number of applications, and created mounting frustration among the refugees. On the other hand, he emphasized the need for the presence of all kinds of organizations, PAIRC and USEP included, as a symbol of concern for the fate of these people. Zachariasiewicz pointed out the inadequacy of the care for newly arrived escapees. He expected a new approach from the new administration, and new energy in dealing with the refugees in Europe.[8]

Zachariasiewicz's report was mailed to congressmen, senators and persons involved in the issue.

Among the Committee's more interesting activities dating from the beginning of the new decade, were the free English language courses offered to new immigrants, and closer cooperation with the National Academy of Sciences and its agencies, particularly the National Committee for Resettlement of Foreign Physicians. This latter initiative was meant to integrate and find employment for newly arrived Polish physicians. The Committee published an instruction booklet on how to verify a diploma, on what the various stages were in the qualifying exams for admission to practice in American hospitals, and on how to open one's own medical practice. In order to properly prepare the immigrant physicians for the exams, the Committee contacted them from four centers in New York, which were run by outstanding specialists, where candidates were prepared for the exams through an intensive course. These were: New York Polyclinic Medical School and Hospital, Downstate Medical Center in Brooklyn, University of Buffalo School of Medicine, and Albany Medical College. The Committee distributed applications, carried on voluminous correspondence, and even assisted in taking care of certain matters. It should be remembered that at that time immigrant physicians could not, as in prior years, work as interns without taking certain exams. Several states had their own requirements. For instance, in Florida, before taking the physician's licensing exam, the candidate had to have been an American citizen for at least five years. In other states, the obstacles to a career began with exhaustive examinations that took several years to complete, and ended with extended hospital internships and residencies. Despite these formidable barriers, a significant number of Polish doctors succeeded in completing all those stages and in getting work in their profession. The heaviest burden of this program fell on 1961, but was also continued after that time.[9]

In addition, the Committee carried on its normal work. In the 12 months up to the middle of 1961, emigration to other countries was arranged for 713 Poles. They departed for resettlement in Canada, South Africa, Australia, England, Sweden, and Switzerland. This number was restricted to people whose emigration was possible because of the PAIRC's direct help. On the other hand, 252 families emigrated from Western Europe to the United States. This second number concerned both individual applications and entire families emigrating on the basis of one assurance. Some families had up to seven members, thus the figure of 252 was, in fact, two or three times as large.

The processing of emigration cases in Europe was done by the PAIRC's European offices in cooperation with the United Nations High Commissioner for Refugees, and with the Intergovernmental Committee for Migration and several consulates and other volunteer organizations, both local and international.

Within its charitable work the PAIRC was able, in 1960, to organize Christmas parties in 28 DP camps in Germany, for about $11,200. The list of

The Brewka family at the airport in Chicago. *Standing from left*: Anna Migoń, executive vice president of the PAIRC in Chicago; *next to her*— Stefania Brewka; Michał, 4 years old; Alfreda, 2; Elżbieta, 7; Maria, 8; Arleta, 6; Ryszard, 7 months; Michał Brewka; Zygmunt Podbielski. *Seated from left*: Hela, 14; Wiesława, 13; Ewa-Danuta, 16.

beneficiaries included people with tuberculosis at the sanatorium in Gauting, and at least 2,836 Polish children. Also, large amounts of clothing were shipped from the United States. Generally speaking, in the reporting year 1960/61, the PAIRC spent $52,154.52 on so-called individual projects. Part of this sum came from federal funds and from other organizations, such as the Lutheran World Federation. A less measurable scope of assistance could be evaluated through the case of the Michał and Stefania Brewka family and their nine children, who, after 21 years in various refugee camps in Germany, finally made it to Chicago in 1961 thanks to the efforts of the PAIRC, to begin a new life.

Another case was the Boryka family, still in Germany:

> We thank you a hundred times over for the wonderful gifts. I received everything on Saturday, March 25. We received 5 pillows, 5 comforters, 4 comforter covers, 10 sheets, 10 pillow cases. I also received all the furniture: beds, dressers, a table, chairs, beds for the children, two small armoires, a couch and a lamp. I also received the sewing machine and thanks a million. The kids are also very happy with everything. We really want to thank all the Poles in the USA who have helped us. God will reward them for this and give them lots of good health. I am happy that I can live a little more like a human being now. I cleaned up all that German dirt, but we would be even happier if we could emigrate somewhere. I feel anguish that my children might end up being Germans and that there is no hope for the future for them.[10]

The Committee received many more "thank you" letters. From October 1961 on, they were received at the Committee's new headquarters at 156 Fifth Avenue in Manhattan, where the somewhat-more-modest, but functional office was located on the 11th floor.

In 1961, an important event was the hearings before the Subcommittee on Refugees and Escapees of the Senate Committee on the Judiciary, where Judge Zaleski made a lengthy statement on July 14. PAIRC Vice President Zaleski focused on the problems of Poles in Western Europe, who were the largest ethnic group among the refugees, estimated at 60,000 persons. He noted that the refugee problem would continue, so it was necessary to continue the work of such organizations as the PAIRC, and the help from federal agencies. Zaleski strongly opposed the rumors about the closing of the United States Escapee Program (USEP), noting the great need to maintain it, especially in light of global East-West rivalries. USEP's propaganda value in that battle was difficult to deny. He also brought attention to the need for legalizing the right to political asylum for victims of political persecution in Communist nations. Previously, cases of that sort were sanctioned on the basis of private bills. According to Zaleski, the so-called Parolee Law was a misunderstanding. Contrary to expectations, it did not expedite, but in fact delayed, immigration procedures, because this law only applied to escapees from some of the West European nations. Connected with the political refugee issue was the danger of repression upon returning to the country of former settlement, therefore Zaleski also opposed the increasing frequency of deportations. As an example, Zaleski cited the case of Budny, a prewar policeman and a soldier of the Polish underground army, whose undoubted membership in anti–Communist organizations most certainly threatened reprisals if he were deported to Communist Poland. Meanwhile, his asylum application of February 8, 1961, was denied. Fortunately, the intervention of Senator Kenneth Keating, who was favorably disposed to the PAIRC, halted the deportation process. This example very well illustrated the heartlessness with which the INS applied procedures after October 12, 1956, with regard to Poles who left Poland after that date.[11]

In his conclusion, Zaleski advised of the need for the long-awaited reform of immigration law. Generally speaking, during calendar year 1961 PAIRC registered 1,104 persons with the INS in Western Europe, of whom 423 emigrated. But 574 refugees either backed out or were denied, and there were 107 applications in progress.[12]

The year 1962 marked the 15th anniversary of the Committee's founding. Many ceremonial events took place to commemorate that event, and the founder, Monsignor Burant, was honored as the grand marshal of the Pulaski Day Parade in New York. Occasional publications noted the enormous work that Monsignor Burant and his Committee had accomplished. It was recalled that thanks to the Committee about 40,000 Poles were able to start a new life, and that about 300 sailors who had abandoned ships flying under the banner of Communist Poland received the right to settle in the United States. All told, about 100,000 Poles had availed themselves of the services of the PAIRC and its branches. There was no way to measure the efforts to unite families that had been torn apart, or to assess immigration and legal advice. The Committee had succeeded in bringing about the emigration of about 1,200 persons in the hard-core case category. On the other hand, the Committee had spent about $12,000 on aid to 400 refugee hard-core cases residing in the refugee camps. It would be negligent not to mention the constant efforts to improve immigration law and the struggle to ensure a proper percentage of Polish participation in all forms of aid offered by federal sources. These accomplishments were noticed both by Poles and others. Senator Philip Hart, chair of the Senate Subcommittee for Refugee Matters, wrote in his telegram on the occasion of the PAIRC's 15th anniversary:

> The Committee's work is not as widely known as the results of its activity deserve to be noted. Apparently the Committee focuses on its work

XI — Swimming with the Tide: Scaling Down 147

without fanfare and in its modesty does not attempt with sufficient energy to gain recognition and accolades.... It is my fervent desire that your Committee continue its work as long as the last refugee from under the communist yoke is not resettled permanently and until such time as there will be no more refugees and escapees, that is, until the communist plague is completely excoriated.

On that same occasion, Senator Keating wrote:

The Polish Immigration Committee was a very effective element in the cooperation of various departments of the administration and the Congress. You can be sure of my permanent interest in the activity of your outstanding organization. In particular I will continue to counteract the harm done to persons who escaped from behind the Iron Curtain and were forced by administrative regulations to return under communist rule.

U.S. President John F. Kennedy also sent a telegram:

Among charitable organizations that care for refugees and the latest escapees and who also work to resettle them, the Polish Immigration Committee has noteworthy accomplishments ... the government of the United States is sincerely grateful to the Polish Immigration Committee for its work in this field.[13]

Praise in this vein came from high officials, including Bishop Edward Swanstrom, executive director of the Catholic Relief Services — National Catholic Welfare Conference, with which the Committee had cooperated for many years, and also from Richard Brown, the director of the Division of Refugee and Migration Matters in the Department of State, who noted the creative contribution of the Committee in resolving many problems. Praise was also showered on the PAIRC during debates of the U.S. Congress. In his address on the occasion of the 23rd anniversary of Germany's and Russia's attack on Poland, Congressman John J. Rooney of New York emphasized the permanence of the problems connected with refugees, which began in 1939. With regard to the PAIRC's mission he said:

The unsolved Polish refugee problem in Western Europe presents mounting difficulties to the nationwide Polish-American voluntary agency, the Polish American Immigration and Relief Committee with headquarters in New York. This institution, observing this year the 15th anniversary of its noble service, represents the interests of the stateless, down-ridden victims of World War II, and victims of postwar brutality and inhumanity at the hands of totalitarian modern barbarians. It is a recognized voluntary agency working in close cooperation with our Department of State, and as such it

A Christmas party for Polish children in Rome organized with the help of the PAIRC. On the right Bishop Szczepan Wesoły seen in profile, and Witold Zahorski is standing next to the staff of St. Nicholas.

well merits continued and substantial U.S. Government assistance.... I for one do not propose to abandon hope for solution of the Polish refugee problem. I for one do not propose to abandon our wartime allies who were first to fight Hitler's aggression; who distinguished themselves mobilizing huge volunteer armies that were on the side of the Western Allies in the Battle of England, in the Norwegian fjord at Narvik, in Tobruk in Africa, Falaise in France, and Arnhem in Holland, and last but not least, at Monte Cassino which they wrested from the Nazi armies. I for one do not propose to let down the compatriots of the 7-million-odd Americans of Polish lineage who have served this country in both world wars, and who are serving it daily in their manifold tasks and endeavors, enriching continuously our great common American heritage.[14]

Lofty praise did not, however, help in the struggle with everyday problems, even with problems that depended on the good will of the U.S. government. In 1962, the Committee strongly backed the proposal for the new immigration law sponsored by President Kennedy. Msgr. Burant expressed his full approval in a telegram to the White House. Although the president's

XI — Swimming with the Tide: Scaling Down

This is the first Christmas Eve abroad for new Polish refugees in the transit camp at Zirndorf near Nürnberg in Germany. Even the greatest optimists among the refugees, those who believed that in a month or two "the Polish Immigration Committee will get us out of here and open wide the door to the world for us," had hung their heads because the candles were lit on Christmas trees in German homes and loneliness in a foreign land had really begun to make itself felt. Just then, Mr. Z. Jędrzejowski, a delegate of the Polish Immigration Committee, invited all the Poles to a Christmas Eve supper — Christmas carols, the Christmas wafer, Christmas greetings, even the traditional Polish straw under the tablecloth to symbolize Christ's birth in the manger ... just like in Poland. At times like this a mysterious force, sometimes called a national bond, creates a miracle: every Pole becomes a brother, and one big Polish family sits down to Christmas Eve dinner. "God is born, and might trembles...," the strains of that old Polish carol sound the same in Warsaw, in Chicago, and in the refugee camp at Nürnberg.

understanding could be counted on, the challenge before the Committee became much more difficult after the president's assassination in Dallas, when part of the suggestions included in Kennedy's proposal were withdrawn. An even more difficult challenge was the effort to delete several provisions of the new law that were discriminatory to Poles concerning reparations for victims of Nazism, approved by the Federal Republic of Germany. The basis for the claims of the refugees was an agreement between the German government and the United Nations High Commissioner for Refugees signed in Geneva on October 5, 1960. The first of the above-mentioned documents had several sections that discriminated against Poles. For instance, the Poles were included in the category based on nationality, but not in the category of those persecuted for political beliefs, which the PAIRC protested. In addition, the Committee voiced its opposition to the expiration date of October 1, 1953, as persons not holding refugee status by that date could not obtain benefits. Through this administrative maneuver, the German side tried to dismiss the claims of those who fled from communist Poland after that date. The Committee attempted to intervene. This dispute went on for quite some time. It took a memorandum from the Committee to the UN High Commissioner for Refugees (UNHCR) to bring about corrections favoring Polish victims of Nazism in the second of the above-cited agreements.

The procedure of applying for claims was based on certain principles. First, in light of the pact, the High Commissioner acted as the spokesman for the injured parties, which in this case also included Polish refugees. In order to get reparation, one had to prove persecution such as imprisonment, beatings or deprivation of other rights. The Committee became a coordinator for the claims of Polish refugees from the moment of filing the application and throughout the entire review process. Under the High Commissioner's aegis, several conferences were held regarding the distribution of the reparations fund, which was established at 45 million Deutsche Marks. The fifth conference, held on September 14, 1964, was devoted to the details and principles of distribution. In all, the Poles submitted 40,229 claim applications; by September 1964 some 11,639 received a positive response, 21,875 applications were rejected as not meeting the criteria, and 1,100 were in the process of being reviewed. Moreover, 5,295 applications were in limbo and 2,898 appeals were admitted for consideration. Ludwik Łubieński did an enormous amount of work in this field. He had formerly been the Committee's delegate for Europe, and had developed excellent relationships in Europe; moreover, he was fluent in German and English. Thanks to him, payments on the first two installments of the reparations (an overall sum of $6,130,750) were made by September 1964, while the third and fourth (and last) installment was paid by December 31, 1964, in the sum of $6,500,000. The Committee's work in this field had enormous significance not only in material terms, but, more importantly, in moral ones. The PAIRC became the spokesperson for those who were deprived of their own country and who found themselves in a country that had brought various injuries and misfortunes on them during the war. The ability to bring the claims to a successful conclusion, and to get the reparations paid, was to the Committee's eternal credit.[15]

The above activity was going on independently of the concurrent relief

XI—Swimming with the Tide: Scaling Down   151

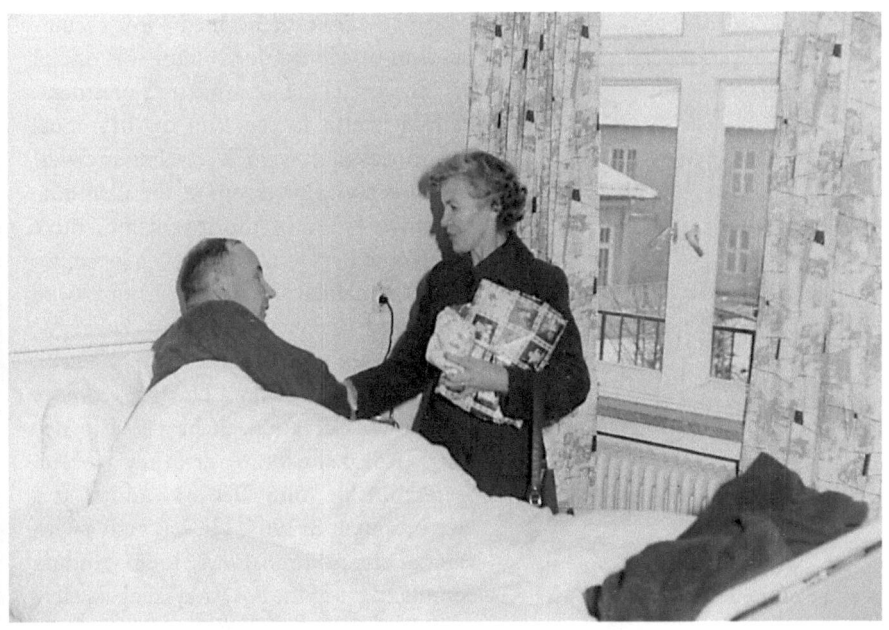

During the Christmas season PAIRC delegates in Europe also remember sick Polish refugees lying in hospitals (1963).

work, which included traditional elements, if they can be called that. In the 1963/64 reporting year, the PAIRC expended $5,000 for charitable work (Christmas parties, parcels, clothing, etc.) which also included aid to the Near East. Help was being rendered ever more frequently in cases of family loss, where the father or some other family provider died due to the stresses of war, age, or disease. In such instances, the PAIRC gave financial assistance. At the beginning of the 1960s one other form of assistance appeared — scholarships for training in the trades. Ewa Kabacińska, the daughter of participants in the Warsaw Uprising of 1944, received such a scholarship. She was born in the Ravensbrück concentration camp in 1945, where her mother was imprisoned. The Committee paid $1,283.06 for a tailoring course for her in 1964, thus giving her access to a useful trade. Also in 1964, the Committee sponsored college studies for seven Polish refugees in Austria, four in Spain, and two young priests at the University of Louvain in Belgium. High school studies were also sponsored, especially for orphans. For instance, the Committee paid for 13 Polish half-orphans from Germany to study in English schools, and paid for the schooling of several girls in Germany to study in French schools. The scholarships were paid for by the PAIRC together with the Polish section of Radio Free Europe.[16]

Ignacy Morawski, executive director of the PAIRC, 1965–1969.

The above-mentioned 1959 memorandum of Monsignor Burant was one of his last acts as the Committee's president. Failing health forced him to shift most day-to-day matters to W. Zachariasiewicz, who was a vice president of the Committee since 1959. In the meantime, there were some personnel changes. Monsignor Burant remained as president from 1961 to 1964, and the vice presidents were: W. Zachariasiewicz, Judge Henry Zaleski, Zofia Dattner, Czesława Durska, Florence Jarzębowska, Franciszek Proch, attorney John Różański, and attorney Joseph Świerzbiński. John Dec was added as a vice president in 1964. He was active with veteran organizations, was a long-standing commandant of the Stowarzyszenie Weteranów Armii Polskiej (SWAP — Polish Army Veterans Association of America). In the meantime, Zofia Dattner, a representative of the Polish Falcons, resigned her post, but then returned again as a vice president in 1966. In 1964, Judge Henry Zaleski died. He had served the Committee with great devotion and was present at its founding. His post was filled by Edward Kurmel in 1965. That same year, Ignacy Morawski, one of the senior Polish journalists in America, became the executive secretary and a director.[17] Before World War II, Morawski had worked in the Polish Consular Corps; later, he was the editor-in-chief of *Nowy Świat* (the New York Polish daily). He replaced W. Zachariasiewicz on the Committee (after Czesław Rawski's interim filling of that post). Zachariasiewicz in 1963 left to work in the federal administration in Washington, D.C., but still maintained contact with the Committee. The Reverend Monsignor John J. Karpiński served as the chairman of the Committee's board of trustees. He served as its chairman. Feliks Popławski remained the financial secretary for many years, and Edward Witanowski was the treasurer.[18]

In 1965, Rt. Reverend Monsignor Francis P. Kowalczyk became president of the Committee. He was the pastor of Holy Rosary Parish in Passaic, New Jersey, a post–Synodal judge of the diocese of Patterson, and the chaplain of many local charitable associations.

The death of the founder and soul of the Committee was a big shock for the organization. Monsignor Burant died on August 25, 1964, after a long illness. In the sea of telegrams with condolences praising the contributions of the deceased, the one from New York City's Mayor, Robert Wagner, stood out:

> It is with deep sorrow that I have learned of the death of Dear Friend Right Reverend Monsignor Felix F. Burant, the tireless worker and spirited citizen in the many humanitarian endeavors which mark his life. The Polish Immigration and Relief Committee, which he founded and guided so ably, helped thousands of homeless victims of Nazi and Communist oppression to find a new life and new opportunity in this country. As Mayor of New York City I salute the passing of one of our most outstanding citizens.[19]

Other civic volunteers also recalled the great personal sacrifice of the deceased and his organizational abilities. The succeeding president, Msgr. Francis Kowalczyk, described him as a "Great alms-giver." Msgr. Burant was buried on August 29, 1964.

The next change was the assumption of the executive director post on September 15, 1963, by Czesław Rawski, who over the five prior years had worked in the PAIRC's branch offices in Europe. He remained the executive director until August 15, 1964.

Both events, especially the passing of Monsignor Burant, marked the closure of a certain stage in the Committee's work. Due to his undoubted organizational talent, and the respect he had in political circles, in the U.S. Congress, and throughout the Polish American community, many of the Committee's proposals, and its many appeals, fund drives, and initiatives could count on support. In this period, the Committee's labors were directed toward the following objectives: (1) facilitating emigration, (2) relief for hard-core cases, (3) helping refugees assimilate in the countries of their resettlement. The Committee

Rt. Rev. Msgr. Francis P. Kowalczyk, president of the PAIRC, 1964–1968.

received funding from federal sources for this work. That help varied, depending on the State Department's budget for the given year. In 1964 PAIRC received $50,800 from USEP, while in 1965 it received $47,850. Financing from this source was designated for European operations, and to pay for offices and personnel there.

To this the Committee added its own funds, such as those collected during the Pulaski Day Parade in 1963 ($3,405.72) or the profit from the annual PAIRC ball in New York ($4,880.10 in 1963) and other enterprises or events such as holiday appeals and radio campaigns. Between July 1964 and the middle of April 1965, the PAIRC sponsored the immigration of 65 refugees to the United States, issued 60 affidavits and 25 assurances. For comparison's sake, from July 1963 to April 15, 1964, eighty refugees were brought to the States, and 42 affidavits and 19 assurances were issued. These figures confirmed the decline in the numbers of new arrivals and cases sponsored by the PAIRC.

Where the situation in Europe was concerned, on December 31, 1964, there were 82 cases pending for 99 persons in Germany, 34 cases for 40 persons in Austria, and in the remaining countries the proportions were as follows: France, 33 cases/45 persons; Italy, 27/47. Together, that totaled 196 cases for 261 refugees. Regarding cases that did not qualify for emigration, there were 7,000 Poles not permanently settled in the Benelux countries (i.e., Belgium, the Netherlands, and Luxembourg), of whom 2,733 were registered with the PAIRC. Of the PAIRC total, 116 had expressed interest in further emigration, and 2,094 wanted to integrate on site. In Austria, of 700 Poles not permanently settled, 266 were registered with the Committee. Forty-six of those registered with the Committee were ready to emigrate further, and 76 wanted to settle permanently where they were. In France, of over 8,000 persons not permanently settled, 2,521 were registered with the PAIRC. Of those, 86 wanted to emigrate further, 55 had decided to seek permanent status where they were, and 35 cases were closed. Of the Polish refugees in Germany, 15,235 were registered with the PAIRC, and 825 of them were ready to emigrate elsewhere, 1,720 sought permanent residence on site, and 45 cases were closed. In Italy, 558 Poles had unresolved permanent residence. Of 465 persons registered with the PAIRC, 9 were ready to emigrate, 23 were ready to integrate, and 9 cases were closed.[20] For the sake of comparison, it is worth quoting the numbers in the Committee's 1966 report. In the European branch offices of the PAIRC, 20,379 persons were registered—15,112 in Germany, 2,218 in France, 2,360 in the Benelux countries, 237 in Austria, and 452 in Italy. In the reporting year, the PAIRC had enabled the emigration or integration of 446 persons, of whom 90 emigrated to the United States, 33 moved to Canada, 19 moved to Australia, 25 moved to South Africa, and 68 moved to West European nations. These were mostly the newest escapees from Communist Poland. In that same year, several hundred Polish children in Germany and Italy enjoyed summer camps thanks to the PAIRC's assistance. In addition to these matters, a lot of effort was poured into 23 proposals for the social integration of hard-core families in Germany and 18 proposals for persons in Austria. Unfortunately, not all of them received the approval of the UN High Commissioner for Refugees, causing enormous disillusionment among the interested DPs.[21]

Coming back to Committee sponsorship, from April 15, 1966, to May 1, 1967, the Committee, through its foreign branch offices, enabled the immigration of 91 persons sponsored by it (in the prior year 101 persons had been sponsored), 16 affidavits were issued (in the prior year 13), and 85 parolees received assurances (versus 44 in the prior year).[22]

The Committee's 20th anniversary year was 1967. The anniversary was utilized to sum up accomplishments and to open up a broader front toward the Polish American community, making it more aware of the need to continue its generosity on behalf of the refugees and escapees. Ludwik Łubieński, the Committee's delegate headquartered in Munich, arrived from Europe and toured Polish communities in the United States and Canada. The aim of his trip was to present the Committee's work in Europe, to appeal to the generosity of the communities, and, also (as already discussed earlier), to try to establish a PAIRC division in Canada. In the United States, Łubieński was accompanied by Msgr. Kowalczyk, as the president of the PAIRC, and by Hieronim Wyszyński. During the jubilee year, the PAIRC president visited Chicago four times, Detroit and Buffalo three times, and Cleveland twice. Thanks to his efforts, the Polish National Alliance in Chicago gave $5,000, the Polish Roman Catholic Union of America in Chicago gave $4,000, and the Polish Women's Alliance in Chicago gave $1,000. With regard to direct assistance, the Committee accepted and guaranteed employment for 507 persons, of whom 58 people got financial aid. According to published reports, 2,850 clients visited the offices at 156 Fifth Avenue, over 10,500 telephone calls for advice were handled, and 43 interventions at the INS offices were carried out. As before, the Committee participated in the work of the American Council of Voluntary Agencies for Foreign Service. During the reporting period, the Committee's European offices registered 446 new refugees, while in that same year 445 refugees departed. These were emigrants who were able to get a visa to the United States or other countries, as well as persons who had settled permanently (i.e., had integrated) or who had interrupted their contacts with the Committee. For instance, 502 persons were registered in Sweden, of whom 307 were refugees (according to the USEP definition) and 157 were other types of emigrants. Thanks to the opening of a new ferry line in 1967 between Ystad, in Sweden, and Świnoujście, in Poland, 121 Poles decided to stay in Sweden. This was a new channel for refugees to that country.[23]

The year 1968 brought several changes. A totally unforeseen blow was the passing away of Msgr. Francis P. Kowalczyk, the PAIRC's president, which happened in Passaic, New Jersey on March 6, 1968. Msgr. John J. Karpiński, pastor of St. Stanislaus Bishop and Martyr Parish in Lower Manhattan, who was the chairman of the Committee's board of trustees, replaced the deceased president. And in Europe, another change was the departure of L. Łubieński from the European delegate ranks for the Polish Section of Radio Free Europe. Paweł Sapieha replaced him on February 5, 1969. From May 1968 to May 1969, the Committee facilitated the emigration of 544 persons as part of the United States Escapee Program, of whom 117 were from Germany, 138 were from Austria, 62 were from Benelux countries, 121 were from France and 106 were from Italy. Forty two persons were helped to emigrate outside the USEP program. Of a total of 586 persons, the Committee's offices in the United States were directly responsible for the placement of 242 immigrants.

In 1968, the Committee's European offices registered 607 Polish refugees, 56 Czechs, 5 Romanians, 5 Bulgarians and 1 refugee from the Soviet Union for a total of 674 persons. Clearly, the Committee had begun to assist refugees from other countries of the Soviet bloc. On the financial side, the cost of running the European network and the subsidy of refugees amounted to $66,908.60, while the costs of upkeep for the New York office and placement of refugees in America cost $52,217.25. In sum, expenses for 1968 amounted to $119,125.85. On the other hand, the PAIRC budget for 1969 foresaw expenditures of $73,245 for Europe and $49,080 for the United States. The general financing rule was that official U.S. agencies financed

Rev. Msgr. John J. Karpiński, president, PAIRC, 1968-1988.

the work and offices of the PAIRC in Europe, while the New York headquarters tried to gather funds for maintenance of its office and for special work directed toward hard-core cases and children.[24]

The following year was marked by the Committee's increased activity. At least 1,710 clients, who were given advice or were assisted in completing claims, came through the New York office in 1969. More than 23,000 Christmas Appeal letters were mailed. The deluge of letters thanking the Committee for its help continued unabated. Approximately 100 to 200 letters per week came to the New York office in this period. A growing portion of them concerned work done in Europe. Here is part of a letter from S.L. Rachocki, who settled in Joliet, Illinois:

> We want to express to the Committee our profound gratitude and admiration for the selfless and devoted work of the Committee's Brussels representative, Mr. Stanisław Merło. From the very first contact with the office of the Polish Immigration Committee in Belgium we were the recipients of Mr. Merło's care and cordiality, which most certainly went far beyond the call of duty. We most assuredly reflect the opinion of many Poles, who at the turning point of their lives come across the Immigration Committee's helping hand in the person of little known, anonymous heroes, of whom the Committee's Belgian representative is an example. Their devoted effort helps Poles in many points around the globe. We want to congratulate the Committee on its selection of people for such responsible positions, because they are the best proponents of your humanitarian and patriotic work.[25]

From May 1969 to August 1970, the Committee placed 286 persons in the United States (versus 242 the year before) both within and outside the USEP program. During that reporting period, about 600 persons were resettled in countries other than the United States. Where the registration of refugees in Europe is concerned, on August 7, 1970, the following numbers awaited visas: 191 persons in France, 59 in Italy, 68 in Germany, 67 in Austria, and 79 in Belgium, for a total of 464 persons. Just as in prior years, interventions were made on behalf of Poles residing in the United States, cooperation continued with institutions engaged in the care of refugees, and with congressmen of Polish descent. In order to reduce the high rent, the office at 156 Fifth Avenue was relocated to 17 Irving Place, i.e., the Soldiers' Home, the headquarters of the SWAP (Polish Army Veterans Association of America). The Committee's staff was also reduced as a cost-cutting measure.

The Committee tried to keep track of refugee issues. In November 1969 a conference on refugees was held in Washington, D.C., with 200 delegates participating. It was chaired by Bishop Swanstrom. Vice President W. Zachariasiewicz led the Committee's delegation, which included Executive

Director Wyszyński and Treasurer F. Popławski. The PAIRC continued to cooperate with the American Council of Voluntary Agencies for Foreign Service and the American Immigration and Citizenship Conference. From 1958 on, the PAIRC maintained contact with the United States Escapee Program, especially in Europe. Conferences such as the one in 1969 helped to define the line of work and to establish the rules of cooperation with various agencies and institutions, as well as to define the amount of financial aid from the State Department for each of the organizations. Participation in these conferences also influenced eventual adjustments to existing law.

In the summer of 1970, Wyszyński went to Europe to coordinate refugee affairs. He visited the camp at Zirndorf in Germany, and camps in Austria and Italy. He also visited the Committee's offices in Munich, Vienna, Brussels, Paris, and Rome. He conferred with Bishop Władysław Rubin in Rome and with Bishop Szczepan Wesoły, as well as with Kazimierz Papée, the last ambassador of the prewar Polish Republic to the Apostolic See, still recognized by successive popes despite the protests of the Polish Communist government. In Geneva, Wyszyński held discussions in the offices of the U.N. High Commissioner for Refugees and with the staff of the United States Mission.[26]

The end of the 1960s and the beginning of the 1970s marked a certain substage in the Committee's activity. This occurred due to serious political changes in Central Europe. It had to do with the 1968 events in Poland and Czechoslovakia, and with the 1970 Gdańsk protests in Poland. Czechoslovakia's fate in 1968 became a classic example of how the Brezhnev Doctrine of nonintervention in spheres of Soviet influence worked in practice, and of the domination of the Communist Party in each of the countries in the Soviet bloc under the threat of armed intervention. Thanks to the election of new leaders, the leadership group of the Czech Communist Party headed by Aleksander Dubček tried to bring about several reforms within the system, including a loosening of censorship and limited economic reform. This was called the Prague Spring. Moscow treated these moves as a *coup d'état* against the "community of Socialist nations," which brought in its wake armed intervention by Warsaw Pact armies in Czechoslovakia on August 20 and 21, 1968. The leaders of the Czech Communist Party were detained, all reforms were blocked, many people with liberal leanings were imprisoned, and liberal periodicals and newspapers were brought to heel. The armed intervention caused a mass exodus of Czechs and Slovaks, mainly to Austria, Germany, and Italy, as well as to Switzerland. The mass emigration was possible because after August 1968 the borders were relatively open. About one hundred thousand Czechs and Slovaks left Czechoslovakia, of whom 50,000 had been resettled by 1970, mainly in Canada, the United States, and Australia. About 25,000 awaited further emigration, while 25,000 remained permanently in Western Europe.

The events described above opened the eyes of the administration in Washington to the problem of national sovereignty and to the scope of democratic freedoms under Soviet domination. Once again it became clear that the refugee problem in the age of globalization along East-West rivalry lines was of a permanent character. Each successive political crisis brought on a more or less massive exodus, which had to be coped with at least for humanitarian reasons, if not for political ones. Observations of this sort became topical even earlier, namely after the March events in Poland. In March 1968, Polish intellectuals protested against censorship, although the real flash point was the staging of Adam Mickiewicz's *Dziady* (*Fore-Fathers' Eve*, a strongly patriotic drama forbidden by the Communist regime), which ignited student meetings and riots in Warsaw and in other academic centers. The Communist authorities headed by Gomułka took advantage of the situation to eliminate their opponents from public life. As a result, several thousand individuals, mostly Jews, emigrated to Western countries and Israel. A small number of these people took advantage of PAIRC's help. The group of émigrés who came independently of the PAIRC that year included well-known names in Polish culture, who continued their academic and artistic careers in many nations of the world. A significant group of scholars, most prominent of whom was Professor Leszek Kołakowski, maintained constant contact with Polish affairs, and with time became a source of support for the burgeoning democratic opposition in communist Poland. The next shock for the Polish authorities came as a consequence of the price hikes on food just before Christmas 1970. That led to organized strikes in Gdańsk and Szczecin. Strike committees were organized and strike bulletins were published. Most importantly, the authorities were confronted with several demands. The authorities replied by unleashing the police and the army, which used force against the workers. Several dozen people were killed.

The December 1970 events conclusively undermined the authority of the Communist rulers. The events opened the eyes of the younger generation to the real face of the system. And even though the team of Gomułka's successor — Edward Gierek, the new first secretary of the United Polish Workers' Party — tried to take a more liberal economic course, many people, including the strike organizers and participants, decided to emigrate. This meant new responsibilities for the PAIRC and new challenges for the Polish American community.

If for no other reasons than the above, the 1970s did not mark a break in emigration to the United States. To the contrary; in the period 1970–1979, thanks to the assistance of the Committee, 2,427 Poles came to the United

States, which meant an average of 263 persons per year. In the first half of that decade, the Committee assisted 1,062 persons (approximately 212 per year), and in the second half of the decade 1,365 persons, an average of 273 per year. Two-thirds were men, usually in the 20–40 age bracket, who were ready to work. Women made up 25 percent of the immigrants, and children only 10 percent. According to observations and statistics, about 90 percent of the Polish immigrants integrated into life on the new continent without any difficulties. This was made easier by the fact that about two thirds of those people had a technical or high school education.

Financial backing was also reevaluated. In the years 1947–1959, Polish American donations to the Committee, including American Relief for Poland and the Polish American Congress, totaled $555,688.76. Federal grants for the years 1954–1957 reached $46,128.05, or less than 10 percent of revenue. In that period, $98,742.31 was spent on help in Europe. The Committee's reserve fund by the end of that term reached $56,644.41. In the decade 1960–1969 as well, the Committee continued to be generously supported by the Polish American community. Not until the second half of the 1960s were large grants received from federal agencies. The Committee's own revenues in that period amounted to $559,753, of which the Committee forwarded $89,900 to Europe. Financial reserves decreased from over $90,000 to $69,900 in 1969.

The 1970s turned out to be equally difficult. Up to 1976, the Committee's deficits forced a continual borrowing from reserves. The reserves fell, by 1976, to barely $22,406. After renewing the government contract that same year, the Committee's reserves jumped to $120,118. Thanks to F. Proch's financial policies in 1981, the reserve fund was increased to $138,221, and that year's budget reached $181,914.

All told in the years 1970–1979, the Committee's own income totaled $523,861, and almost $300,000 was received in grants from federal sources. In the meantime, expenditures for direct aid to refugees shaped up as follows. In the years 1947–1959, $321,254 was earmarked for this purpose. In the decade of the 1960s $452,706 was expended for the same purpose, while in the 1970s that sum reached $617,860. It should be noted that the increasing expenses were in inverse proportion to the number of persons entering the country for permanent residence. The reason for the disproportion was the increasing per capita cost of bringing immigrants to the United States and the decreasing participation of volunteers in the resettlement process. In the 1950s a significant percent of costs was reduced by the work of volunteers.[27]

But absolute numbers can be misleading. In certain years the situation was so tenuous that rumors surfaced about the possibility of closing the Committee. Bishop Szczepan Wesoły reacted to one of those rumors:

XI—Swimming with the Tide: Scaling Down 161

Recently information has reached us that the ever more difficult financial situation of the Committee might cause it to completely shut down its operations. If this were to happen, it would be an enormous loss for the refugee cause. The issue of refugees is constantly alive and topical. Recently their number has increased, because escapes from Poland are more frequent and more numerous. These refugees are placed in various camps where they live in onerous and unpleasant conditions. The situation is becoming ever more difficult, because of longer stays in the camps, and lack of opportunities to emigrate. This situation is to the great detriment of the refugees, who are demoralized by prolonged encampments.

The Committee's work in past years has helped thousands of people to organize their lives anew, giving them a new start on life in the different American conditions. Aside from the political aspect of the issue, the Committee's activity is a humanitarian action. The liquidation of its operations would be a great loss to many refugees.

Without a doubt there are financial difficulties. Maybe they are partially connected with slack in the Committee's activities. An increase in activity might bring more funds. The one somehow is intertwined with the other.

We are writing of this to you out of a sense of concern that the help for refugees not be halted, both for those refugees already in the camps and those who will yet swell the camp ranks, so long as the existing political situation continues.[28]

The Committee's difficulties, of which the bishop wrote, occurred at a time when the Committee was deprived of federal funding. As has been noted above, with the increasing thaw between Washington and Moscow, the Committee's political functions broadened. This made its continuation all the more crucial.

The Committee's thirtieth anniversary, celebrated in 1977 and 1978, became an opportunity for summing up and reflection. Many congratulations and expressions of gratitude poured in to the Committee's office on this occasion. Bishop Władysław Rubin's letter best characterizes the atmosphere of these achievements, in which this spiritual shepherd of the émigrés also wrote:

> The work that the Polish Immigration Committee has done in the thirty years of its activity is worthy of great recognition. In that period the Committee rendered needed aid to fifty five thousand Polish émigrés, who thanks to that support found the opportunity to settle in new countries, especially in the United States of America and Canada, and also in Australia and New Zealand. The Committee provided not only emigration opportunities for these many thousands of people, but also found them housing, jobs, and money to tide them over in the first stage of residence in the new country. Rendering this necessary assistance was accompanied by a great effort to take care of many burdensome formalities which require a lot of time, patience

and appropriately trained staff. The Committee has been devotedly performing this onerous work for thirty years and for this reason has earned the gratitude not only of those who were helped, but also of those who know of this charitable activity. The objectives of the Polish Immigration Committee continue to be relevant. Though thirty years have passed from the end of World War II, the waves of emigration of our countrymen flow unabated in greater or smaller dimensions so that the Committee's existence is constantly needed all the more so that in the current period of economic crisis the difficulties of emigration have disproportionately increased.[29]

This letter came in handy during the Committee's annual fund drive. The 1970s and 1980s brought the next generational changeover in the

Members of the PAIRC board and representatives of the Department of State pose for a photo after the conclusion of sessions of the American Immigration and Citizens Conference at the Plaza Hotel in New York (beginning of the 1970s). *Seated, from the left*: W. Piłat; President Monsignor J. Karpiński; B. Watson, the administrator of Security and Consular Affairs of the Department of State; F. Kellog, the assistant secretary of state for Migration; and R. Murthy, executive vice president of the AICC. *Standing from the left*: F. Popławski, J. Świerzbiński, T. Maksymowicz, Kaye Kafka-Kowal, I. Morawski, J. Jabłoński, the Reverend L. Makulec, and PAIRC Executive Director H. Wyszyński.

staffing of the committee. Monsignor John J. Karpiński served as president since 1968. He was the pastor of St. Stanislaus Parish in Manhattan, and was a distinguished priest and social activist well known throughout the Polish American community. Thus the tradition was maintained that at the head of the Committee stood a priest from a parish that was known for immigrant care. Monsignor Karpiński served as the PAIRC's president for 20 years, until his death in 1988. After that date, the Reverend Monsignor Joseph A. Marjańczyk, P.A., was elected president. He served as the pastor of Our Lady of Mount Carmel Parish in Bayonne, New Jersey. He is a priest with many prestigious titles: apostolic protonotary of His Holiness, canon of the Metropolitan Chapter of the Archdiocese of Warsaw, vicar emeritus of the Metropolitan Archbishop of Newark, laureate of the "Chluba Polonii" (Pride of Polonia) award of the Polish Apostolate in the USA, officer of the Order of Polonia Restituta, and later, also of the Order of Merit of the Republic of Poland. The monsignor is known as the chaplain of many organizations, and is the initiator of many social campaigns, which both energized and united the entire Polish American community. He is the president of the Committee to this day.

Rev. Msgr. Joseph A. Marjańczyk, P.A., current president of the Polish American Immigration and Relief Committee.

Returning to the position of executive director, on January 23, 1969, the board of trustees elected Hieronim Wyszyński to this post due to the illness of Ignacy Morawski, which in the summer of 1968 made it impossible for him to continue as the executive director. Wyszyński was a veteran of the Polish Home Army, an inmate of Hitler's prison camps, and president of the Związek Polaków w Ameryce (United Poles in America) in Perth Amboy, New Jersey. He served as Morawski's assistant since 1966. Joseph Świerzbiński, an attorney, remained the executive vice president. He was one of the most senior volunteers on the Committee. His legal advice was doubly significant, especially considering the passing of Judges Zaleski and Bayer. Among vice presidents whose responsibilities barely had a titular character, the following names were to be found: Jan Dec, SWAP (Polish Army Veterans of America) commandant; Stanisław Gierat, president of the SPK (Polish Veterans of World War II — SPK); Vincent Kiejna, Polish American activist from Connecticut; Rev. Ludwik Makulec; Ignacy Morawski; Franciszek Proch; and attorney Francis Wazeter, the president of the New York Chapter of the Polish American Congress. Also notable are: Jennie Widlicki, the widow of an industrialist who was an active sponsor of the Committee; and Władysław Zachariasiewicz, who despite his job in Washington maintained contact with the PAIRC. Successive vice presidents were Walter Borzęcki, a Polish American journalist and activist; Ruth Żebrowski, the wife of a funeral home owner and, like Widlicki or Świerzbiński, a longtime Committee volunteer; and Feliks Popławski, who was also the treasurer. Some of the above-mentioned persons were also on the board of trustees. Bolesław Wojewódka should be mentioned as well. He was a social activist and the president of the Paratroopers Circle, who in later years, after the death of Stanisław Jordanowski in 1993, played an active role in the Committee's work as its treasurer.

There also were Kaye Kafka-Kowal, who was active for many years in organizing the Committee's balls; Dolores Regal; and Stanisław Rzetelski, the president of the Polish Home Army. On the other hand, the Advisory Council reflected the Committee's territorial scope to a certain degree. Its members included: Judge T. Adesko, A. Migoń, S. J. Kusper, Jr., Chester Sawko, Z. Radoniewicz, and Dr. E. Różański, all from Chicago; further, T. Wieniawa Dziekanowski, the owner of Teddy's Provisions; the earlier mentioned H. Korab-Janiewicz; M. Labowski; W. Marut; W. Sosulski, a SWAP activist in New Jersey; C. Szafrański; and E. Warlikowski, all of New Jersey; H. Budny of Connecticut, C. Polak of

Hieronim Wyszyński, the executive director of the Polish American Immigration and Relief Committee, 1969–1975.

Yonkers, and several others. By virtue of this fact, as also by personal invitation to New York events, efforts were made to connect the field more closely with the central office. Also, various promotional materials were sent to the field offices, which gave individual attention to these generous volunteers.

Nonetheless, certain differences in the style of operations became evident as compared to the period when Msgr. Burant was president. While the Committee's founder tried to directly influence the Committee's work, his successors moved most of the responsibilities onto the shoulders of the executive director, and to a lesser degree onto the executive vice president. For that reason, the filling of that post was crucial. At the moment of taking over the job from Czesław Rawski in 1964, Ignacy Morawski was already advanced in age. Fortunately for the Committee, many programs were moving forward on their own momentum; thus, Morawski's weak health did not affect the tempo of the Committee's work. In addition, as has already been mentioned, the Committee's board gave him the assistance of Hieronim Wyszyński, who had the opportunity to familiarize himself with the executive director's duties, which he later fulfilled until 1975. Franciszek Proch succeeded Wyszyński as the executive director. Proch was a law school graduate and a former prisoner of the Dachau concentration camp, was president of the Polskie Stowarzyszenie Byłych Więźniów Politycznych Niemieckich i Sowieckich Obozów Koncentracyjnych w Ameryce (Polish Association of Former Political Prisoners of Nazi and Soviet Concentration Camps), was president of the New York Chapter of the Polish American Congress, and was author of a well-known book about the fate of Poles during World War II titled *Poland's Way of the Cross*. He came to the United States in 1949, thanks to help from the PAIRC. Up to that time he was a refugee camp delegate to UNRRA. After its liquidation, and when he obtained his license from the German authorities, he represented Polish refugee cases in the German courts. The new director had a broader vision of change, particularly regarding methods of financing the Committee's work. He proposed the formation of an endowment fund of at least $250,000, and a permanent membership base. The PAIRC ought to get steady dues-paying members, he believed, just like the Kościuszko Foundation. He also brought attention to the need for obtaining bequests, particularly from those persons who had come to the United States thanks to the Committee's help. Proch's successor as executive director, and next also as executive vice president was, as of June 1981, Janusz Krzyżanowski. He completed his Ph.D. at Columbia University, concentrating in management and industrial economics. He is a former prisoner of the Soviet gulags, a former officer of the Special Unit of the General Staff for cooperation with the Home Army, is president of the Stowarzyszenie Polskich Kombatantów (SPK) in the USA and is vice president of the Polish American Congress. Earlier, he had worked at the Committee as treasurer; later, as vice president; and then as the executive director. The second large immigration of Poles to the United States after the strangling of Solidarity occurred during his tenure.

The day-to-day work of the New York office was carried on by Ewa Konikowska, Zofia Wełdycz, and Eleonora Witanowska. There were staff changes later on. But at this point, Elżbieta Truszkowska-Marciak ought to be mentioned, as well as Zbigniew Sygnarski, who worked there for 10 years, and Daniela Ptak, who worked for 13 years in the Committee's office, almost to the conclusion of its operations.

With regard to the offices abroad, in 1970 the entire European delegation, with its headquarters in Munich, continued to be overseen by Paweł Sapieha. His deputy continued to be M. Tyszkiewicz. Wacław Suchanek-Suchecki, on staff for several years already, played an important role and was responsible for matters connected with the office of the UN High Commissioner for Refugees, as well as for reparations and police cases. Mrs. Aleksandra de Notto was responsible for finances, banks, and personnel matters. Mrs. Evelyn Lasko was responsible for the secretariat, the archives, and registration matters.[30] Further staff changes occurred in the 1980s. The older workers, who lived in Germany since the war, were replaced by newcomers, who gradually took over the responsibilities. It should be noted, however, that from the 1980s on, the tenure of staff members working in Germany became shorter. With the passage of time, the workers assimilated more and more easily, melted into the mainstream of life in the country of resettlement, and undertook new employment outside the Committee. The Munich office was located at 46 Augustenstrasse.

The manager of the Munich office, which was the largest of all the offices abroad, was Wacław Dziewulak, whose administrative domain consisted of documentation for registered Polish refugees in all of Europe (for USEP) and of all refugee

Franciszek J. Proch, executive director of the PAIRC, 1975–1981.

From the left: member of the PAIRC Advisory Council Michał Preisler (whose daughter Ewa taught English for some time at the PAIRC), Executive Director Franciszek Proch, ball Chairman Alfred J. Bartosiewicz, and ball committee Treasurer Walter Bobrek — in conference before the PAIRC ball in 1977.

matters in Germany. Antoni Kokot was in charge of administration, and of accounting for the PAIRC's entire European operation. The secretary was I. Guzy, and administrative duties were carried out by Charlotte Andrzejewska. Zygmunt Jędrzejowski worked alone in the camp at Zirndorf. His duties included reception of refugees, and their initial registration and care.

Austria, traditionally important for the Committee, was staffed by Andrzej Balko, who lived in Vienna. In addition to the reception and registration of refugees, he also maintained contact with the INS and with the missions of other countries that were accepting refugees. He was assisted by Józef Podoski, who worked out of the camp at Treiskirchen, near Vienna. Podoski worked part time for the PAIRC, and the other half of his employment was with the Tolstoy Foundation. Work for the PAIRC's office in Austria's capital, located at 14/2 Postgasse, was soon begun by J. Barycza in the secretariat, and by Roman Rogoyski, the former secretary of Józef Beck, prewar Poland's minister of foreign affairs.

Beginning with 1968, Jerzy Złobicki managed the office in France. He was a former member of the prewar Polish government's consular staff. He was assisted by Wanda Grużewska. Złobicki was in charge of registering refugees and of relations with the office of the INS, the UNHCR, and the missions of nations that were accepting Polish refugees. The office was also responsible for contact with the local police, when necessary. The Paris office was located at 20, rue Legendre. Stanisław Merło indefatigably continued his mission in Brussels. The Benelux countries remained the region of interest of this office.

In Italy, as in Austria and Belgium, no staffing changes occurred. Witold Zahorski continued to represent the Committee in Rome, with offices in the SPK quarters at via Licia 19. His situation in the Eternal City was unique. As an active member of the SPK, Zahorski assisted the Committee with various social matters almost from the beginning of its existence. When the Refugee Year was announced in 1960, the center in Geneva, which was the hub of the network bringing aid to refugees in Europe, agreed to engage Zahorski for special projects carried out together with the UNHCR and the U.S. Mission. These programs included special help for various categories of refugees, including the hard-core cases. In time, he went to work for the Italian Caritas (UCEI) which cooperated with the Committee in sponsoring Polish refugees. The Committee did not have to strain its own resources, as it received very productive and needed assistance. Since the number of tourists and refugees coming to Italy kept growing, the decision was made in 1971 to move J. Podoski from Austria to Triest, where he worked simultaneously for Caritas and PAIRC. The reason for this state of affairs, namely the increased traffic in this area, was the easing of passport restrictions for trips out of Poland to Warsaw Pact countries. While on a trip to Hungary, it was easy to slip into relatively liberal Yugoslavia, and from there to continue on to the Adriatic shore and Triest, where the Italian consulate and a refugee camp were located. Thus, the representative of the Committee in Rome was interested in the refugees from the camps at Trieste and Latina. In Trieste, there were 102 Poles and 26 Gypsies from Poland in 1971.

Generally speaking, 165 refugees came to West Germany and 90 left in 1970. At the same time, 113 refugees arrived in Austria and 141 departed from it, while 84 came to Belgium and 48 left. On the other hand, 170 persons seeking refugee status arrived in France, while 122 departed.

The numbers for 1971 were as follows: 56 refugees came to Germany, and 54 left; 59 came to Austria, while 57 departed; 53 arrived in Belgium, and 18 emigrated; and 107 refugees entered France, with 76 emigrating from it. The figure of 107 included 17 Gypsies.

The cited figures show an astonishing trend. The number of escapees entering Germany was smaller than the number entering France. Second of all, Austria, equally popular as an escape destination, pretty much balanced out arrivals and departures; and as the statistics for 1970 show, more refugees left it than entered it. The raw numbers were not very impressive, but this did not at all signify less work. Refugees sometimes waited several years for emigration; besides, the PAIRC was still caring for well over ten thousand hard-core cases, which turned out to be the most lasting and difficult problem to resolve. Aside from this, the cusp of the 1960s and 1970s was an unnatural period for escapes from Poland in terms of numbers. After March 1968, intellectuals rarely took flight in "classic" form, that is, illegally across the border; more frequently they defected to the West during a scholarly or tourist trip. Many of those who wanted to escape were simply thrown out of Communist Poland. They also did not seek the PAIRC's help. Second of all, the statistics did not include the increase in traditional escapes, which showed up after the December 1970 events on Poland's seacoast.[31]

The Committee's ongoing work at the threshold of the 1970s did not basically differ from the prior several years. Its tasks continued in the same vein. The PAIRC enabled emigration for Polish refugees to Western Europe, the United States, and other countries. It continued to extend humanitarian aid to seniors, invalids, children, and other persons in the hard-core cases category through financial, material, and spiritual support. It helped fresh arrivals in the United States to adjust to the new living conditions, and helped secure employment and other life necessities for them. The Committee found itself increasingly involved in intervention with the INS on behalf of Poles. This resulted from the broader participation of tourists in the general number of arrivals. Many of them tried to remain permanently, others found jobs or extended their visas for other reasons. In the 1971–1972 reporting year, the Committee sent out 550 affidavits and guaranteed jobs for 650 persons, received 453 refugees from Europe and other countries, gave advice and instructions to 7,000 people, and conducted 30 successful interventions at the INS. Several dozen people were able to take advantage of the opportunity to extend their stays in the United States.

In the 1972–1973 reporting year, several proposals seemed to have prospects for improving the Committee's financial situation. First of all, it was decided to establish individual membership in the Committee. It was thought that this type of connection with a larger group of people would help popularize the Committee, and that the annual dues would fill the budget gap and also add to the reserve fund. Next, it was decided to publish a bulletin that would provide information on topics of current interest and that would report on the Committee's work. Another project was to get permission from the administrators of Catholic dioceses in America to conduct collections in front of Polish churches throughout the year. Appropriate letters were prepared for mailing. Finally, there was a plan to engage Polish lawyers in the Committee's affairs. The aim was to obtain bequests on behalf of the Committee.[32]

These measures had been employed for years by other organizations. But the Committee was a totally different kind of entity. The attempt to introduce these kinds of innovations, after decades of existence, was doomed to failure. Throughout the prior years, the Committee had been supported by an environment of its own creation, which consisted of parish groups, veterans' organizations, and social institutions which themselves had the support of their own membership base. In other words, the Committee was trying to get another dues payment out of people who already were members of other organizations that were generously supporting the Committee, and whose own financial resources were not that large. On the other hand, reaching the new Polish American community, or the entire Polish American community in the United States, was virtually impossible in the 1970s. The refugee issue was not page one news and did not arouse the kind of emotions it used to. The Polish American community was busy with entirely different issues. The only thing that could be done was to do long-term groundwork through the bulletin. But that, too, did not materialize because the costs of editing, printing, and mailing were higher than the potential revenue in the immediate future. Even church-front collections seemed to bring on more problems than benefits. The automatic agreement of diocesan administrators could no longer be counted on because the problem of Polish refugees paled in comparison to the human tragedies that were playing out in the world. Then there was the question of the direction of the Polish American community's generosity. The community was offered many other options from other quarters — often more attractive, closer to the particular community — in contrast to the distant and unknown reality of the refugee camps. The fund drives could no longer be conducted in an atmosphere of alarming need, or under the aegis of a great rescue mission. There were no such opportunities any more. Those campaigns also could not compete in terms of effectiveness with collections at the Pulaski Parade, which heightened the mood and opened the hearts and pockets of participants. But even there, the sums collected were minor in the overall financial picture. Generally taken, the ambitious plans to motivate the community on behalf of the Committee met with only partial understanding.

One of the obstacles, from the broader perspective, was the changed viewpoint of the entire American society. The first signs began to appear of a negative attitude toward mass immigration, especially of the illegal kind, which, as the argument went, took jobs away from American citizens. It should be remembered that after the oil crisis at the beginning of the 1970s there was an economic recession in the United States, inflation rose, and prices increased markedly. Immigrants, flowing in from everywhere, burdened the federal budget; but most importantly, they competed in the job marketplace. In the middle of the decade still another problem arose, motivated by political considerations. As a result of the conclusion of the Vietnam War, hundreds of thousands of Asians declared their readiness to emigrate to the United States. This pertained to residents of South Vietnam, an ally of the United States, and to several categories of people, such as children and the spouses of American citizens, members of broken families, and officials on various levels of the South Vietnamese government. And it was not just about Vietnam. The war in Southeast Asia created a problem consisting of hundreds of thousands of refugees. In 1981 alone, over 131,000 Asians were admitted to the United States. By the end of the 1970s, 325,000 persons from that region were waiting to emigrate.[33]

In the second half of the decade, the issue of illegal immigrants also became a serious problem. This especially concerned immigrants from Mexico, who crossed the southern U.S. border en masse. The issue ballooned to such proportions that on August 4, 1977, President Jimmy Carter proposed the amnesty and legalization of illegal aliens who had crossed the border before January 1, 1970. This was connected with specified health, security, and what was described as "moral" requirements. Those who crossed the border prior to January 1, 1977, were offered temporary resident status in the United States.[34]

Regardless of the long road to legalization that stood before this proposal, the existing situation was evidence of a shift in immigration policy priorities. Only a violent political crisis, bringing with it humanitarian problems on a grand scale, could restore the treatment of Polish refugees to priority status. From the Polish point of view, the events on the Polish seacoast in the summer of 1980 were a godsend, the consequence of which influenced policy on a global scale.

In the second half of the 1970s, the Committee continued its activity within the scope defined by existing conditions. During the first six months of 1975, 158 Poles arrived thanks to the Committee's efforts. For January 1 of that same year, the Committee's offices in Europe registered 954 political refugees, of whom 364 were in Germany, 233 were in Austria, 168 were in Belgium and 189 were in France.[35]

The report of Executive Director Franciszek Proch, for the June 8, 1976, meeting of the board of trustees, best reflects the transitional character of that decade for the Committee. The report had the title "A Year of Transition," and covered the period April 1975 to May 1976. One of the reasons for this mood was the pressure from Washington to close certain offices in Europe or to merge them with other ethnic organizations. The Tolstoy Foundation, whose headquarters were also in New York, was suggested as a partner. This is an old organization, established in 1939, with a stronger financial base than the Committee's base, operating in Europe on principles similar to those of the PAIRC. Its main clientele were escapees from East Central Europe, with Russians forming the largest portion.

The situation was discussed at the May 12, 1976, board of trustees meeting. It was decided then to gather more information from France, Belgium, and Switzerland before taking any steps concerning the offices in Europe. Nonetheless, during the discussion the trustees leaned more toward downsizing staff, rather than closing offices. It could never be assumed that in the coming years a given country wouldn't become a popular destination for escapees from Communist Poland. At the root of the plans to limit the presence in Europe were also financial difficulties, which could have helped spawn the idea to close offices. The idea to merge with the offices of other organizations in Europe did not win board approval.[36]

Financial matters were the main item on the agenda at the annual meeting of June 8, 1976. The Committee's financial crisis mainly happened because the Committee was unable to raise enough money to match the funds received from the USRP (United States Refugee Program — the successor to the USEP), which in consequence placed the existence of that part of the program in jeopardy. Second of all, donations from the Polish American community were relatively smaller. For that reason, at the abovementioned meeting the transfer of $17,665 from the Building Fund to the Committee's general account was approved, as was the sale of $5,000 worth of stocks to buttress the PAIRC's budget. It was also decided to intervene directly with the State Department in Washington to get back the funding for the Committee. Aloysius Mazewski, the president of the Polish American Congress, was to support these efforts. The proposal to energize outlying chapters of the Committee in Detroit and Jersey City, and to establish one in Philadelphia was in the same vein, that is, toward the improvement of the financial situation.[37]

The $25,000 grant from the State Department formed a large part of the budget. Mazewski and Proch went to Washington, where they were promised a positive review of the matter. The question of cooperation with the European offices was more broadly discussed at the board of trustees meeting held on December 14, 1976. Stanisław Wujastyk, the successor to Paweł Sapieha, and Michał Tyszkiewicz, as head of the PAIRC's European operations, participated in the meeting.

At the meeting, Wujastyk was sharply upbraided for operating on his own without consultation with headquarters. Among other things, he was criticized for taking an unapproved trip to Canada (he stopped in New York along the way) and also for presenting a budget proposal (regarding salaries) directly to Geneva, which in turn reflected on the amount of the matching

XI — Swimming with the Tide: Scaling Down

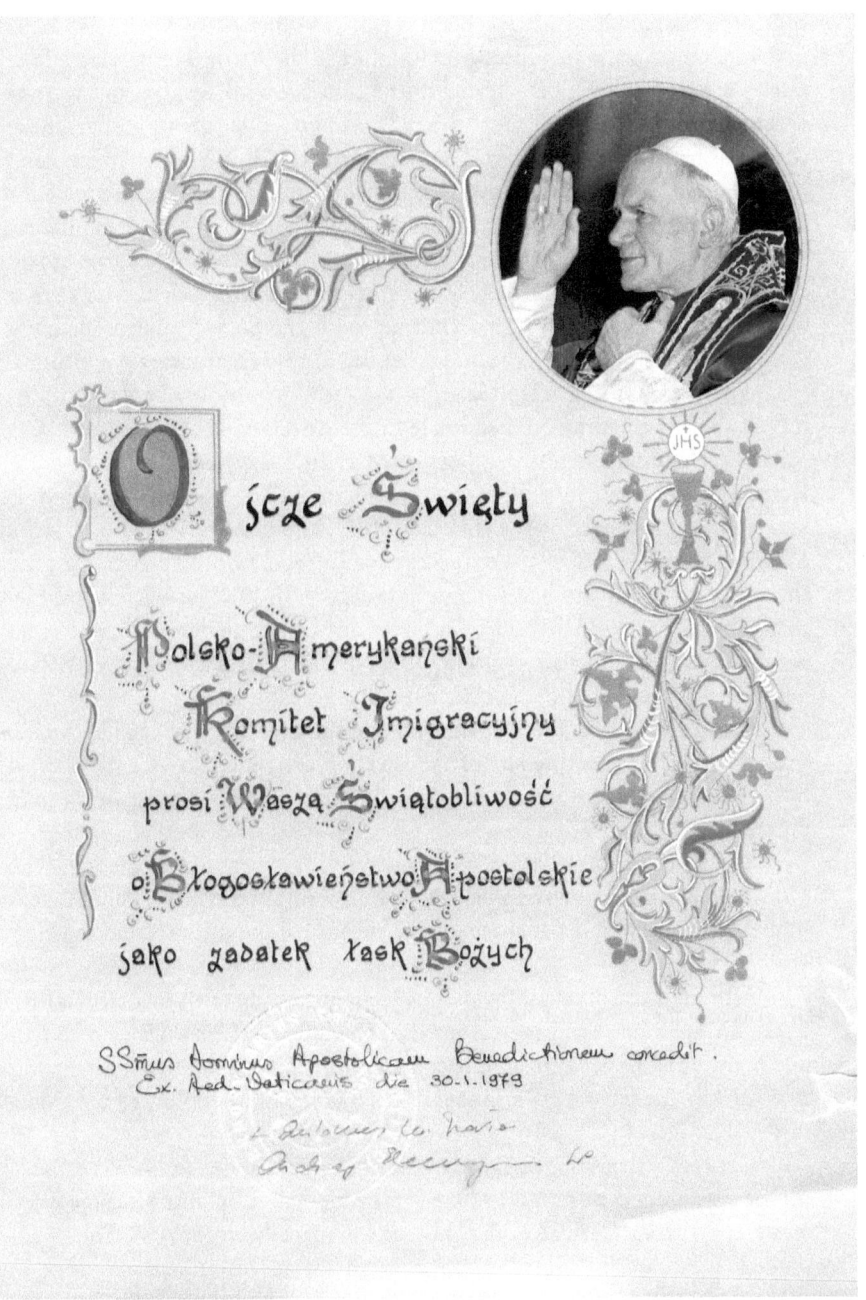

A papal blessing for the Polish American Immigration and Relief Committee from Pope John Paul II.

funds required, and which the PAIRC had to additionally pay in the midst of its financial crisis in order to maintain the matching funds ratio stipulated in the contract. This referred to the contract with agencies of the State Department, in which the Committee had to guarantee about 25 percent of the funds from its own sources. The staff of the PAIRC's Munich office, once the Committee's first and only European outpost, and at the moment the European headquarters, felt that they had the right to some independence, as they received their operating funds directly from the State Department offices in Geneva. They evidently did not notice that it was the New York headquarters that had to sign a contract with the State Department every year, on the basis of which the budget of the European offices was approved.

The situation that resulted from the rather caustic exchange of opinions at the aforementioned meeting led to tense relations between the Committee's headquarters and Wujastyk. In 1978 a new deputy director for Europe was chosen, in the person of Andrzej Balko, who up to that time had been the manager of the Austrian office (the director of the New York office was also, nominally, the director for Europe). Unfortunately, shortly thereafter he fell ill and had to undergo surgery. In 1979 he was replaced by the manager of the PAIRC office in Germany, Dr. Ludwik Frendl, and from that time on both functions were handled by the same person. The PAIRC's new site was located at 6 Zwibruckenstrasse in Munich.

In 1978 the Committee opened an office in Sweden, managed by Marek Trokenheim, and the director of the Paris office, Żłobicki, was superseded by Mieczysław Josz de Dulmen. He, in turn, was succeeded by Wanda Grużewska.

The opening of a branch in Houston, Texas, was a real success. The Houston contingent even had plans to start a credit union under the PAIRC's umbrella. But that did not come to pass because of opposition from the New York headquarters.

Although the above information seemed to indicate a favorable prognosis, on the other hand the Committee was surprised by a decision to halt payments of $250 per person to partially cover resettlement costs, which was refunded by the federal government. This was yet another blow to the Committee's budget.[38]

Generally, according to the executive director's report, in 1977 the Committee was able to bring 203 refugees to America, of whom 86 came from Austria, 84 from Germany, and 33 from France. Moreover, 47 Poles succeeded in emigrating from Italy. Although the registrations were done in that country by Caritas, PAIRC participated as the sponsor. The Committee received a partial refund of the expenses connected with those operations.

Where financial matters were concerned, 1978 presented a better picture. The Committee regained the full measure of Washington's trust, and renewed its registration with the American Council of Voluntary Agencies for Foreign Service, Inc. The Committee received $170,000 for maintaining its offices in Europe and $53,750 for helping immigrants with resettlement in the United States.[39]

The issue of the contracts with the USRP was difficult to resolve quickly. The European visit of the Committee's executive director, Franciszek Proch, was to serve that end. His main partner in the negotiations was Charles Stein, the chief of the U.S. Mission to Humanitarian Organizations in Geneva. One of the problems was the high cost of PAIRC operations in Europe. In 1972 the cost per registered refugee was $118, but in 1977 it was already $232. Meanwhile, the average for all organizations registered with the American Council of Voluntary Agencies for Foreign Service was $175 per refugee in 1977. In other words, federal funds were not being used sparingly enough. Besides this, the matching fund was not doing too well. It was successful with other organizations, but weak in the Polish American community.

The situation in Italy also had its difficulties, in that Polish refugees were registered outside PAIRC structures; therefore, from the point of view of the State Department funding, the PAIRC there missed the point. In response to the above, Director Proch received approval for the 1978 budget, but with stronger emphasis on matching funds from the Polish American community. After his return, Proch suggested a series of staff cuts in the European PAIRC, and moving the European headquarters from Munich to Vienna. The main reason for this move was that the PAIRC office in the camp in Zirndorf, where the most active center for registering Poles in Germany was located, was marked for closing because the camp director needed the space. That, in turn, shifted the main burden of the work to Austria. Also, there was an oversized staff in Germany, which had caused the difference of opinion with S. Wujastyk, the prior director.[40]

It was a bold plan, which adjusted the main sponsor's work style requirements, and also cut personnel expenses in Europe to fit the measure of existing limitations. At that time, there were 14 full-time employees in Europe. This represented a big chunk of the budget. The most important achievement of Proch's European trip was the continuation of the contract, which was the main item in the PAIRC's budget. Equally promising was the possibility of cooperation with Canadian centers for aiding immigrants through the Polish Canadian Congress. In the light of legal restrictions, the establishment of a branch, or the subordination of Canadian organizations to the Committee in New York, was no longer considered viable. But having an ally in another country that accepted Polish immigrants was, clearly, a big plus.[41]

The number of refugees brought to the United States did not decrease; 187 of them arrived in the first seven months of 1979. A larger number could be expected, especially in light of the sharper conflict that was growing between the budding democratic opposition in Poland and the authorities, but financial limitations were an obstacle. This problem was also discussed during the Committee's annual meeting on July 28, 1979. A ceiling on European costs was established (without inner resources) of $20,000 to the end of the fiscal year (September 30, 1979), a promotional fund was established, not to exceed $5,000, and a review of the salaries of the Committee's employees in Europe was conducted. Once more there was a discussion concerning the State Department's suggestion to share the administrative costs of the European offices with another organization. It was finally decided that the Committee could not accept that proposal because it was feared that in such a situation there might be problems connected with the registration of refugees and that in the future that might even lead to loss of organizational independence.

The Committee experienced several positive changes, in terms of the social cross-section of the escapees. There were more educated people, who were ambitious to advance in the country of their resettlement, and who easily adjusted to their new environment. One of them was Ludwik F. Zon, who wrote in his letter to the Committee:

> I am writing this letter in connection with a change of address, which I made in the last several days. Up to now I lived in Philadelphia, where I worked as assistant to the technical director in Transcontinental Leather Inc. At first I studied English, and since the beginning of 1978 I studied chemistry at Drexel University. According to my professors I was a good student, so decided to take a shot at applying to Harvard University in Cambridge. At the beginning of May I had to take four exams, which allowed the selection committee to ascertain my level. In this totally unexpected way I became a student in Harvard University's chemistry department. I am in the doctoral studies program and if I don't meet with any larger obstacles along the way, I should be getting my Ph.D. in chemistry at the beginning of 1981. At the present time my daily schedule is rather tight, as I have to hold down a job in addition to my studies. For your information I would like to add that I came to the United States from Austria on March 17, 1977, flight Number TW833, permit number 117 5655, Visa A21 365 889. Once again I want to thank you and the entire Committee, and especially Mr. Balko in Vienna, for the help rendered, which assistance was and is the basis of all of my successes.[42]

This kind of correspondence reflects yet another trend, namely the emigration of a growing group of intellectuals from Poland, who had no opportunities for scientific development under the censorship and research limitations present there. Equally important was the adjustment of the remaining immigrants, who entered the mainstream of life in the United States. Władysław Malinowski of South River, New Jersey, wrote in August 1978:

> I want to cordially thank the Polish American Immigration Committee in New York for the financial support given me, as also for the personal involvement of many of its members in enabling the emigration of fellow countrymen who cannot stand the Socialist doctrine. My aim was not to make a fortune, but freedom of the soul and conscience. Here, in the States, I found both. So now I can be optimistic about my children's future, I can start a family, and I don't have to fear about bringing it up, as I feared earlier, and I can be an actively devoted Pole, for whom America is his second homeland, but I will never forget that first one, victimized as she is, whose freedom ought to and must be fought for. Having no family here, and without knowledge of English, thanks to your help I gained a firm footing on this promised land. I currently have a good construction job, I am a siding man, and I have a decent apartment. With time I will learn the language and will become a fully contributing citizen, grateful to you and America for this opportunity to live. Concluding these few words I wish continued productive work to the entire team of the Polish Immigration Committee.[43]

Stanisław Gierat, head of the SPK, wrote accurately about the matters raised in both the letters in one of his articles for *Kombatant w Ameryce*:

> Emigration from Poland will always exist. The Communist Party's boasts that it is able to employ all idle hands in Poland and secure jobs and apartments for young people, has proven to be fictitious. Poland continues to be a materially impoverished country, little attractive to more dynamic individuals, does not augur any chances for unfettered development and for achievement of a position in line with one's talents. Everything depends on the Communist Party, which gives jobs to those who serve it, and not to those who deserve them based on their knowledge and their professional qualifications. Poland has a gross national product growth three times lower per capita than the United States, and two times lower than West European nations.[44]

According to one of the Committee's outstanding activists, regardless of political factors, economic considerations will continue to make emigration from Poland a constant problem. Meanwhile, the American authorities did not want to share that viewpoint. For example, the continued operation of the offices in Belgium and France was defended with the utmost difficulty. The Americans pressed hard to get them closed. On top of that, they demanded a merging of the offices on the Munich-Vienna line. Janusz Krzyżanowski, the Committee's vice president, went to Europe in order to examine the situation on site. He was there during the first two weeks of September 1979. He visited London, Germany, France, Belgium, Austria, and Italy.

The most important discussions took place in Geneva, with Minister Stephen E. Palmer; John A. Buche, the deputy chief for humanitarian affairs of the U.S. Mission to International Organizations; Douglas R. Hunter, humanitarian affairs officer; Paul Hodara, the chief accountant; and Vera Steiner, the financial auditor. As a result of the discussion held in the presence of Dr. L. Frendl, Mr. Buche declared that the contract with the Committee would be signed together with the unamended preliminary budget for 1979–1980. Both Belgium and Paris were placed in this preliminary budget, which was a sizable success.

Regarding the general activity of the Committee's offices in Europe, Krzyżanowski determined that Dr. Frendl would be the acting deputy director to the end of 1979, because of the aforementioned illness of A. Balko in Vienna. With time, more precisely from December 27, 1979, Frendl became the deputy director of the PAIRC for Europe to the end of the fiscal year. Appointment to the next term occurred each year at the beginning of the next fiscal year.

As of January 1, 1980, the European headquarters was to be located either in Munich or Vienna, depending on Balko's health. Observation showed that the Munich site, where the Committee's European headquarters was located, worked productively under Dr. Frendl's leadership. In addition to him, the employees in that office included A. Kokot, bookkeeper Charlotte Andrzejewska (part time), and Henryk Królicki, who serviced the Zirndorf refugee camp and was contracted on an as-needed basis. There was also a part-time position paid for by the UNHCR for a person in charge of integration. The visitor-inspector from New York, in his report, suggested moving to cheaper quarters, organizing the documentation, and getting rid of some of the furnishings. All this was in order to trim expenses and was in response to the plans to move the headquarters to Vienna. In that case, the workload of the entire office would have had to undergo reorganization. A case in point was that only Królicki worked directly with the refugees, receiving and registering Poles in Zirndorf. Krzyżanowski saw one and a half positions for Munich and one position in Zirndorf, should the headquarters be moved to Vienna.

Meanwhile, the Vienna office was running with the help of Balko, who was slowly regaining his health, and with Lidia Berezka, an American who knew Polish, as well as with Mr. Szenderowicz. In case the European headquarters was to be moved there, the office would get an additional part-timer. Wanda Grużewska at that time headed the Paris office, and her work was evaluated as very good. The report stated:

Newly arrived refugees are directed to the police, after which the PAIRC takes care of them for two weeks, giving them 15 Francs per diem and in case of need a room in space contracted for with local small hotels. After two weeks the French social welfare agency takes over, and the Committee's office takes care of the legal and immigration formalities.[45]

The procedure was somewhat different in Belgium.

The Belgian police has our office address in Brussels (together with others). When a refugee goes to the police, they contact Mr. Merło by phone, who then offers the refugee moral support and takes care of the emigration formalities. From the very first day the refugee receives material support (food, living quarters, and even employment) from the social welfare department.

The problem in Belgium was the small number of registering refugees, which influenced the attempts to close that site. Thus, the idea arose to register refugees in Great Britain at the Brussels office, because the Committee did not have an office in London. Another solution, in case the office closed, was to have the headquarters in New York finance the Belgian site, which would cost about $6,000 per year.

In Italy the Committee's office was not independent in registering refugees. It worked in contact with UCEI, the Italian Caritas, and that in turn caused the reluctance of federal agencies to finance that branch. Krzyżanowski proposed placing Italy on the same level as the branches in France, Belgium or Austria, that is, to make this site fully independent in order to obtain federal funding. The matter required further deliberation. Among the conclusions from his inspection tour, Krzyżanowski proposed requesting a list of names in New York of every transport arriving in the United States. He also recommended turning to the Committee's European headquarters for a copy of the list of names of the transports sent from Italy by the ICM. He also recommended publishing specific instructions concerning the categories of persons for whom the Committee would be able to provide assurances. In addition, there was a series of practical suggestions to make operations more productive. One of the results of that trip was the establishing of contact with R. Treister in London, a member of the five-member Australian Commission for Emigration Matters, who expressed interest in organizing an émigré affairs office in Australia to work with the PAIRC.[46]

Generally speaking, the trip had some very positive results in terms of a closer familiarity with the operation of the Committee's European branches. Most importantly, it resulted in an extension of the Committee's contract, which meant the ability to have a presence on the Continent on the eve of serious events in Poland. Several months later, it allowed certain reforms to be carried out in the operation of the Committee's European branches.

The next step in improving the effectiveness of operations, and also in broadening emigration opportunities, was a proposal for an agreement between the Polish Canadian Congress and the Committee. It was proposed to open an office in Toronto, which was to:

1. carry on efforts with the Canadian authorities to broaden the immigration law in order to include as many Polish immigrants as possible.
2. receive emigrants at the Toronto airport who were directed to Canada by PAIRC's European branches, and to help them in finding housing, jobs and in taking care of formalities in government agencies.
3. retrieve from the arrivals (within a year or so) the loan received by them from the Intergovernmental Committee for European Migration (ICM) for transportation to Canada. So long as the law was in force, the Polish Canadian Congress could keep 25 percent for the needs of the Polish Information District Center, and forward 75 percent according to PAIRC instructions either to New York, or directly to ICM in Europe (as per the proposed agreement between PAIRC and ICM);
4. keep funds received from Canadian sources at the disposal of the Polish Information District Center[47]

The PAIRC declared its readiness to support the office's operations with an annual $1,000 grant until the center obtained its own funds from Polish Canadian community sources. In addition, PAIRC reserved the right to use the statement that it was resettling refugees in Canada in cooperation with the Polish Canadian Congress, whose agency was the Polish Information Center. Such a statement was needed in order to get the direct contract with ICM for transportation loans for the refugees. ICM required that the contracting agency place refugees in at least two countries and that is why the Committee, which placed refugees in only one country, did not have such a contract. It was only able to get loans for refugees from ICM on the basis of an agreement with ICMC (International Catholic Migration Commission) and the USCC — Migration and Refugee Service in the United States. The Committee's interest in an organizational connection with a Polish institution in Canada was also due to the fact that refugees could be resettled in Canada who did not have adequate political reasons for emigration, according to U.S. immigration authorities. Emigration to Canada could take place on the basis of economic usefulness, and not due to political persecution, which was also true of Australia. As mentioned before, the Canadian foothold never materialized, but contact was made between the PAIRC's European branches and chapters of the Polish Canadian Congress, which later on turned out to be helpful in many instances.

In July 1980 the first strikes began in Poland, first in Świdnik and in Mielec. In August, Anna Walentynowicz was fired at the Lenin Shipyards in Gdańsk, which sparked the strike at the shipyard. Soon the strike spread to other workplaces in the Tri-City region (Gdańsk, Gdynia, and Sopot) and to Szczecin. Following in the footsteps of the seacoast cities, strikes broke out in Śląsk (Silesia), where strike committees were also organized. The organization and the strength of the protests surprised the authorities to such an extent that they did not decide to use force as they had done in 1970. The strike committees also presented a number of political demands. In Gdańsk, the interplant Strike Committee with Lech Wałęsa, Anna Walentynowicz, Andrzej Gwiazda, and Bogdan Lis presented 21 demands, including the legalization of an independent professional union and pluralization of public life. Access to the mass media and liberalization of censorship were also demanded. The need was stated to guarantee basic democratic freedoms and freedom of religion, including the right to transmit Mass over Polish radio. On August 31, 1980, an agreement was signed between Solidarity and government representatives, which signaled legalization of the new labor union. But soon there were changes. In September, First Party Secretary Gierek stepped down and was replaced by Stanisław Kania. In February 1981, that post was filled by General Wojciech Jaruzelski, who was also the minister of defense. In September 1980, the Communist authorities began preparations to introduce martial law and to eliminate Solidarity from public life. At the same time, a list of people to be imprisoned was prepared. There was a serious confrontation in March 1981 when a general strike announced by Solidarity was cancelled. As a result, the Communist authorities gained needed time to complete preparations for martial law, which took effect during the night of December 13, 1981. In consequence of widespread arrests, tens of thousands of Solidarity members and sympathizers were detained and imprisoned. Among the detainees were the leaders of the movement, with Lech Wałęsa at the head, and also individual leaders of the union at the plant level. Even potential strike leaders or leaders of underground configurations of the union were detained. One of the basic tactics used by the Communist authorities against the strikers was encouragement for them to emigrate. They were promised immediate release from prison and issuance of a passport for one-way transport for the prisoner together with members of the immediate family. Thus, the Communist Party wanted to get rid of the most active opponents of the system. The prisoners held a broad spectrum of opinions about the possibility of leaving Poland. The most outstanding activists almost single-mindedly refused to leave, though some of Solidarity's rank and file took advantage of the opportunity. Moreover, there was a group of people — tourists and scholars — in the West at the time martial law was declared. Surprised by the events, they decided to remain in Western Europe. It is generally believed that about 100,000 Polish citizens found themselves beyond Poland's borders in December 1981, all of them potential emigrants. Some sources even cited the number at closer to 200,000.

The throttling of Solidarity was not only a blow to the aroused hopes of East Central European nations, it also confronted the governments of NATO member nations with a serious humanitarian problem. The decided majority of nations in the alliance eased the residency requirements for all Poles who were surprised by the introduction of martial law while they were in the West. With regard to the United States, amendments to the law did not have any direct connection with the events in Poland; nonetheless, the legislators had foreseen the possibility of adjustments if exceptional circumstances were to occur. On March 17, 1980, the Refugee Act of 1980 was passed (PL 96-212). This was the first legal act that confirmed the attitude of the United States toward refugees on a permanent basis. For it should be remembered that all prior legislation had a temporary character and addressed specific geographic regions or specific refugee groups. It was also the first law that incorporated the UN's 1951 definition of refugees into American law. Most importantly, the 1980 law provided a permanent basis for the regular influx of refugees regardless of nationality, race, or creed. The new law included an interesting stipulation that secured two immigration tracks for refugees. The first, called normal, set a ceiling for immigration. The limit for 1980-1982 was 50,000 persons. But in each of those years, the president of the United States could raise that figure if unexpected circumstances demanded it. The 1980 law established a new office: United States Coordinator for Refugee Affairs, with the title of ambassador at large, nominated by the president. The duties of this office included setting policy on receipt and resettlement of refugees with clearance from the State Department and the U.S. Congress, and representing the United States before the governments of other nations and international organizations dealing with the problem of refugees. The March 17, 1980, act nullified the differentiation between the Eastern and Western hemispheres. Up to that time, the ceiling for immigration from the Eastern Hemisphere stood at 170,000, while for the Western Hemisphere it stood at 120,000. From that time on, the ceiling was set at 270,000 immigrants annually. However, the limit of 20,000 immigrants per year from any one sovereign nation remained as before. Several corrections were made in preference groups, and there were six of them. Two of them concerned professionals, artists, and highly qualified scholars, in both cases 27,000 could immigrate per year. The others defined preferences for persons related to U.S. citizens. The above categories had nothing to do with the 50,000 visas annually reserved for refugees. But only 10 percent of that number was allowed on the basis of political asylum, thus no more than 5,000 in the first year. The differentiation between refugees, aside from other elements, had to do with the fact that the asylum seeker was already in the United States or at its border, while the refugee was applying for the right to enter the territory of the United States from a third country.

An important element in the new law was the renewed definition of a refugee. According to the Refugee Act of 1980 a refugee was:

> ... any person who is outside any country of such person's nationality, or, in the case of a person having no nationality, is outside any country in which such person last habitually resided, and who is unable or unwilling to return to, and is unable or unwilling to avail himself or herself of the protection of that country because of persecution or a well-founded fear of persecution on account of race, religion, nationality, membership in a particular social group or political opinion.[48]

A spirited legal debate developed around the definition of persecutions and a well-founded fear of persecution. There was no generally accepted definition of what constitutes persecution. Threat of loss of freedom was an even looser concept, allowing freewheeling interpretation or outright rejection of a given refugee. For instance, one argument was that the limitation of freedom of movement constituted limitation of freedom. And such a situation presented itself in all the nations of the Soviet bloc, where the privilege of owning a passport or the ability to move freely within the given country's borders was restricted. Discrimination was another dilemma. For this reason, attempts were made to refer to the Bill of Rights and also to the Universal Declaration of Human Rights, which only partially satisfied the two sides of the dispute. For in various countries the same rights and limitations were variously defined. For instance, in certain countries discrimination had a racial character, but in Communist countries people who were not members of the Communist Party were not allowed to advance to higher positions in their profession. This also could be viewed as discrimination. No less controversial was the question of burden of proof with regard to danger to the refugee. In case of a sudden escape or a natural catastrophe there was the possibility that the refugee was not able to present adequate evidence of the threat to his or her freedom or persecution in the country of prior residence. In such instances the INS was inclined to treat oral statements as sufficient, if other statements or the general situation of the given country supported the statements.[49]

In general, this discussion related to Poland. It was known that the oppressiveness of the Communist system in Poland in the 1970s and later was not like what it had been in the Stalinist era. Only a negligible percent of refugees could prove direct persecution. On the other hand, a decided majority were able to declare the danger of loss or actual loss of specific freedoms, which was sufficient for an application for political immigration.

From the Polish point of view, it was important to leave up to the president the possibility for increasing the number of persons allowed to immigrate above the 50,000 per year limit. In light of the possible obliteration of the freedom movement led by Solidarity, this was a way out for potential refugees. The relevant section in the 1980 law stated:

> If the President determines, after appropriate consultations, that (1) an unforeseen emergency situation exists (2) the admission of certain refugees in response to the emergency refugee situation is justified by grave humanitarian concerns or is otherwise in the national interest, and (3) the admission to the United States of these refugees cannot be accomplished under subsection (a), the President may fix a number of refugees to be admitted to the United States during the succeeding period (not to exceed twelve months) in response to the emergency refugee situation and such admissions shall be allocated among refugees of special humanitarian concern to the United States in accordance with a determination made by the President after the appropriate consultation provided under this subsection.[50]

On this basis, Poles who found themselves in the United States prior to December 13, 1981, and did not want to return to Communist Poland, were enabled to stay by President Reagan.

The new law obligated the secretary of state to initiate language and professional courses for refugees waiting for immigration. The second assignment was help in initial settlement for the arrivals, known as the Reception and Placement Program. The law also safeguarded a broad program of aid administered by the Office of Refugee Resettlement in the Department of Health and Human Resources by means of officials who supervised the coordination of the expenditure of public funds in the refugee resettlement process.

In 1982, certain changes were made in the Refugee Act of 1980 which centered on the disposition of the Congress to quicken the employment of refugees by better coordinating cooperation between the private sector and state and local agencies. Secondly, a directive was introduced which limited resettlement to areas more densely populated by immigrants. It was advised to improve communications with volunteer organizations (like the PAIRC) where notifying the refugee of employment was concerned. Guidelines were also set for carrying out a study on the possibility for an alternative resolution of the issue of financial aid for newly arrived refugees.[51]

Despite appearances, the number of emigrants from East Central Europe to the United States did not change much. In fiscal 1981 (October 1, 1980, to September 30, 1981), 6,704 persons came from East Central Europe (it had been estimated that 6,900 would come); in fiscal 1982, 10,780 came and 11,000 arrivals had been planned for. In 1983, there were 12,083 arrivals as against 15,000 planned visas, and a year later only 11,000 arrived. In 1985 there were 2,000 less.[52]

When we compare the number of Poles within the general number of East Central European immigrants, the picture is clearer still. For instance, in the years 1975–1981, 6,078 Poles came to the United States as refugees, and 355 were political asylum seekers. All told, 6,433 persons arrived. In 1982 alone, that is, after the closing down of Solidarity, 7,504 refugees came to the United States and 200 asylum seekers. A year later the number of Poles was already lower, 4,625 and 805, together 5,430 persons.[53] This means that the number of Poles who emigrated to America after the abolition of Solidarity was not impressive. For the sake of comparison it is worth noting that in 1981, 131,139 Asians came to the States, while for that same period 33,000 visas were set aside for the Soviet Union, but only 13,444 were used. In the latter instance, the difference in the number of unused visas resulted from the opposition of the Soviet authorities to releasing Russian Jews to the West. There were more Romanian refugees than Polish ones. In the years 1975–1981, 11,309 Romanians emigrated, and in 1983, 4,346, or barely a thousand less than Poles.[54]

It should be generally noted that in the overall mass of refugees coming to America, the Poles did not represent a significant percentage. Nonetheless, their number grew dramatically in comparison to the immigration from several years before, which signaled greater responsibilities for the Committee.[55]

This is confirmed by the fiscal year 1981 report included in the report of the Office of Refugee Resettlement and of the Social Security Administration to Congress of January 31, 1982:

> Due to the extremely volatile and dangerous political situation in Poland, since August 1980, the number of people seeking political asylum has quadrupled. The refugee camps in Europe, particularly in Austria are swelling with Polish refugees, and there is no relief in sight; if anything, their numbers will increase this coming year. The PAIRC has already experienced a significant increase in the latter part of 1981. Usually, the agency alone handles about 300 refugees a year. In the period 1980/1981, out of a total of about 4,000 Polish refugees entering the U.S.A., 458 were relocated by the PAIRC. At the present time there are about 15,000 Poles awaiting

emigration visas, mostly to the United States, and that number is sure to continue to grow as long as the situation in Poland does not improve. The PAIRC most certainly is prepared to handle its share.[56]

The *New York Times* also wrote about this in the first half of 1981. According to the article of April 7 of that year, 1,400 Poles awaiting asylum arrived in Austria in the first quarter of the year:

> The Intergovernmental Committee for Migration (ICM), which is involved in the resettlement of refugees, said the Poles made up the majority of the 1,678 East Europeans who registered from January and March. In the first three months of last year, 650 East European refugees registered in Austria.[57]

It is clear from this that both the federal authorities and the Committee were aware of the oncoming wave of refugees independent of the direction that events by the Vistula River might take, which the date of the document confirms. In analyzing the above statistics, one more thing ought to be remembered. Namely, of the overall number of Polish refugees who came to the United States from 1981 to the end of May 1986, only 3,000, or 10 percent of the total number, were real members of Solidarity. This was a significant, but not an impressive number.

XII
Activity in the Years 1980–1990

The decade of the 1980s was marked by vigorous activity and by several internal changes. At the quarterly meeting of the Committee on February 23, 1980, salaries were set for the staff in Europe, with several changes. The salaries of Balko and Zahorski in Italy remained the same, but Frendl, as the new deputy director, got a raise. The overall budget for Europe was $132,482, of which $107,158 was covered by a federal grant and $25,324 was contributed by the Committee. At the end of 1979, the Committee received about a $30,000 increase in its budget thanks to a large donation from the Barbara Piasecka-Johnson Foundation. The foundation also supported the Committee in the following years.

As a result of the new division of work, there was to be a return to the function of office manager. The executive director was to focus on maintenance of relations with government institutions and on general planning. The reason for the anticipated changes was the announced departure of Franciszek Proch after a five-year term. The reason for his decision was his departure from New York for health and family reasons. The aim was to make the office work more effective during the absence of an experienced director. On the other hand, the 40 percent increase of the Committee's rent as of March 1 by the Soldier's Home forced the Committee to cut costs and look for other quarters.[1]

The remaining elements of the proposed reorganization of the office in New York took up the next two meetings, on August 26 and September 8, 1980. According to the new plan, the board of trustees was the lead body of the Committee, to which the Executive Committee and the executive director reported directly. The executive director, in consultation with the above two organs, controlled contacts with refugee and federal organizations, and also controlled the finances. Moreover, he was responsible for the New York office, outlying branches and the PAIRC's European offices. Within the parameters of his administrative responsibilities, the executive director managed the office and supervised the work of the secretariat through his office manager. The office manager maintained documentation and financial materials, did promotion, and monitored the refugees after their arrival in the United States. He also coordinated the receipt of immigrants at the airport or some other port of entry and took care of transportation arrangements to the final destination. The resettlement counselor was responsible for securing housing, for job counseling, for advising on professional schooling, and for change of place of residence in the United States. Both the immigration counselor and the resettlement counselor were responsible to the office manager.[2]

The responsibilities thus defined guaranteed a better organization and were a departure from the practice of having the executive director responsible for virtually everything concerning the day-to-day functioning of the Committee. The ambitious reorganization plan, even though it was not put

JFK airport in New York, October 5, 1987. A group of refugees sponsored by the PAIRC is met by Dr. Elżbieta Tracewicz (*in the middle*), at one time an employee of the Committee's New York office, and currently a volunteer, who escorted everyone to their hotel.

New York, December 13, 1985, the emblem room [sala herbowa] in the Polish Veteran Home, next to the Committee's office. Executive Vice President Janusz Krzyżanowski holds his "informational talk" with a group of refugees that had arrived in the United States on December 12 and was to be resettled in the New York metropolitan area. The visible face is that of office worker Ewa Korzińska. Other refugees located beyond the metropolitan region received the PAIRC brochure by mail with all the essential information. (David Reiss/The Media Group)

into practice in the end, was evidence of the Committee's resourcefulness. An even more important necessity which kept hanging over the Committee was the issue of a more complete integration of the European branches in line with the requirements of State Department agencies. For this reason, the next emissary of the Committee's board, Jerzy Werner, went on a trip to Europe in the summer of 1980. He visited Munich, Vienna, and Geneva. His visit occurred in August 1980 while strikes were developing in Poland, which was reflected in the issues that he discussed. During his stay in Vienna, for the first time in the history of the PAIRC's branch there, the U.S. consul in that city came by for a visit, and "for a few hours we discussed all the refugee problems in Vienna. The American authorities were particularly interested to obtain information if whether in connection with the strikes in Poland a greater number of immigrants ought to be anticipated. We of course replied that only the development of events in Poland could bring the answer to that question."

After the talk, the refugees receive their first assistance, which is paid out by PAIRC staff member Ewa Korzińska in the presence of Executive Vice President Janusz Krzyżanowski. After that formality comes the assignment of lodging and a discussion about the first job. (David Reiss/The Media Group)

In a further part of his report Werner wrote:

"Observing the over-all work of the Vienna office I was pleasantly surprised with the contacts that Mr. Balko had made in Vienna with the Austrian and American authorities. He is the only representative of refugee offices like ours who is regularly invited to all the official ceremonies in the American Embassy and Consulate."[3] But the Viennese branch had one nagging problem, namely, lack of a Committee representative in the Treiskirchen camp near Vienna. Austria's political neutrality caused that camp to be the goal of many "tourist" trips from Poland for those who planned to emigrate to Western countries. Thus, many Poles were registered by alien organizations. This problem could not be handled without a representative in that camp.

A heretofore unknown element was the growing emigration trend to Australia, which at certain times was stronger than emigration to the United States. The reason was the difference in expectations of those two countries. Whereas the emigration admitted to the United States was of a political character, Australia and Canada did not create difficulties for nonpolitical emigrants. The only more serious requirement was that the candidates not have been convicted of any crime. In addition, the refugees were encouraged by the shorter bureaucratic path, that is, a shorter waiting period and better conditions offered during the primary period of adaptation. Where numbers are concerned, the PAIRC office registered 603 persons in Vienna between January 1 and August 14, 1980, of whom 19 emigrated to Canada, 114 went to the United States and 154 went to Australia. As Werner reported:

> Emigration to Australia is a peculiar phenomenon in Vienna. The Australian authorities presented the refugees with excellent terms, guaranteeing them employment, transportation, and English language courses, and what is most important, a wait, at first, of no more than 3 weeks for emigration. Later that stretched out to about 5 weeks, but in comparison to other countries that is such a short time that many new refugees, who were thinking of going to the United States or Canada, decided to go to Australia. This primarily concerns people who are young, healthy and believe that they do not have the opportunities in Canada or the United States that Australia is creating for them by facilitating the quickest possible departure for them.[4]

Of course, the Committee had little to say about how long the bureaucratic procedures took. The Australian authorities did not refund the Committee the expense of preparing each emigrant's case, and these emigrants were not included in the budgetary statistics of the USRP. The lack of a Committee representative in Treiskirchen allowed other factors to influence the Polish refugees. Fortunately, Werner promised Balko that the appropriate items would be included in the following year's budget to allow the placement of a PAIRC representative in the above-mentioned refugee camp.

In Geneva, Werner met with Sievers and Hodara of the U.S. Mission to humanitarian organizations. Both of them served notice about possible cuts in the future budget, nonetheless they were open to the need for a part-time position in Treiskirchen. In Geneva, Werner also spoke with Carlin, the chief of the Inter-governmental Committee for Migration (ICM). The main item on the agenda was that the Committee wanted to get an independent contract for carrying out its obligations connected with the transportation of refugees from Europe to the country of final destination. Werner received an assurance that the appropriate application by the Committee in this matter would reap positive results.[5]

In their search for funds, PAIRC Treasurer Kazimierz Rasiej and Director Franciszek Proch decided to turn to the United Way, which had its headquarters at 99 Park Avenue in Manhattan. This organization raised funds and then distributed them in the name of the donors, usually large corporations. An appropriate letter from the Committee was prepared and sent on May 8, 1981, and was signed by Executive Director Proch. The Committee's work over several decades was highlighted, as were the needs of the moment, which was a clear allusion to Solidarity's fight in distant Poland. The letter said:

> Since 1977 the Committee has a contract with the United States government, a resettlement grant for refugees coming under our auspices from Austria, Belgium, France and West Germany, which covers approximately one half of our expenses per person. All political asylees processed in the United States are not covered by this grant. Over 70 percent of PAIRC's expenses constitute direct aid to refugees such as rent for the first month, food, medical and travel expenses, as well as English courses. Due to the present economic situation, with spiraling inflation and curtailment of federal grants, we are forced to seek new sources of funds.[6]

The efforts made in this matter by Proch's successor dragged on for almost two years and were finally crowned with success in 1983. From that time on, the United Way supported the Committee with a modest donation to the end of its activity. A negative aspect of the new sponsor was the requirement for detailed accounting. On the other hand, gaining United Way help was important in that a larger wave of emigrants was approaching, connected with the founding of Solidarity and the increased flow across borders. It should be pointed out that there were fluctuations in the amount of support that federal institutions gave to the Committee. The federal grants for the New York headquarters were mainly Resettlement Grants, that is, funds to assist the immigrant in integrating during the first phase of life on American soil, up to the moment of getting a job. It was calculated on a per person basis, and then multiplied by the number of arrivals. In the years 1964–1976, the grants amounted to an average of $25,000 per year, ranging from $16,666 to $45,000, depending on the year. In the years 1975–1976, the Committee received no grant, although it resettled almost 450 refugees. On the other hand, in the years 1977–1979 the grant amounted to an average of $250 per capita, although that barely covered 40 percent to 50 percent of the costs. The other problem was that the funds had to be expended before they were refunded by the federal government. Aside from this, the Committee lost a lot of money because the total sum of expenses did not include the costs incurred for refugees arriving from Italy during these years. Not until 1979–1980 was the Resettlement Grant raised to $350 per person. This raise came at the moment when the first of the increased wave of immigrants appeared on the horizon. During the Committee's board of trustees meeting of April 4, 1981, it was unanimously approved to increase staff in case of sudden needs connected with the anticipated wave of refugees.[7]

This matter was discussed during the Executive Committee meeting of May 12, 1981:

XII — Activity in the Years 1980–1990 193

The matter was first viewed from the ability of the organization's constitution and it was the view of the undersigned and others present that assistance could be rendered for persons emigrating to places other than the USA. Upon that note it was voted that the Director may authorize an expenditure of $15,000.00 for this increased activity. Included in the $15,000.00 would be a portion of up to $3,000.00 for the immigration of Poles to Sweden if such materializes.[8]

Pursuant to the above resolutions, the Committee tried to interest other sources in funding the anticipated refugee wave. On March 3, 1981, the PAIRC's president, the Reverend Monsignor J. Karpiński, sent a letter to the Barbara Piasecka-Johnson Foundation requesting additional funds, and on April 17, 1981, Director Proch sent a letter to Polish American Congress President Aloysius A. Mazewski asking him to try to get the Committee into all possible federal relief programs in Washington that might appear in connection with the new political situation. The goal was to hook the Committee up with new federal programs, since in prior years a series of political crises produced increased aid to refugees from Hungary or Cuba. By the middle of 1981 there was no such reaction yet. On the other hand, a negative situation crept into the Committee's work with the resignation of Dr. Frendl as deputy director for Europe, formally as of September 1, 1981. In fact, however, Frendl left his post in June. The cause was his poor health. The Committee thanked him for two years of productive effort. Stanisław Liptak took over for Dr. Frendl, and two years later the post was filled by Ryszard Rudnicki, the Committee's emissary from New York. Another change that year was the resignation of Franciszek Proch from the function of executive director. In his place the board appointed Janusz Krzyżanowski, who was already the Committee's first vice president. In order not to duplicate functions the newly elected director proposed to eliminate the post of executive director and combine all of those responsibilities in the person of the executive vice president, which was approved. Krzyżanowski agreed to accept the function for a term of three years with the right to cancel earlier.

The new executive vice president took on practically the entire current activity of the Committee as of June 1, 1981. He had an appropriate professional education and appropriate organizational experience. He sat on the Committee's board for many years, and independently of that he was the long-serving president of the Polish Veterans of World War II — SPK, a nationwide organization. In contrast to many local civic activists, he was very well aware of the complexities of Poland's political situation, which was of great help in the existing circumstances. The ability to explain many complex issues was key to receiving funding, and also was crucial in protecting the Committee from unwanted refugees, or possible political provocations.[9]

At that same meeting, the Committee's board decided to look for living quarters for the anticipated immigrants. It further decided to analyze the possibilities for the emigration of Poles living in various West European nations, to other nations. The objective was to avoid the time-consuming U.S. immigration process and to utilize the opportunity for emigration to Australia and New Zealand, which had been signaled earlier from Vienna. The European branches were also on the lookout for a possible exodus from Poland. Ludwik Łubieński, the longtime Committee staff member, wrote to F. Proch in a letter of June 4, 1981:

> Please remember that today the Polish question is on the lips of the entire world, so PAIRC's activities in Europe ought to be increased easier and more effectively. As word has it from Sweden, huge preparations are being made there in case of a massive Polish exodus, and the same in Austria. Therefore, increasing the staff in these offices ought to be considered already now. The INS ought to be pressured through Washington that it should apply other criteria toward the Poles in their emigration to the USA, because as it looks right now, they don't want to accept hardly anyone, and the procedure takes months. There ought to be pressure on the Canadian and Australian authorities to more quickly and effectively review the applications of Polish refugees, mainly in Germany, especially now, when there are difficulties with the INS. I know that there are efforts being made to have the INS also include Sweden in its operations, because there are a lot of refugees there, and there might be considerably more.[10]

Alarms in a similar vein were sent to the Committee from Munich. Dr. Frendl confirmed that Poles were emigrating to Australia and Canada in increasing numbers, due to the difficulties and the extended administrative procedure of the American INS. Increased activity and asylum applications could already be felt in Germany. Frendl wrote:

> In a paradoxical way, in contrast to the very difficult political situation in Poland, the authorities in communist Poland have liberalized passport regulations and the practice of issuing passports. The increased tourist flow from Poland is already apparent, of whom part is choosing asylum and wants to emigrate. That also increases our workload, and quite significantly; we are literally buckling under the flood of telephone calls and letters.[11]

Fortunately, an answer came from Geneva on May 5, 1981, concerning staff positions and salaries of PAIRC workers in Europe. They were increased by 10 percent, and a new position was funded in Munich and Treiskirchen. Simultaneously, it was demanded that the office in Brussels be shut down and that another position be eliminated in Rome.[12]

On the other hand, there were signals from Sweden, which was treated as a marginal point of immigration, that preparations were under way for receiving a broader wave of refugees. The signals were even made public. In the March 27, 1981, issue of *Svenska Dagbladet* (the *Swedish Daily*) there was an article about the preparation of boarding houses in southern Sweden, and even military camps, with the appropriate material and medical support for the refugees. In Gotland, military units were readied for assistance; even translators were brought in. What is more, the article stated that the Swedish Army would give the Polish Army help in Sweden, if the latter were attacked by other armies of Warsaw Pact countries. An armed response was prepared for any attempts at encroaching on the territory, airspace, or territorial waters of Sweden. It was a far-reaching declaration with serious political consequences. Also, Marek Trockenheim, the PAIRC representative in Sweden, reported on his meeting with two U.S. vice consuls in Stockholm on March 24, 1981, who declared the possibility of opening an INS office in Sweden for processing refugee applications. Up to that time those matters were taken care of in Frankfurt, Germany. The vice consuls received detailed replies to their questions concerning the scope of the PAIRC's operations in Scandinavia.[13]

Further news on the changing conditions in Europe was brought to New York by the following Committee members: Executive Vice President Janusz Krzyżanowski and board member Zbigniew Konikowski, who participated in the Congress of the Polish Diaspora of the Free World in Rome. On this occasion they visited, among others, the camp in Latina in order to seek advice on the wisdom of having two part-time positions in Italy. As it turned out, due to the camp's multinational character, the conditions there were poor. Nonetheless, the necessity of the PAIRC's presence in Italy was not subject to discussion. Moreover, Krzyżanowski and Konikowski visited the U.S. Mission in Geneva on November 17, 1981. In Geneva they were able to convince Mssrs. J. Buche and D. Hodara that the PAIRC would cover office expenses in Italy, which would guarantee the budget at the existing level.

This argumentation was convincing, and saved the life of that office. Geneva's proposal had been to merge the existing position in Italy with the Munich office, which could have been a preliminary step to elimination.[14]

On February 2, 1982, the Italian Ministry of the Interior granted permission for the official conducting of business in Italy of an independent office of the PAIRC on behalf of refugees.

These and earlier examples indicate that the Committee was aware of the changing situation and tried to prepare appropriately for it. Meanwhile, the Polish crisis had an internal character, and did not cause an armed intervention as in the case of Czechoslovakia and earlier Hungary. Nor were any signs of a mass exodus noticed; thus, one can understand the restrained reaction of federal elements. Yet, the example of the conversation of Trockenheim in Sweden was evidence that various options for a reaction to the Polish situation were taken into consideration.

Meanwhile in New York, the effects of a growing incoming wave of refugees from Poland was beginning to be felt. This led to certain difficulties in terms of proper housing and employment. In addition, certain newspapers and periodicals in New York, as well as in Chicago, tried to take advantage of the arrivals' difficult situation, by running articles attacking the PAIRC for inadequate assistance, in their opinion.

It should be noted here, however, that many arrivals had too optimistic a view of living conditions in the United States. Certain persons anticipated paid quarters in a hotel for many months and employment at unreasonably high hourly wages, despite lack of a knowledge of English and lack of professional qualifications. Many were shocked when they compared American conditions with social welfare in European countries. Moreover, not everyone could get employment in his or her profession. As is usual in such situations, individuals who were more active, independent, and streetwise assimilated more quickly, and found jobs and their own place more easily in the new environment. Some of the immigrants ignored the suggestions of the Committee and even gave up the resettlement conditions and employment offers, and decided to look for themselves. Such efforts did not always end successfully. Many then tried to return under the Committee's umbrella, but after the passage of a set amount of time the Committee was unable to support old cases.

Committee volunteers went out of their way for the difficult cases. Despite lack of funds, the hotel bills for many arrivals were paid for beyond the established period, and medical expenses were paid, as were telephone bills and other similar expenditures. How to take care of basic matters was patiently explained, official correspondence was translated, and assistance was rendered in city agencies. Meetings were also organized for young immigrants. Thanks to meetings with the arrivals, which were organized in the second half of 1981, the Committee finally succeeded in straightening out the image of America that the immigrants had constructed in their minds on the basis of movies and stories.[15]

In order to properly take care of the more numerous immigrants in that period, it was decided to reactivate the outlying branches of the Committee in America. Chicago was targeted in particular as having big housing and employment possibilities, as was the Houston chapter where Barbara Tomaszewska worked. The Chicago chapter was also important from the point of view of financial donations. In 1980 it was anticipated that $6,000 could be obtained from that source. Meanwhile, a new staff member was added to the New York office, and one other position was created. It was decided to purchase a telex machine in order to make communications with Europe more efficient. At the Committee board meeting of March 20, 1982, the budget was amended upward, from $215,700 to $311,000. All this was done in anticipation of the effects of martial law in Poland.[16]

Executive Vice President Janusz Krzyżanowski was to go to Geneva and Munich in October 1982 to check out the situation in Europe. Moreover, the Committee's longtime resident in Zirndorf, H. Królicki, retired, and a replacement had to be named for him. A couple, Mr. and Mrs. T.E. Kieniewicz, took on the job in Munich. There was also a change of guard in Belgium, although the flow of refugees in that region was moderate. The already mentioned Ryszard Rudnicki departed for Munich in the spring of 1983. He was a member of the Committee's council, and was designated to take over the responsibilities of deputy director and coordinator of the office for one year. In the meantime, the Committee was looking for a permanent replacement for that very important function. But due to lack of an appropriate successor, Rudnicki's contract was extended to 1986.

In fiscal 1982, the Committee resettled to the United States 160 refugees who had left their immediate families behind in Poland. Thus, the Committee was additionally burdened with cases of uniting families. Moreover, 245 persons in Germany who were approved by the INS in Frankfurt were waiting to depart, and another 230 were waiting for approval.

The report for fiscal year 1981/1982 stated:

The year 1981/82 was the most difficult period in the Committee's history. It was a time of increased Polish immigration, so not only did assurances and correspondence with Europe have to be dealt with, but also refugees had to be resettled, work and housing had to be found for them, and they had to be assisted with Medicaid, Social Security and similar formalities. In this period, with almost super human effort, we were able to place 958 persons (Sept. 1, 1980–May 31, 1981: 132; 1979/1980: 339 persons; 1978/1979: 328 persons) everyone is working and living on their own. The entire American refugee resettlement system, with the cooperation of government and charitable institutions, is going through a period of reform. This means that it is necessary to write reports to government departments, participate in conferences at the Department of State, at the INS, at Human and Health Services and in conferences with State agencies, which is a huge burden on the management.

The financial crisis in the United States is also reflected in policies regarding the refugee issue and mainly concerns the great limitation of the number of refugees admitted. Whereas four years ago the number of admitted refugees approached 200,000, in the last year (1981/82) only 90,000 were admitted, and for the current year the numbers are set at 55,000, of which about 15,000 from East Europe, including Russia and Romania. Seven thousand visas are set aside for Poland, but most of them are being used for Solidarity — and they are not registered in our office in Germany. In the last fiscal year the cost to the American government, connected with 90,000 refugees, was $2.3 billion. Hence the system reformers came to the conclusion that the refugee issue should become an international one, so that all countries participate in the costs. But in connection with this Washington wants to change the existing registration system in Europe and eliminate independent organization offices by withholding the so-called European budget for the independent operation of those offices. Among others this will especially impact PAIRC, Tolstoy and the Czechs, which organizations totally depend on funding from Washington. In this matter we expressed our negative attitude toward these plans in a letter to Undersecretary of State R. Funseth and in direct conversations with officials of the Department of State, and most recently, on December 30, 1982, in conversation with the President's Coordinator of Refugee Affairs.[17]

Faced with the possible elimination of funding, the Committee intended to undertake preparations for independent financing of its European offices. At any rate, the indicated limitations resulting from the difficult economic situation further hampered the Committee's work. Fortunately, the Committee could count on the support of other Polish organizations, including the Polish American Congress. The board of directors of the PAC discussed immigration matters at its meeting on August 6, 1982, in Chicago. Several postulates addressed to the federal authorities were approved. The Congress counted on opening broader immigration opportunities for Poles and on eliminating numerous bureaucratic obstacles in that regard. One of the resolutions concerned the PAIRC:

> In view of the continuing large influx of Polish refugees from Europe there is an urgent need to strengthen the resettlement activities of the Polish American Immigration and Relief Committee (PAIRC). To this end PAIRC should broaden its organizational base and widen its representation to fully reflect its national scope and purpose. In these efforts PAIRC should count on the support and cooperation of the Polish American Congress.[18]

The initiators of the resolution thought about opening one more chapter, in Colorado, which would be manned by Franciszek Proch. But this, due to reasons independent of the Committee, never happened.

Forecasts for 1983 did not augur a slowing down of the tempo of registration and the influx of new emigrants. The Committee's report forecast that:

The refugee problem in Fiscal Year 1983 will be as acute as it was in the previous year because of the extremely volatile and repressive situation in Poland. The situation of the Polish refugees became less serious in Austria, where according to semi-official estimates the number has dropped from 50,000 to some twenty odd thousand (out of which 8,000 Poles are already registered and awaiting emigration). These people have been stranded here by Poland's martial law and many of them are registering as political refugees. If last year's quota of visas allotted to West Germany will prevail, only a very small number of them will be able to reach this country, creating an untenable situation, especially for families with small children.[19]

The issue of reorganizing the system of registration and admitting refugees was alive for at least the next twelve months, which is attested to by the minutes of several successive Committee meetings. They show that the federal government had concluded that the creation of a centralized, monolithic organization for refugees and immigrants from outside America would be a more effective and less expensive solution than relying on a series of ethnic organizations which were funded by Washington for the most part anyhow. Nonetheless, the Committee felt that even if those intentions were to materialize, there would still be the need to maintain at least a skeleton crew in Europe in the event of further political changes. Undoubtedly the continued tensions in Poland and the persisting repressions against Solidarity raised PAIRC's rank in its relations with Washington and with regard to other similar organizations. At any rate the Committee decided to commit an additional $18,000 for fiscal year 1984 to support its European offices. It was expected that the offices in Belgium and probably also in France would close in 1985.[20]

The Committee's own assessment of the situation, based on tours of Western Europe and on reports from PAIRC offices on the continent, formed the framework for a memorandum titled "Problems Regarding the Admission of Polish Refugees to the USA," dated September 8, 1981. It contained data on 9,000 Poles who had come to Austria in recent months due to a loosening of passport policy and to both internal and external pressure on Polish society after August 1980. The huge financial burden caused by the presence of so many refugees inclined the Committee to recommend to the federal authorities the need for reforming immigration policy with regard to East Central European refugees:

> To cope with this new situation, it would be useful to review the present definition of "political refugee" and to modify it to include the new type of econo-political refugee from communist-ruled East Europe. The quota for immigrants from these countries should be expanded or, at the very least, the quotas from the whole region (Eastern Europe, Romania and the USSR) should be combined and re-allocated on an as-needed basis.[21]

The next opportunity to present the needs of Polish refugees occurred at an international conference in Geneva, on November 29 and 30, 1983. Krzyżanowski gave a lengthier paper there titled "Refugees from Poland," which contained an extensive historical sketch and also an analysis of the current situation. Many of its conclusions were identical with those in the prior document.

> The old definitions which differentiate between political and economic refugees can no longer apply to those leaving Poland. The repressive system of government is responsible for the econo-political conditions, and therefore for the mass exodus. The communist system is, first and foremost, an economic system but one which requires a police apparatus to enforce compliance, thus combining concepts of economics and politics completely and therefore permeating the everyday life of every citizen in every way.... In order to alleviate the distressing situation of those homeless people and assume the traditional American policy of welcoming the oppressed, the United States should recognize the unique qualifications of these future citizens. They are young (generally between 20 and 40 years old), well educated and anti-communist. Because of their good background, these people have the potential to be quickly assimilated into the mainstream of American life....

Among recommendations which were included at the end of this paper there were suggestions as to the need for preparing a general guide concerning the principles of qualifying applications, with a chapter on the political leanings of the applicants. Second, it was suggested to place an office of the INS in Sweden, due to the proximity of that country to Poland. Third, the PAIRC demanded the retention of subsidies for refugees who came to the United States by way of Belgium and France, where, due to the already mentioned decisions, PAIRC office funding from federal sources was suspended. Another postulate was that the waiting period in West Germany for an American visa should be shortened to less than 12 months, which was an exception even with regard to the waiting period for similar visas in Austria and Italy. Several technical changes were also demanded, as for instance notification about coming to the United States for participants in the Visa 93 program, and ensuring better orientation as to current conditions in the United States for emigration candidates who were members of Solidarity.[22]

Both presentations can be treated as one element of an organized campaign by the Committee on behalf of refugees from the Solidarity era, though they themselves were not then aware of the role played by the Committee in their efforts to emigrate to the United States, Canada, or Australia. In order to supplement the postulates directed to the outside, the Committee made an effort to activate its base in America. The first priority was for the chapters in Chicago and Houston, as well as securing financial sponsors, and adding new members to the board. With regard to the latter, Edmund Sułkowski was elected to the board. He was a World War II veteran, an emissary to occupied Poland, an active SPK member, and president of the Polish American Congress for the northwestern part of New York. Another candidate was E. Witanowski, who did not accept the nomination. He was to have joined the board in 1985. Edwin Gorski, an attorney with law offices in midtown Manhattan, played a significant role in the Committee, to which he rendered many services. Gorski became secretary and later was elected a vice president. In 1986, Jadwiga Kawa joined the board. She was a widely respected social activist from Brooklyn, a state vice president of the PAC, president of the Ladies Circle of the SPK, a member of the Pulaski Parade Committee, and a member of several other associations.

With regard to Europe, the Committee decided at its December 14, 1984, meeting to increase the staff in the Austria office and considered the possibility of increasing its services for Czechs, Hungarians, and Iranians. The latter became numerous in the refugee camps after the Ayatollah Khomeini's revolution. The departure from a program of assistance to a single ethnic group could have a positive effect on the Committee's position in the eyes of the authorities in Washington.[23]

At this meeting it was also noted that in fiscal year 1984 the Committee assisted 591 refugees in emigration, while in fiscal year 1985 the figure was 529. This was lower than the record year 1982, when the Committee brought and resettled 640 refugees; nonetheless, 1984 and 1985 belonged to record years in that decade. On September 30, 1986, the PAIRC had a list of 1,692 registered Poles trying to gain entry into the United States and 555 seeking to enter other countries. Between October 1, 1986, and June 30, 1987, the Committee registered 1,215 new refugees in Europe for emigration to the United States and 183 for emigration to other countries.[24]

The situation of Polish refugees had changed in that after 1984 Austria closed its border to Polish refugees. An exception was made for those who had documentation for further emigration. In general, according to Committee and Catholic organization estimates, there were about 30,000 Polish refugees in Western Europe. Meanwhile, in 1986 the U.S. Congress and also the State Department made several changes to existing immigration law, which was connected with a greater centralization of federal aid and higher reporting requirements for individual organizations. The practical aspect of resettling refugees also changed because of those new guidelines. For instance, the government now demanded that arrivals be resettled no farther than within a 100-mile radius from the Committee's offices, which was to facilitate communication with the immigrants. It was assumed that in case of a problem, the organization would be in a position to send a representative by car. This was exceedingly harmful to the Committee, as some of the refugees registered in Europe by Committee branches had private sponsors who were farther away from the Committee than the mandated 100 miles. Thus, many refugees registered by the PAIRC had to be handed over to other organizations for resettlement in the United States. The next disposition of the State Department introduced a total separation of registration sites from resettlement offices. According to this system, all the refugees were distributed by the Refugee Data Center in New York, according to preset percentages, among voluntary agencies regardless as to which of the organizations had registered and prepared the refugee's departure to the United States. The next change concerned the competency of the Mission to Charitable Organizations of the United States in Geneva (which was the direct supervisor of all offices of organizations that registered refugees) regarding the approval and financing of their budgets. As of fiscal year 1986, the budget proposal had to be submitted directly to Washington, and organizations received their money from there for European operations and for the placement of refugees in the given European country. Washington also announced a series of budget cutbacks for the coming years.

As for Europe, in the middle of the decade the Committee was maintaining an office in Munich and agencies in Zirndorf and Hamburg. SPK activist Maksymilian Pelc worked on a volunteer basis in the latter city, which had a growing influx of refugees. In the middle of 1983, the PAIRC office in Zirndorf was moved out of the refugee camp and into the private apartment of P. Paschek, who took over Królicki's function, and which was active until the middle of 1987. In turn, Austria as of 1984 was a country almost totally off-limits to Poles, thus registrations there were less than twenty annually. For this reason one of the workers in the Vienna office left in 1986, and further eliminations were being considered due to lack of higher registration numbers. At that time, the Committee's office in France was being maintained solely with Committee funds. The annual cost was about $5,000. There were few registrations, and many Poles were being taken over by other organizations, including Catholic ones, which offered better material conditions for the period prior to departure to the final destination. The PAIRC's Paris office went out of business in 1988.

On the other hand, there was a continuous increase of refugees in Rome. One of the channels was the frequent pilgrimages to the Vatican, from which many people split off in order to choose emigration. This phenomenon was on such a large scale that the *Kronika Rzymska* (Roman Chronicle) and the Parisian *Kultura* wrote about it. However, the PAIRC office in Rome was not able to entirely cope with the situation; there were delays and backlogs.

The fate of the staff there was ever more dependent on the effectiveness of further work.[25]

The Committee reacted to the attempts to change immigration law and its financing. One of the best opportunities to present a position was the memorandum of Executive Vice President Janusz Krzyżanowski to the House Sub-Committee on Immigration, Refugees and International Law of November 2, 1989. Perceiving the possibility of political changes in Poland, which in the future might eliminate the political refugee category, the Committee's vice president noted the presence of 20,000 persons scattered all over Western Europe who deserved a helping hand. The Committee was pleased at the separation of the Soviet Union refugee category from the overall number of visas designated for Eastern Europe, although Krzyżanowski felt that the ceiling of 6,500 visas annually for Poles was too low. That number corresponded to the infamous quotas and was as low as it had been several decades earlier. An important part of the presentation was devoted to explaining to the legislators the essence of the changes that had occurred in Poland. The Committee vice president highlighted the contrasting character of the elections to the Seym (Polish Parliament) of June 4, 1989, and the fact that General Wojciech Jaruzelski, General Czesław Kiszczak, and General Florian Sawicki still controlled key government posts, such as the presidency, and posts at the Ministry of Internal Affairs and National Defense. In light of this, it was still necessary to carefully evaluate the depth and irreversibility of the changes that took place. Therefore, the Committee's representative appealed to Congress to treat refugees who had left Poland prior to April 1989, that is, before the end of the Round Table discussion in Poland, as the conditions at that time called for.[26]

The looming political changes coincided with another change in quarters for the Committee. Due to the projected renovations at the Soldiers' Home, the Committee rented a place in 1989 at 140 West 22nd Street. This site served the Committee to the end of 1997, at which time the office was moved to the Polish National Alliance building at 180 Second Avenue in lower Manhattan, where the Józef Piłsudski Institute was already located.

Another important event was the opening, in the late 1980s, of another emigration channel, this time to South Africa. That country offered quick visa processing and attractive employment terms, which caused a number of refugees, who had tired of waiting, to go to Africa instead of to the United States.

XIII

A Review of Immigration Law in the Years 1980–1990

After the passage of the Refugee Act of March 17, 1980, several amendments to it were introduced. One of them was the Refugee Education Assistance Act of October 10, 1980, which provided for financial assistance on the state level toward the education of the children of refugees. There were also prohibitions resulting both from budgetary limitations, and from concern about obeying the law. For instance, financing opportunities were curtailed for several categories of refugees with regard to housing in properties administered by HUD (the act of August 13, 1981). In further amendments passed on December 20, 1981, INS officials were authorized to impound vehicles that were suspected of engaging in legally prosecutable procedures, regardless of whether the given foreigner directly participated in those illegal acts. The objective here was drug trafficking across borders and along certain routes, as for instance from Florida to New York. Nor was the INS held liable for any legal expenses. The next act, of October 2, 1982, greatly curtailed the categories of immigrants with the right to take advantage of the Legal Services Corporation.

Even greater changes were introduced with the Immigration Reform and Control Act of November 6, 1986. First of all, it authorized the legalization of the resident status of all those who did not have legal status, and who lived in the United States before January 1, 1982. This included a sizable group of Poles, who had arrived as tourists and subsequently had stayed without trying to obtain legal status, as well as those who had been denied political asylum. The act of November 6 also introduced sanctions against employers who consciously employed illegal aliens, and created a new category of immigrants for retired workers of certain international organizations. This included, among others, persons employed by the U.N. Also, a pool of

5,000 visas was created for certain categories of individuals who planned to visit the United States. In addition, the ceiling on preferential categories was raised from 600 to 5,000, beginning with fiscal year 1988. In addition to several other stipulations, it was also announced that borders would be better patrolled.

In November of that year the problem of fictitious marriages was raised, which were arranged for the purpose of getting permanent residence. It was decided that a marriage had to have existed for at least two years before permanent resident status could be granted. In the meantime (on September 28, 1988), border crossing restrictions were eased and employment restrictions between Canada and the United States were removed on the basis of reciprocity. From the Polish point of view, the effect was that it became easier to obtain legal resident status for Poles from the United States in the more liberal Canada. In time, it became apparent that the Canadian-American border was yet another channel for the transport of illegal aliens. Fortunately, it only concerned a small number of Poles. Further acts that concerned Polish immigrants were: the law of November 15, 1988, and the Immigration Nursing Relief Act of 1989 enacted December 18, 1989. They granted legal resident status for specific categories of nurses regardless of nationality and irrespective of their overall number, provided they fulfilled the guidelines, which included work in their profession during the prior three years. The law of November 29, 1990, closed out the Congress's busy immigration issues schedule. It raised the ceiling on all categories of immigrants admitted to the United States. The issuance of between 675,000 and 700,000 visas annually was provided for with the following internal division: 480,000 family-sponsored immigrants, 140,000 for immigrants in certain job categories, and 55,000 diversity immigrants. The latter concerned the so-called visa lottery. Illegal immigrants or the citizens of other countries living outside the United States participated in the lottery drawing of a certain number of visas assigned to a given country. This helped to partially solve the problem of illegal immigrants and also to attract valuable, determined candidates.

Simultaneously a revision was made of regulations concerning deportation and visa denial on the basis of specified political conditions. For example, the provision denying entry to Communists was eliminated, because of the fall of the Soviet Union. Political considerations could no longer be a reason to deny a visa or a reason for deportation. Employment visa categories were amended, both in terms of quantity and of quality (H-1 (b) and H-2 (b) visas). Also, a number of corrections were made in the operation of various immigration departments and the border patrol.[1]

From the Polish point of view, a key decision was the closing of registration for Polish refugees by the State Department retroactively as of November 22, 1989. That decision did not include persons with families in the United States. Still it was a huge blow for the Committee's activists, because their continued work was now under a big question mark. After all, the heart of PAIRC operations was assisting political refugees from Communist Poland. As for the timing of the decision, it should be noted that it occurred after the formation of Tadeusz Mazowiecki's government, but without any significant changes in Poland's internal situation. The Warsaw Pact still existed, and Soviet troops were still stationed inside Poland. It was most clearly an issue of deleting what was believed to be a redundant item in the budget and opening up the path for immigrants from other countries.

XIV
Political Changes in Poland: The Committee's Activity in the Years 1990–2000

The last of the cited laws was enacted after the Round Table discussions in Poland and after the formal abolition of the Polish People's Republic. After many postponements the Round Table discussion began on February 6, 1989, and ended on April 5 of that year. Without going into a broader presentation of the details, it is enough to state that they led to a division of power between the opposition and the Communist authorities. In consequence of the agreements that were hammered out there, elections to the Seym and Senate were held on June 4 and 18, 1989, and on July 19 the National Assembly elected General W. Jaruzelski president. On August 24, 1989, the Seym elected Tadeusz Mazowiecki to the post of prime minister of the first non–Communist government in over 40 years. At the end of that year, on December 28, the name of the state was changed back to Republic of Poland, and its emblem, once again, was the crowned eagle. Despite several defects, such as the continued presence of Soviet troops, and the continued enforcement of the former constitution, there was no doubt that Poland was on its way to becoming a sovereign state. A milestone on this road was the presentation on December 22, 1990, of the insignias of the Second Polish Republic by Ryszard Kaczorowski, the president of the Polish Republic in London, to Lech Wałęsa. The general presidential elections ended on December 19, 1990, with the victory of Solidarity's leader. Poland was no longer perceived as a source of emigrants; to the contrary, it was believed that it would play an ever-greater role in reviewing refugee issues and assistance for them due to its geographical location between East and West. This situation is reflected in the State Department's analysis from the beginning of 1992:

> In 1991 Poland completed the transition from a refugee generating country to a refugee receiving one. In light of continuing democratic reforms in Poland, Western countries found virtually no Pole eligible for refugee status in 1991. Germany, where most Polish asylum seekers applied, denied all but a handful of the 3,448 applications — the ones approved consisted of family members joining a previously adjudicated refugee. Moreover, significantly fewer Poles sought asylum in the West. In Germany, for example, 3,448 Poles applied, compared to 9,155 in 1990 and 26,092 in 1989.
> Despite its economic problems, Poland began to attract scores of asylum seekers, especially from the former Soviet Union. In all of 1990, two Soviet citizens applied for refugee status in Poland; in 1991 over 1,400 persons applied. This number does not include the hundreds of Soviets who approached Poland's refugee center the week of the Soviet coup. In 1991, Poland received 2,236 applications for asylum. Prior to September, Poland referred all non–European applications to UNHCR for adjudication.
> Plans to deal with a growing number of would-be refugees resulted in the creation of the Office of the Plenipotentiary for Refugee Affairs in January 1991. This office supervised the building of two refugee accommodation centers that could house several hundred refugees. The United Nations High Commissioner for Refugees (UNHCR) provided $250,000 in 1991 to complete the main reception and accommodation center in Nadarzyn. In September, Poland consummated the legal framework for processing refugees by signing the 1951 UN Refugee Convention and its 1967 Protocol. This done, Poland took over adjudication of refugee applications, which had formerly been referred to UNHCR. Despite mechanisms in place to handle refugees, Poland recognized only 35 refugees from two countries in 1991, none of whom were from the former Soviet Union.
> ... Because of its location on the threshold of Europe, Poland can expect to continue to receive asylum seekers. Poland's financial situation, however, will influence its ability to confer status to even legitimate refugees. Poland will likely continue to rely on UNHCR for help in resettling approved refugees. A UNHCR liaison office, which was to open in Warsaw in January 1992, will provide resettlement assistance.[1]

The results of those observations had, clearly, a significant influence on the treatment of Polish refugee status applications by the authorities of the given countries and, by the American federal government, and also on the work of the PAIRC. In the case of countries accepting Polish refugees, the problem was that tourist entry into certain countries was made easy. Austria was an example, to which tourist entry was nonproblematic as of 1988. During the first three months of 1987, when visas were required to enter Austria, only 97 Poles filed asylum applications. But from the beginning of the new year to May 1988 there were over 1,000 such applications. Due to the mass arrival of Poles and Hungarians, Karl Blech, Austria's minister of internal affairs, declared on May 4, 1988, that there would be a two-week verification period for Poles and Hungarians from that point forward, after which those who did not deserve political refugee status would have to return to their country.[2]

With regard to the Committee, the changes discussed above signaled a smaller influx, and in consequence a shifting of the burden of work to on-site immigration advice and assistance for cases in process.

The final decade of the twentieth century brought several changes which were the result of Poland's political transformations and of the Committee's diminishing role as an entity registering and assisting the emigration of Polish refugees from West European nations. The Committee's problems were of a twofold nature. First, the enormous influx of applications for departure was overlaid by the gradual restrictions on refugees in Austria, Germany, and the other European countries. For example, Germany's attention shifted toward escapees from behind the Berlin Wall. It was anticipated that the next breakthrough would be the unification of Germany, and in this connection the authorities of the Federal Republic tried to remove alien refugees from their own territory and, moreover, they restricted financial resources for assistance. Second, the Committee sustained several budget cuts, which in consequence left a skeleton structure in Europe in 1989 and the following years. Instead of full-time positions, work was now doled out on demand only. As has already been cited, the offices in Belgium and France were eliminated. By 1989 in Germany (Munich), barely two positions remained and the need was looming to eliminate one of the workers. Also, in Austria there was barely one position left, filled by Lidia Berezka. The Rome office could be maintained only by the Committee's strenuous efforts.[3]

The issue of the Committee's European offices returned to the agenda at the March 1990 board meeting. The decision was made then to eliminate the Austrian office because only tourists were coming to Vienna. And there were big difficulties with the registration of new political refugees. The closing of that office was to take place with three months' notice, in accordance with local regulations. Where Munich was concerned, which after Rudnicki's departure was managed by Adalbert Grabowski, it was anticipated that the office there would function to September 1990, that is, to the end of the government contract. After the State Department's decision of November 29, 1989, to cease registering Polish refugees in Europe, maintaining offices there just made no sense anymore.

It slowly became obvious to everyone that the functions of the Committee would have to undergo a dramatic reorientation. The only people left in Europe were those whose cases had been registered before the watershed year of 1989 and who were only waiting for the conclusion of their administrative-visa processes. It was known that there would not be many

New York, November 6, 1998. A meeting of the board of the PAIRC in the Portrait Hall of the J. Piłsudski Institute, where the matter of concluding PAIRC operations was discussed in the presence of former PAIRC executive directors. *From the left*: Franciszek Proch, Władysław Zachariasiewicz, Franciszka Szczygielska, Edwin Gorski, Janusz Krzyżanowski, the Reverend Monsignor Joseph Marjańczyk, Hieronim Wyszyński. (Photograph by Edmund Sułkowski).

political refugees; besides, there was no way to register them, as the repressions in Poland had ceased. During the discussion at the March 8, 1990, board meeting, a reorientation of the Committee's work was undertaken in the direction of counseling on immigration matters and employment services. Someone even introduced the idea of helping the homeless, and to open a shelter for that purpose at St. Stanislaus Parish on 7th Street in Lower Manhattan.[4]

The question of the Committee's European offices was answered the following year. In line with the announcement, the Munich office was closed in September 1990. The office in Rome was also closed, where, after the death of longtime staff member Witold Zahorski, the work was continued on a part-time basis by Elżbieta Zahorska. As if all those changes weren't enough, the Committee's office in Chicago was closed in the spring of 1991. It had been managed since 1983 by Krystyna Hussar-Litwińska. That was tantamount to the closing of the Committee's chapter there (in the spring of 1993), which, after the late Zbigniew Radoniewicz, had been managed in its final years, once again, by the president of the SPK chapter, Dr. Feliks Krzan.[5] Somewhat earlier, another Chicago organization conducting emigration work in Chicago closed its doors. The Self-Help Association of the New Emigration (Stowarzyszenie Samopomocy Nowej Emgracji), which had been established in 1949, concluded its mission in the immigration sector in 1990. From the very beginning to its final days, it was directed by Jan Bieżanowski, a former officer of the First Armored Division of General Maczek. The Association assisted in asylum cases and in finding employment and housing, maintained relations with the INS office, and represented new Polish arrivals there in relevant matters.

In addition, there were financial problems. The elimination of federal subsidies had quite an impact on the Committee's budget. There were attempts to rescue it through a series of internal cost-cutting measures recommended by Treasurer Stanisław Jordanowski, but despite this, the deficit for the year 1989–1990 was $53,723.

The new tasks of the Committee were revisited during the board meeting of April 19, 1991. The participants focused attention on the presence of large groups of homeless Poles in the area of Tompkins Square on Manhattan's Lower East Side and in the vicinity of the shelter in Greenpoint, Brooklyn, a neighborhood inhabited mostly by Poles. These were frequently alcoholics to whom the Committee had resolved to lend a helping hand. It was decided to try to persuade them to take up employment or to return to Poland. In certain cases the visa application process was simplified for the closest family members of the alcoholics, or for persons who were unable to stand on their own two feet and had given in to depression or dependency. That was the case of Krzysztof S., who was fired from several jobs in a row and broke off contact with his family. The Committee's address was the only one that his mother had. She therefore tried to find her son through that channel, and afterwards to seek help in obtaining an American visa in order to take care of her son on site. There were more cases like this one.[6]

Another group the Committee decided to help was Poles who had illegally crossed the U.S.–Mexico border. Because those who were detained there had to pay high security deposits, the Committee deliberated whether it should help them. Another innovation was advice rendered in connection with the visa lottery (the diversity immigrant visa), which required that the application be filled out in a particular manner and also needed clarification of a number of fuzzy points. Finally, of matters that had been impossible before due to political considerations, there were now requests for material assistance, counseling, and a more extensive correspondence with Poland. Most frequently the letters requested explanations regarding existing immigration law or a search for loved ones.[7]

All these plans seemed necessary in light of the de facto halt to the influx of refugees emigrating with the Committee's assistance. The report for the year 1990–1991 mentions 24 Poles who had immigrated to the United States with the Committee's help.[8] During the 1991 Christmas season, the Committee's president, the Rev. Msgr. Joseph Marjańczyk, sent out an appeal for help, directed to the Polish American community, which already contained the signs of change:

> Today there are no more political refugees but, among those already here, are people requiring our continued guidance. Those with emotional problems have difficulty learning English, suffer nervous breakdowns because of family difficulties, or become dependent on alcohol. The majority of these are single people who are unable to hold steady employment or even a temporary job.
> The Polish Immigration Committee is often the only place where these people are sure of acceptance, a sympathetic hearing and understanding. Within our limitations, we try to help them with replacing lost documents, placing them in shelters or hospitals, rendering emergency financial assistance, finding suitable housing or helping with rent payments until they receive public assistance. We try to find jobs for those who are unable to work, but for those who are unable to adjust, we attempt to facilitate a return to Poland.
> We take care of all the people who turn to us for assistance. We help those who have dealings with various agencies, we translate documents, help place children in school, provide information about immigration law, and help with family reunification.
> We do not charge for any of our services; therefore all who need help will find it here, regardless of their financial situation.[9]

The various proposals that had been discussed since the beginning of the 1990s materialized in 1995. At that time a scholarship contest was announced for the children of immigrants who had come to the United States in the prior years. A two-year scholarship was for $500 per year and was automatically renewed for the school year commencing in September 1996. This contest, as with the ones that followed, met with the interest of both parents and children. In 1997, 10 children received such a scholarship for a total of $5,000. Scholarships of various amounts were granted up to the year 2000.[10] For many families, a scholarship for a child in school was a significant boost. That was the case with Bogumił Misiuk of Newark, New Jersey. He was attending St. Casimir Catholic School in Newark, but his parents were unable to come up with the tuition. His mother had breast cancer and had undergone complicated surgery and was only able to work two hours per day. The father, despite a severe hernia, worked as a physical laborer. He was the only breadwinner in the family.

XIV—Political Changes in Poland 213

The Committee recognized the gravity of the situation and gave the boy a scholarship.[11] Each such decision on the part of the Committee was the extension of a helping hand to the newest immigrants. The parents clearly understood the importance of the program. Ilona Polkowska, the mother of Piotr, who also tried for a scholarship, wrote to the Committee as follows:

> Regardless of the outcome of the lottery, we would like to praise your organization for the idea and the desire to render aid in this manner to the new emigrants. Thank you and please accept our words of respect.[12]

On the other hand, it was clear that the granting of scholarships, or aid for the homeless, only had an indirect connection with the basic objectives that had brought about the founding of the Committee in 1947. The danger of losing another funding source loomed over the Committee in 1997. An informational conference convened that year by the United Way served as a harbinger of changes to come. It was feared that the United Way would stop supporting organizations of a similar profile that did not agree to the

One of the last meetings of the PAIRC board took place on June 22, 2001. *Seated from the left*: Jadwiga Kawa, President Rev. Msgr. Joseph Marjańczyk, P.A., Secretary Franciszka Szczygielska. *Standing from the left*: Edmund Sułkowski, Treasurer Deacon Bolesław Wojewódka, Vice President Edwin Gorski and Executive Vice President Janusz Krzyżanowski.

proposal to merge in order to cut administrative costs (some time before that, the State Department had wanted to institute a similar system in Europe). A discussion on this subject took place at the Committee's board meeting of November 17, 1997. After that discussion, the board decided to jump the gun on the United Way and announce the conclusion of operations. At that time the fate of the archives was also discussed.[13]

That was the last meeting at the old site on 22nd Street. Thanks to the favorable attitude of Edward Moskal, the president of the Polish National Alliance, the Committee obtained a modest but inexpensive office on the fourth floor of the PNA building at 180 Second Avenue in Manhattan. That is where the board's November 6, 1998, meeting took place, during which the further fate of the Committee was discussed. At the beginning of the session a conference was held with former Committee directors W. Zachariasiewicz (1951–1962), H. Wyszyński (1968–1975), and F. Proch (1975–1981). Once again the question of the placement of the archives upon the dissolution of the Committee was discussed. Taken into consideration were: the University of Minnesota in Minneapolis, Minnesota; Orchard Lake near Detroit, Michigan; the Polish Cultural Foundation in Clark, New Jersey; the Polish Institute of Arts and Sciences; the Piłsudski Institute; and the SWAP Foundation. The University of Minnesota gained the most adherents because the archives of other ethnic groups are already located there in the Immigration History Research Center, as is the Polish American Collection. In order to protect the fate of the archives, an appropriate agreement was to be signed and a personal visit was to be arranged by Executive Vice President Krzyżanowski. The final decision in this matter was made at the November 1999 board meeting. A decision was also made at that time as to which materials were to be saved and which were to be destroyed. On the basis of correspondence with the above-mentioned university, essential information was obtained regarding the conditions for storing the archives. The Committee's board also decided to relinquish the United Way donation as of June 30, 2000. A letter in this regard, addressed to Ralph Dickerson, Jr., the president of United Way of New York City, was sent by Committee President Reverend Monsignor Joseph Marjańczyk on May 6, 1999. The final shutdown of Committee operations was slated for the middle of 2000, and the transfer of the archives to Minnesota was to take place after that date.[14]

XV
A Summing Up and Conclusions

The Committee's activity took place during watershed events in the history of Poland and the Polish emigration. It could be said that it began operations the day after independence was lost in order to decrease the effects of human tragedy on a massive, unprecedented scale, and it concluded operations when it became evident that the mass exodus caused by political or economic persecution had, in fact, ceased. The Committee was there for the Polish nation and the emigration from the end of World War II through the 1956 revolt, the 1968 and 1970 protests, the rise of Solidarity, and finally the regaining of sovereignty in 1989. Through its efforts, it ameliorated the social and individual effects of the mass migrations, which were a result of persecutions and social experimentation on a grand scale. According to many reports, the Committee assisted the impressive number of about 70,000 Poles in immigration to various countries, not including a huge throng of those whom it served with advice and material assistance.

If one were to attempt an internal division into substages of activity, it would be easy to observe that they coincided with political watersheds in Poland and the world. The first stage was undoubtedly the period 1947–1958, from the commencement of operations up to the Poznań and Hungarian events and their direct consequences. At that time, help for the victims of war residing in Western Europe dominated, as did the fight for a change in U.S. immigration law. The Reverend Monsignor Feliks Burant, the Committee's founder and moving spirit, spread his dominant influence over its work. That is why the next stage of activity, enclosed by the years 1958 and 1970, has the additional break of 1964 when the Committee's founder passed away. The fourteen years between June 1956 in Poznań and December 1970 was marked by a decreasing flow of refugees, an internal strengthening of the Committee and further battles for refugee legislation with a consideration of Polish postulates, and a broadening of the Committee's presence in major refugee centers of Western Europe. This was accompanied by the development of outlying chapters in the United States combined with an attempt to expand into Canada.

The 1970s brought a gradual globalization of the refugee issue, in other words, a departure from the treatment of Europe as the fundamental commitment of the United States with regard to humanitarian matters, and by the same token a marginalization of the Polish refugee problem. In this period the Committee tried to continue its work with emphasis on the care of those left behind in the escapee camps, and of new refugees, with the support of increasing federal funding. The rise of Solidarity was a serious watershed for the Committee, as was the second large wave of refugees from Poland in the postwar period. The Committee's new team struggled with it, with Janusz Krzyżanowski as its executive vice president, the Rev. Msgr. Jan Karpiński as its president, and the Reverend Monsignor Joseph Marjańczyk, who took over the post of president after Rev. Karpiński's death. The result was the resettlement of several thousand Polish refugees in the United States, Canada, and Australia. When Poland regained independence, the Committee was able, once again, to reorient its mission toward serving refugees in their adaptation to America. The lack of a reason for continued operations after Poland regained its sovereignty allowed for a gradual phasing out of its mission.

There is no doubt that the Polish Immigration and Relief Committee fulfilled its assignments well. As a social service organization, it was able to elicit from the Polish American community significant moral and financial support, and was able to spark interest in its work and to compel appropriate sectors of the federal administration in Washington to support it. The Committee's position as the only Polish organization focused on refugees was unquestioned, and its affiliation with the State Department was treated as a confirmation of this exceptional position. The Committee's presentations in refugee matters before the appropriate committees of the House and Senate were treated with due attention. They influenced many immigration law regulations, which facilitated the emigration of tens of thousands of Poles to the United States.

During a half century of activity, the Committee had the privilege of benefiting from the generosity of the entire Polish American community, and of hundreds of volunteers, thanks to whom its achievements exceeded expectations. It should be noted here, as well, that those successes would not have been possible without the group of self-sacrificing activists who represented the full cross section of the Polish American community and the newest emi-

XV—A Summing Up and Conclusions

gration. All these groups managed to set aside their prejudices and group ambitions. Another attribute of the Committee was its competent management, which gave it direction and incited it to self-sacrifice. The most outstanding of the many presidents and directors ought to be mentioned: the Rev. Msgr. Feliks Burant, Władysław Zachariasiewicz, Franciszek Proch, Janusz Krzyżanowski, the Rev. Msgr. John J. Karpiński, and the Rev. Msgr. Joseph Marjańczyk. At the most difficult turns of history, the Committee had at its helm exceptional personalities who guaranteed the maintenance of a high work standard and an effective defense of Polish interests. Meant here are not just refugee interests, but also the representation of independent Poland. This aspect of the Committee's mission ought to be clearly emphasized.

Despite all the qualities mentioned above, the Committee's work remains surprisingly little known. This is true in equal measure both of the "old country" and of the Polish American Community. The Committee did not engage in advertising its accomplishments. It was convinced that its

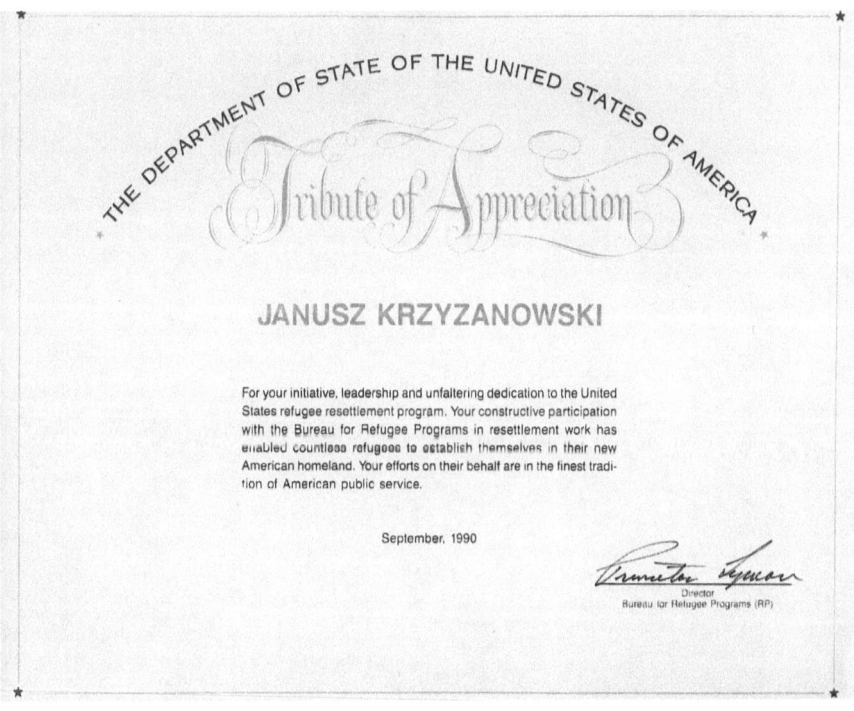

Krzyżanowski feels that these words of recognition refer in full to the many current and former activists of the Polish American Immigration and Relief Committee.

priority was to serve the Polish refugee. In Poland, on the other hand, its assessment, or the writing of a credible history of this organization, was rendered difficult by a lack of access to source materials and due to the political conditions that dominated in Poland up to 1989. This book claims for itself no more than the humble right to lift the veil of silence resting on the story of one of the most outstanding organizations of the Polish Diaspora.

Notes

Chapter I

1. *St. Joseph's Home for Polish Immigrants, Church of St. Stanislaus, B&M, 1874–1954* (New York, 1954), 19–20: Franciszek J. Proch, *Polski Komitet Imigracyjny — PKI. Polish American Immigration and Relief Committee — PAIRC, the Years 1946–1981.* MS, 3–5.

Chapter II

1. *Immigration Laws of the United States* (Indianapolis, 1955). Charles Gordon, Ellen G. Gordon, *Immigration and Nationality Law* (New York, Frank L. Auerbach, 1979). Edward P. Hutchison, *Legislative History of American Immigration Policy, 1798–1965* (Philadelphia, 1985). John F. Kennedy, *A Nation of Immigrants* (New York, 1963). Charles B. Kelly, *U.S. Immigration: A Policy Analysis* (New York, 1979). *Selected Readings on U.S. Immigration Policy and Law,* A Compendium Prepared at the Request of Senator Edward M. Kennedy, Chairman, Committee on the Judiciary, United States Senate, for the use of The Select Commission on Immigration and Refugee Policy. Prepared by The Congressional Research Service, Library of Congress, Washington, 1980. U.S. Department of Justice, Immigration and Naturalization Service, *1992 Statistical Yearbook of the Immigration and Naturalization Service* (Washington, 1993) A.1-1-A1-21.

Chapter III

1. John L. Snell, *Illusion and Necessity; The Diplomacy of Global War, 1939–1945* (Boston, 1963), 45.
2. *Nowy Świat*, New York, September 2, 1939.
3. Karol Wachtl, *Polonia w Ameryce* (The Polish American community) (Philadelphia, 1944), 404.
4. Wojciech Białasiewicz, *Pomiędzy lojalnością a serc porywem. Polonia Amerykańska we wrześniu 1939 roku* (Between Loyalty and the Call of the Heart. The Polish American Community in 1939), (Chicago, 1989), 13.
5. *Ibid.*, 15.
6. Piłsudski Institute in New York, *Consulate General of the Polish Republic in New York*, File 17–19.
7. Wojciech Białasiewicz, op. cit., 26.
8. Official Minutes of the XXVIII Convention of the Polish National Alliance held September 10–16, 1939, at the Book Cadillac Hotel, Detroit, MI, 34–35.
9. Donald E. Pienkos, *PNA: A Centennial History of the Polish National Alliance of the United States of North America* (East European Monographs, Boulder, Colorado, 1984), 151.
10. "Pod Hasłem Jedności; Sprawozdanie ze Zjazdu Amerykańsko-Polskich Zrzeszeń na Wschodzie w Nowym Yorku w dniach 11 i 12 marca, 1944" (Under the Slogan of Unity; Report on the Convention of American-Polish Associations in the East, in New York on March 11–12, 1944) (Coordinating Com-

mittee of American-Polish Associations in the East, New York, 1944).

11. Rev. Kazimierz Kucharski, S.J., "Pomoc Rady Polonii Amerykańskiej dla Wileńszczyzny w okresie 1939–1941," in: "Sprawozdanie Delegata na Europę Rady Polonii Amerykańskiej" (Aid of the American Relief for Poland for the Vilnius Region in the Period 1939–1941, Report of the American Relief for Poland Delegate for Europe); *American Polish War Relief for the period 1941–1958* (Geneva, 1958), 45–50.

12. *Ibid.*, 5.

13. John J. Olejniczak, *American Relief for Poland — Auditor's Report for the Period November 1, 1939 to September 30, 1948*, Buffalo, 1948, 5–11; Report of the delegate for Europe of the American Relief for Poland; *American Polish War Relief for the Period 1941–1958*, Geneva, 1958, 5.

14. *Ibid.*, 9.

15. Thaddeus Theodore Krysiewicz, *Polish Immigration Committee in the United States*, "A Historical Study of the American Committee for the Relief of Polish Immigrants: 1947–1952," New York, 1954, 9.

16. Mark Wyman, *DP, Europe's Displaced Persons, 1945–1951* (The Balch Institute Press, London and Toronto: Associated University Presses, Philadelphia, 1989), 24–25.

17. The Reverend Alexander Jurisson, *Operation Good Samaritan: The Resettlement of Displaced Persons, 1949–1952* (New York, nd), 1–8.

18. "Documents on Return of Poles to Poland," Polish Press Agency, Edinburgh, April 1946, 1–2.

19. *Ibid.*, 7.

20. "To All Members of the Polish Armed Forces," an appeal issued by H.M. Government, London, 1946.

21. Mark Wyman, op. cit., 62–63; also see *Foreign Relations of the United States. Diplomatic Papers; The Conferences at Malta and Yalta 1945*, United States Government Printing Office, Washington, 1955, 413–420, where also, "Soviet Draft of an Agreement Regarding the Treatment of Soviet Citizens and British Subjects Liberated from the Germans."

22. *Ibid.*

23. *Ibid.*

24. U.S. Army, *Displaced Persons, Occupation Forces in Europe Series, 1945–1946*, Training Packet 53, Frankfurt am Main, Germany, nd, 67–68.

25. *Catholic Herald*, London, February 1, 1946.

26. Thaddeus Theodore Krysiewicz, op. cit., 9.

27. Ignacy Matuszewski, "Teoria i Praktyka" (Theory and Practice), *Dziennik Polski*, Detroit, April 6, 1946.

28. *Dziennik Polski* Nr 26, London, January 30, 1946.

29. Ignacy Matuszewski, "Dlaczego nie chcą wracać?" (Why Don't They Want to Return?) *Dziennik Polski*, Detroit, April 10, 1946.

30. *Ibid.*

31. "Memorandum of conversation of Minister Tarnowski with Senator Vandenberg held in London on January 29, 1946," Piłsudski Institute in New York, Personal Archives, Sen. A. Vandenberg File, 116–119. Re: Vandenberg's views on Polish issues, also see: "Address by Senator Arthur H. Vandenberg upon the Occasion of the 40th Anniversary of the *Polish Daily News*," Hotel Book-Cadillac, Detroit, MI, April 2, 1944; Arthur H. Vandenberg Jr., Joe Alex Morris (eds.), *The Private Papers of Senator Vandenberg*, Houghton Mifflin Company, Boston 1952.

32. "Factual Report on the Plight of Displaced Persons in Germany. Observations made by a Delegation of U.S. Citizens on Behalf of the Polish American Congress, Inc.," *Bulletin*, Polish American Congress, vol. 3, no. 6, Chicago, February 1947, 36–43.

33. "Report to Byrnes in Paris," *Bulletin*, Polish American Congress, vol. 3, no. 6, Chicago, February 1947, 13–16.

34. *The New York Times*, November 11, 1946.

35. Thaddeus Theodore Krysiewicz, op. cit., 5.

Chapter IV

1. "Polski Komitet Imigracyjny w New Yorku. Działalność Komitetu w okresie od 4 lutego 1947 do 31 października 1948" r. (Polish Immigration Committee in New York. Committee Activity for the Period February

4, 1947 to October 31, 1948) New York, 1948.
2. Piłsudski Institute in New York, Personal Archives, file of the Rev. Feliks Burant; Rev. Francis Bolek, *Who's Who in Polish America. A Biographical Directory of Polish-American Leaders and Distinguished Poles Resident in the Americas* (New York, 1943), 61; Piotr Kardela, "Polskę w sercu noszę" (I Carry Poland in My Heart), *Nowy Dziennik — Przegląd Polski*, New York, April 28, 2000.
3. Thaddeus Theodore Krysiewicz, op. cit., 14–15.
4. "Program of the XXVI Annual Charity Ball," November 23, 1974; F. J. Proch, *Polski Komitet Imigracyjny — PKI. Polish American Immigration and Relief Committee — PAIRC, Years 1946–1981*, MS, 5.
5. "Polski Komitet Imigracyjny Rady Polonii Amerykańskiej. Działalność Komitetu w okresie od 4 lutego 1947 do 17 maja 1948" (Polish Immigration Committee of the American Relief for Poland. The Committee's Activity from February 4, 1947, to May 17, 1948), New York, 1948, 17, MS in archives of the PAIRC (this is the typescript of a brochure which, in changed format, including a longer period of time, was published by the PAIRC).
6. "Polski Komitet Imigracyjny w New Yorku. Działalność Komitetu w okresie od 4 lutego 1947 do 31 października 1948r." (Polish Immigration Committee in New York. The Committee's Activity from February 4, 1947, to October 31, 1948), New York, 1948.
7. "Charter of the Polish Immigration Committee"; also compare: Thaddeus Theodore Krysiewicz, *Polish Immigration Committee in the United States. A Historical Study of the American Committee for the Relief of Polish Immigrants: 1947–1952* (New York, 1954), 38–39.
8. Excerpt from minutes of a meeting of the Immigration Committee of American Relief for Poland, held in its own offices at 25 St. Marks Place, New York, NY, on June 24, 1948. MS in PAIRC archives in New York
9. F. J. Proch. "Polish American Immigration and Relief Committee — PAIRC, the Years 1946–1981," MS, 9.
10. "Polski Komitet Imigracyjny Rady Polonii Amerykańskiej. Działalność Komitetu w okresie od 4 lutego 1947 do 17 maja 1948 r.," New York, 1948, 9.
11. "Polski Komitet Imigracyjny w New Yorku. Działalność Komitetu w okresie od 4 lutego 1947 do 31 października 1948 r.," New York, 1948.
12. F. J. Proch. op. cit., 7.
13. "Sprawozdania Zarządu Wykonawczego Poszczególnych Komisji i Komitetów oraz Biur w Chicago i Washingtonie na Trzecią Krajową Konwencję Kongresu Polonii Amerykańskiej w Atlantic City, N.J. w dniach 30–31 maja i 1 czerwca 1952 r." (Reports of the Executive Committees of Individual Commissions and Committees and Offices in Chicago and Washington at the Third National Convention of the Polish American Congress in Atlantic City, N.J. May 30–31 and June 1, 1952), 12–13.
14. The letter of July 21, 1950, with confirmation of donation in the amount of $1,000, was reprinted in the program: "Bal Dwóch Edwardów, 15 września 1950, Hotel Statler" (The Two Edwards' Ball, September 15, 1950, Hotel Statler) New York, 1950.
15. PAIRC archives, file: General Correspondence 1945–1952; Report of the Executive Secretary for the period June 1, 1957 to December 1, 1958.
16. Excerpt from minutes of the meeting of the Immigration Committee of American Relief for Poland, held in its own offices at 25 St. Marks Place, New York, NY, on June 24, 1948. MS in PAIRC archives in New York.
17. "Memoranda by the Reverend Col. Felix F. Burant, the Chairman of the Immigration Commission at the Convention of the Polish American Congress at Philadelphia, PA, on May 29, 30 & 31, 1948," PAIRC archives in New York, MS, 3.
18. *Ibid.*
19. *Displaced Persons Act*, Public Law 774 — 80th Cong., Chapter 647 — 2nd sess., 2242.
20. "American Council History," Part II, 37, MS in PAIRC archives in New York.
21. PAIRC archives in New York, text of agreement signed on February 6, 1952, by the Rev. Edward Swanstrom, executive director of WRS–NCWC and president and director of ACRPI, Inc., the Rev. F. Burant; also see: Thaddeus Theodore Krysiewicz, *Polish Immigration Committee in the United*

States: A Historical Study of the American Committee for the Relief of Polish Immigrants: 1947–1952, (New York, 1954), 24.

22. "Sprawozdania Zarządu Wykonawczego Poszczególnych Komisji i Komitetów oraz Biur w Chicago i Washingtonie na Trzecią Krajową Konwencję Kongresu Polonii Amerykańskiej w Atlantic City, N.J. w dniach 30–31 maja i 1 czerwca 1952," 2–3.

23. *Ibid.*, 22–23.

24. *Ibid.*, 24–27.

25. Józef Wyrwa, *Pamiętniki partyzanta* (Memoirs of a Guerilla) (Ampol Books, Chicago, 1951), 160–162.

26. "American Immigration Policy. Selected Statements," American Immigration Conference, New York, 1957, 15.

27. T. Katelbach, "Co Przed 20 Laty Obiecywali Stevenson and Eisenhower" (What Stevenson and Eisenhower Promised 20 Years Ago), *Dziennik Polski i Dziennik Żołnierza—Tydzień Polski*, nr. 44 (258), London, 28 October 1972; "Gen. Sosnkowski Meets Ike," *Polish-American Journal*, Vol. XLI, nr. 46, Buffalo, November 15, 1952.

28. Statement of the Rev. Msgr. Felix F. Burant, president of the Polish American Immigration Committee before President's Commission on Immigration and Naturalization, October 1, 1952.

29. *Ibid.*

30. Text of an editorial concerning proposed changes, from *Kuryer Zjednoczenia* (Alliance Courier), published in Cleveland, Ohio; PAIRC archives in New York.

31. Letter of the Rev. Msgr. F. Burant, New York, March 12, 1953, in PAIRC archives in New York.

32. Statement of the Rev. Msgr. Felix F. Burant, president of the Polish Immigration Committee before President's Commission on Immigration and Naturalization, October 1, 1952.

33. "Eisenhower Urges U.S. Admit 240,000 Above Alien Quota," *The New York Times*, April 23, 1953.

34. Statement of the Rev. Msgr. Feliks F. Burant, president of the Polish Immigration Committee before the Subcommittee on Immigration and Naturalization, June 10, 1953, regarding emergency immigration legislation.

35. "President Signs Bill for More Aliens," *The New York Times*, August 8, 1953; Department of State, Information Regarding the Refugee Relief Act of 1953.

36. "Citizens to Press for New Alien Act. Substantial Revision Sought, Lehman Says—He Reminds President of Pledges," *The New York Times*, January 12, 1954.

37. "More Hope for Refugees," *The New York Times*, November 20, 1954.

38. "President Scores U.S. Refugee Act. Law too Awkward, he tells Governor's Representatives in White House Talk," *The New York Times*, August 3, 1955.

39. PAIRC archives in New York.

Chapter V

1. "Polski Komitet Imigracyjny—Polish Immigration Committee, 17 IX 1949—15 IX 1950," in the *Ball Journal*: "Bal Dwóch Edwardów" (Two Edwards' Ball), Hotel Statler, September 15, 1950; also: "Third Annual Ball of the Polish Immigration Committee, September 22, 1951, Hotel Statler," New York, 1951.

2. F. J. Proch, "Polski Komitet Imigracyjny—PKI—Polish American Immigration and Relief Committee—PAIRC, the Years 1946–1981," MS, 8.

3. "100 Wdów i Niezamężnych Polek z Dziećmi Sprowadza Polski Komitet Imigracyjny. Wdowi grosz Polonii rozjaśni życie jeszcze jednej grupie tułaczy polskich" (One hundred widows and unwed Polish women with children brought to America by the Polish Immigration Committee, the Polish American Community's widow's mite will light up the life of one more group of Polish wanderers), in the *Ball Journal*: "Third Annual Ball of the Polish Immigration Committee, Hotel Statler, September 22, 1951," New York, 1951.

4. Letter of the Polish Refugee Alliance in Germany, November 1957, PAIRC archives in New York, Correspondence 1956–1958.

5. Letter of Rt. Reverend Bishop W. Rubin to the Rev. Msgr. Burant, Rome, August 11, 1956. PAIRC archives in New York; file: Korespondencja Ogólna (General Correspondence).

6. A Bill for the relief of certain Polish sailors, House of Representatives, H.R. 5756, October 16, 1951, 82 Cong., 1st sess.

7. *A Bill of Mr. Heller*, May 11, 1953, House of Representatives, H.R. 5120, 83rd Cong., 1st sess.; *A Bill for Mr. Graham*, House of Representatives, H.R. 476, March 18, 1954, 83rd Cong., 2nd sess.; *A Bill of Mr. Anfuso*, House of Representatives, H.R. 6923, June 20, 1955, 84th Cong., 1st sess.

8. Text of the telegram from the Rev. Burant published in the *Ball Journal*: "Piąty Doroczny Bal Polskiego Komitetu Imigracyjnego w Plaza Hotel," (Fifth Annual Ball of the Polish American Immigration and Relief Committee) September 12, 1953, New York.

9. Józef Piłsudski Institute, Personal Archive, Jarecki file; also there: Józef Lipski Archive; Władysław Zachariasiewicz, "Polski Komitet Imigracyjny i Pomocowy," MS, PAIRC archives in New York. Also: "Piąty Doroczny Bal Polskiego Komitetu Imigracyjnego w Plaza Hotel" (Fifth Annual Charity Ball of the Polish Immigration Committee at the Plaza Hotel), September 12, 1953, New York (also contains text of the presentation by Impellitteri).

10. "Polski Komitet Imigracyjny; Siódmy Doroczynny Bal, 17 września 1955 roku, Hotel Plaza," (Polish American Immigration and Relief Committee; Seventh Charity Ball, September 17, 1955, Hotel Plaza), New York, 1955.

11. "Instrukcja dla odbiorców paczek "Care" — Food Crusade ("Instructions for recipients of CARE parcels — Food Crusade); "Paczki "Food Care Crusade" — individual distribution ("Food Care Crusade Parcels), PAIRC archives in New York, file: Korespondencja Ogólna (General Correspondence).

12. "Apel Serdeczny Ks. Prał. F. Buranta, Prezesa Polskiego Komitetu Imigracyjnego o Pomoc w Zbiórce Ulicznej z okazji Parady Pułaskiego," (Heart's Appeal of the Reverend Monsignor F. Burant, President of the Polish American Immigration and Relief Committee, for Help in a Street Fund Drive at the Pulaski Day Parade) *Nowy Świat*, September 30, 1963.

Chapter VI

1. PAIRC archives in New York. The Committee's staff roster was printed in such occasional publications as, for instance: "Bal Dwóch Edwardów, 17 wrzesień 1949, Hotel Statler," New York, 1949.

2. W. Zachariasiewicz, "Szkice z dziejów Polonii Amerykańskiej 1945–1990; Polski Komitet Imigracyjny i Pomocowy (*Sketches from the History of the Polish American Community 1945–1990*; Polish American Immigration and Relief Committee), *Dziennik Związkowy*, Chicago, September 29 — October 1, 2000; "Oświadczenie Prezesa Polskiego Komitetu Imigracyjnego, Ks. Prałata F. Buranta. O szkodnikach społecznych i ich kreciej robocie" (Statement by the President of the Polish American Immigration and Relief Committee, the Reverend Monsignor F. Burant, About Social Pests and Their Underhanded Work), *Nowy Świat*, April 26, 1951.

3. "Oświadczenie Prezesa Polskiego Komitetu Imigracyjnego, Ks. Prałata F. Buranta. O szkodnikach społecznych i ich kreciej robocie," *Nowy Świat*, April 26, 1951.

4. PAIRC archives in New York. Piotr Kardela. *Stanisław Gierat 1903–1977/Działalność społeczno-polityczna (Stanisław Gierat 1903–1977/Socio-political Activity)*, (Szczecin, 2000), 261.

5. W. Zachariasiewicz, "Szkice z dziejów Polonii Amerykańskiej 1945–1990; Polski Komitet Imigracyjny i Pomocowy" (*Sketches from the History of the Polish American Community 1945–1990*; The Polish American Immigration and Relief Committee), *Dziennik Związkowy*, Chicago, September 29–October 1, 2000.

6. Letter of the Rev. Msgr. F. Burant to the board of the Association of the Sons of Poland, April 30, 1964, PAIRC archives in New York, file: Appeals.

7. Letter of Julian Zbytniewski to the Rev. Msgr. Burant, September 27, 1962, PAIRC archives, file: Appeals.

8. Ks. Franciszek P. Kowalczyk do Zarządu Głównego ZPRK, 30 czerwca 1966 (The Reverend Franciszek P. Kowalczyk to the Board of Trustees of the PRCUA, June 30, 1966), PAIRC archives in New York, Correspondence 1956–1958, file: Appeals.

9. PAIRC archives in New York, file: General Correspondence 1945–1952.

10. Archbishop John Król to the Rev. F. Burant, December 26, 1961, PAIRC archives, file: Clergy.

11. Archbishop John Król to the Rev. L. Makulec, December 21, 1964, PAIRC archives, file: Clergy.
12. PAIRC archives, file: Clergy.
13. Janusz Krzyżanowski, *Żołnierski program stałej walki o Wolną i Niepodległą Polskę* (The Soldier's Continuous Battle for a Free and Independent Poland) Przemówienie wygłoszone 18 sierpnia na Święcie Żołnierza Polskiego na Polance Sokolej w Somerville, N.J. (Speech delivered at the Falcon's picnic area in Somerville, New Jersey) *Nowy Świat*, New York, August 31, 1957.
14. W. Zachariasiewicz, Executive Secretary of the Polish Immigration Committee in New York, *Survey of the Polish Refugee and Emigrant Centers in Europe*, MS, PAIRC archives in New York, 58.
15. W. Zachariasiewicz, Executive Secretary of the Polish Immigration Committee in New York, *Survey of the Polish Refugee and Emigrant Centers in Europe*, MS, PAIRC archives in New York; W. Zachariasiewicz, "Szkice z dziejów Polonii Amerykańskiej 1945–1990; Polski Komitet Imigracyjny i Pomocowy" (*Sketches from the History of the Polish American Community 1945–1990*; Polish American Immigration and Relief Committee), *Dziennik Związkowy*, Chicago, September 29–October 1, 2000.

Chapter VII

1. Minutes of the annual meeting of PAIRC in New York of June 8, 1957, at the Kosciuszko Foundation, MS, PAIRC archives in New York.
2. F. Burant, "The Fruitful Years," PAIRC, "Dziewiąty Dobroczynny Bal w Dziesięciolecie Pracy na rzecz Polskich Uchodźców," September 28, 1957 (Ninth Annual Charity Ball on the Tenth Anniversary of Work in Behalf of Polish Refugees), Hotel Plaza, New York, 1958.
3. F. Burant, "In Search of Milestones," 5, MS in PAIRC archives in New York.
4. *Ibid.*
5. PAIRC archives, file: General Correspondence.
6. *Ibid.*
7. F. Burant, "In Search of Milestones," 5, MS in PAIRC archives in New York.

8. "Sprawozdanie Sekretarza Wykonawczego Polskiego Komitetu Imigracyjnego za okres 1 czerwca 1957 –1 grudnia 1958" (PAIRC Executive Secretary's Report for the period June 1, 1957–December 1, 1958), 21–22, MS in PAIRC archives.
9. PAIRC archives in New York, Correspondence 1956-1958.
10. PAIRC archives in New York, file: General Correspondence.
11. *Ibid.*
12. PAIRC archives in New York. Correspondence 1956-1958.
13. Letter of C. A. Konopacki to W. Zachariasiewicz; London, April 26, 1956, PAIRC archives, file: General Correspondence.
14. "Ryszard Eibel's Story," *Polish American Immigration and Relief Committee — Polski Komitet Imigracyjny — Charity Ball Book 1958, September 20, 1958, Hotel Plaza*, New York, 1958 (a fuller description of the case and the Committee's intervention).

Chapter VIII

1. Report of the PAIRC executive secretary for the period June 1, 1957, to December 1, 1958, New York, December 1958, 27–28, MS in PAIRC archives in New York.
2. Letter of Z. Łosowski to W. Zachariasiewicz, November 29, 1958, PAIRC archives, file: Correspondence 1958.
3. PAIRC archives in New York, file: PAIRC Buffalo Chapter; "Group is Created Here to Aid Polish Escapees," *Buffalo Courier Express*, May 13, 1958.
4. Letter of the Reverend F. Burant to J. Bogdanowicz, May 5, 1958, PAIRC archives in New York, file: Cleveland Chapter.
5. PAIRC archives in New York, file: Cleveland Chapter.
6. "Polski Komitet Imigracyjny, Dziesiąty Dobroczynny Bal, 20 września 1958, Hotel Plaza" (Polish American Immigration and Relief Committee, Tenth Charity Ball, September 20, 1958, Hotel Plaza).
7. Letter of M. Kalinowski to the PAIRC, September 3, 1957; PAIRC archives; file: PAIRC New York, 1957; Report of the Committee's activity from July 16, 1964, to April 15, 1965.

8. Letter of Msgr. F. Burant to T. Adesko, December 24, 1958; PAIRC archives, file: PAIRC New York, Correspondence 1958.
9. Report on the committee's activity from July 16, 1964, to April 15, 1965.
10. "The Polish-American Immigration and Relief Committee, Inc., Chicago Chapter. First Annual Charity Ball, Ambassador West Hotel, Saturday, April 22, 1961," Chicago.
11. Report of the PAIRC executive secretary for the period June 1, 1957–December 1, 1958, New York, December 1958, MS in PAIRC archives in New York.
12. Letter of W. Zachariasiewicz to M. Święcicki in Dunellen, March 25, 1963, PAIRC archives; file: PAIRC–New Jersey.
13. Report on the Committee's activity from July 16, 1964, to April 15, 1965.
14. PAIRC archives, file: PAIRC — New Jersey; Report of the PAIRC executive director for the period May 14, 1968, to May 24, 1969.
15. Report of the PAIRC executive director for the period July 22, 1972, to June 30, 1973.
16. PAIRC archives, file: PAIRC — Yonkers.
17. Report on the committee's activity from July 16, 1964, to April 15, 1965.
18. *Ibid.*; also, Report of the executive director for the year 1967, PAIRC archives in New York.
19. Story of Jan Niebrzydowski from New Britain, CT, employed in the Budny family factory for almost 30 years, November 4, 2000.
20. PAIRC archives, file: PAIRC — Connecticut chapter.
21. Report of the PAIRC Executive Director for the period May 14, 1968, to May 24, 1969.
22. "1944–1994, Polish American Congress. Anniversary Banquet," October 22, 1994, Buffalo, NY; PAIRC archives in New York, various files.
23. L. Łubieński to Z. Jarmicki, Munich August 3, 1967, PAIRC archives in New York, file Canada: Montreal, Winnipeg, London, Hamilton.
24. I. Morawski to Col. S. Sznuk, May 10, 1967, PAIRC archives in New York, file Canada: Montreal, Winnipeg, London, Hamilton.

Chapter IX

1. "Report of the Delegate for Europe of American Relief for Poland — for the period 1941–1958," Geneva 1958 (Annex No. 9).
2. Report of the PAIRC executive secretary for the period June 1, 1957, to December 1, 1958, MS in PAIRC archives in New York, 2–3.
3. T.L., July 12, 1958, Engres am Rhein, Germany, PAIRC archives in New York, Correspondence 1956–1958.
4. PAIRC archives in New York, Correspondence 1956–1958.
5. PAIRC archives in New York, General Correspondence, 1958, letter of November 17, 1958.
6. Report of the PAIRC executive secretary for the period June 1, 1957, to December 1, 1958, 5–9, MS in PAIRC archives in New York.
7. PAIRC contract for the year 1969, PAIRC archives in New York.
8. *Ibid.*
9. "Wskazówki dla szukających azylu uchodźców" (Guidelines for Refugees Seeking Asylum), UN High Commissioner. Office of the Representative in Germany (informational brochure); information of Janusz Krzyżanowski, PAIRC executive vice president.

Chapter X

1. "American Immigration Policy, Selected Statements," American Immigration Conference, New York, 1957, 18.
2. *Ibid.*
3. *Ibid.*, 33.
4. "Rewizja Ustawy Imigracyjnej" (A Revision of Immigration Law); *Polish Immigration Committee, Charity Ball, 1957, Hotel Plaza, September 28, 1957.*

Chapter XI

1. Report of W. Zachariasiewicz, executive vice president, Polish American Immigration and Relief Committee (PAIRC)

on his European tour of duty, June 3–July 5, 1962.

2. F. J. Proch, "Polish American Immigration and Relief Committee — PAIRC, Years 1946–1981," MS, 11, PAIRC archives in New York.

3. Letter of T. Finucane from the Board of Immigration Appeals, U.S. Department of Justice, November 17, 1958, to W. Zachariasiewicz, PAIRC archives in New York.

4. Report of the PAIRC executive secretary for the period June 1, 1956, to June 1, 1957, MS, PAIRC archives in New York.

5. Report of the PAIRC executive secretary for the period June 1, 1957, to June 1, 1958, MS, PAIRC archives in New York; The Polish American Immigration and Relief Committee, Twelfth Annual Charity Ball, 24 September, 1960, Plaza Hotel, New York.

6. *Lagerschule Mariental-Horst. Unsere Fahrt an die Ostsee Travemunde — Priwall, vom 20.08.1960–28.08.1960*, in the PAIRC archives in New York.

7. Memorandum by the Reverend F. Burant, New York, March 12, 1959, MS in PAIRC archives in New York.

8. "The Polish American Immigration and Relief Committee. Thirteenth Annual Charity Ball, Statler-Hilton Hotel, 33rd Street & 7th Avenue, New York City, November 4th 1961."

9. "Proposal Concerning Foreign Physicians" in the PAIRC archives in New York, also instruction manual *Dotyczy lekarzy imigrantów* (Concerning Immigrant Physicians) of March 29, 1961, in PAIRC archives, N.Y.

10. "The Polish American Immigration and Relief Committee. Thirteenth Annual Charity Ball, Statler-Hilton Hotel, 33rd Street & 7th Avenue, New York City, November 4th 1961."

11. "Excerpts from the Statement of Judge Henry M. Zaleski, Vice-President of Polish American Immigration & Relief Committee, Before the Subcommittee of Refugees & Escapees of the Senate Committee on the Judiciary at its Hearing on World Refugees, July 14, 1961," in: "The Polish American Immigration and Relief Committee. Thirteenth Annual Charity Ball, Statler-Hilton Hotel, 33rd Street & 7th Avenue, New York City, November 4th 1961."

12. Report of Cz. Rawski for W. Zachariasiewicz, January 29, 1963, PAIRC archives in New York.

13. All telegrams in the PAIRC archives in New York.

14. PAIRC archives in New York.

15. Report of L. Łubieński of September 17, 1964, PAIRC archives in New York.

16. Activity of the Polish Immigration Committee — 1963/64. Report of the executive director at the annual meeting of July 15, 1964; Report on the Committee's Activity from July 16, 1964, to April 15, 1964.

17. Józef Piłsudski Institute, personal file of Ignacy Morawski, information of Dr. Frank Mocha.

18. PAIRC archives in New York, file: PAIRC, Board of Trustees, 1959–1966.

19. *In Memoriam, Late Rt. Rev. Msgr. Felix F. Burant, Pastor of St. Stanislaus Parish in New York from March 10th 1924 till August 25th 1964.* (occasional brochure published by St. Stanislaus Parish, 101 East 7th Street in Manhattan); "Ksiądz Prałat Burant nie Żyje" (Rev. Msgr. Burant Is Dead), *Nowy Świat*, vol. LXVII, no. 200, August 26, 1964; "Pogrzeb Honorowego Kapelana ZNP Potężną Manifestacją Żałobną. Tysięczne rzesze Polonii złożyły Hołd ś.p. Prałatowi F. F. Burantowi" (Funeral of PNA Honorary Chaplain a Powerful Funereal Manifestation. Thousands from the Polish American Community Paid Their Respects to the late Monsignor F. F. Burant), *Czas*, vol. 59, no. 36, New York, September 4, 1964; *Srebrny Jubileusz Kapłaństwa Ks. Feliksa F. Buranta, 10 września, 1944* (Silver Jubilee of the Reverend Feliks F. Burant's Priesthood, September 10, 1944), New York, 1944 (among others, contains a general biography of the monsignor).

20. Report on the committee's activity from July 16, 1964, to April 15, 1965.

21. Report of the European representatives for 1966, given at the General Assembly of the Polish American Immigration and Relief Committee on May 13, 1967, in New York.

22. "Sprawozdanie ogólne z działalności Polskiego Komitetu Imigracyjnego Sekretarza Generalnego i Dyrektora (Ignacego Morawskiego) za okres 15 kwietnia 1966 po 1-szy maja 1967 roku. (Odczytane na Walnym Rocznym Zebraniu, odbytym w sobotę, dnia 13 maja 1967 roku w Sali Roof Terrace Hotelu George Washington w New Yorku)."

[General Report by the Secretary General and Director (Ignacy Morawski) on the PAIRC's Activity for the period April 15, 1966 to May 1, 1967. (Read at the Annual General Assembly held on Saturday May 13, 1967, in the Roof Terrace Suite of the George Washington Hotel in New York)]

23. Executive director's report for 1967.

24. PAIRC executive director's report for the period May 14, 1968, to May 24, 1969.

25. Letter quoted in the journal of the PAIRC's 21st annual ball: "Twenty First Annual Charity Ball, Statler Hilton Hotel, Saturday, November 1, 1969."

26. Annual report of the PAIRC executive director for the period May 24, 1969, to August 29, 1970"; 22nd Annual Charity Ball, Statler-Hilton Hotel, Saturday October 24, 1970.

27. F.J.Proch, *Polski Komitet Imigracyjny — PKI, Polish American Immigration and Relief Committee, the Years 1946–1981*, MS, 15–16.

28. Letter of Bishop Sz. Wesoły to F. Proch in New York, April 1, 1977, PAIRC archives, letter quoted in: *F. Proch, Polski Komitet Imigracyjny — PKI. Polish American Immigration and Relief Committee, the Years 1946–1981*, MS, 15–16.

29. Letter of Bishop Rubin to PAIRC, Rome, April 6, 1978, PAIRC archives.

30. "PAIRC — Europe, 1970," PAIRC archives in New York.

31. "The Polish-American Immigration and Relief Committee. XXV Silver Jubilee Annual Charity Ball, Statler-Hilton Hotel, Saturday November 24, 1973." PAIRC archives in New York.

32. Report of the PAIRC executive director for the period July 22, 1972, to June 30, 1973; PAIRC archives in New York.

33. Henry Kamm, "A Confrontation on refugees. Southeast Asian Nations Want to Know How Far West Will Go in Taking Their 325,000 Indochinese," *The New York Times*, June 28, 1979.

34. Charles B. Kelly, *U.S. Immigration: A Policy Analysis* (New York, 1979), 53–54.

35. "Sprawozdanie z Walnego Zebrania PAIRC w dniu 27 czerwca 1975" (Minutes of the General Assembly of the PAIRC of June 27, 1975), PAIRC archives in New York.

36. "Minutes from the Meeting of the Board of Trustees of the Polish American Immigration and Relief Committee Inc., held on May 12, 1976, at PAIRC's Headquarters 17 Irving Place, NY," PAIRC archives in New York.

37. "Minutes of the Annual Meeting of the Polish American Immigration and Relief Committee, Inc., held on June 8, 1976, at the Headquarters of the Committee, 17 Irving Place, New York, NY 10003," PAIRC archives in New York.

38. "Protokół z posiedzenia Prezydium Polskiego Komitetu Imigracyjnego odbytego 3 sierpnia 1978 w biurze PKI" (Minutes of the PAIRC Presidium meeting of August 3, 1978, in the offices of the PAIRC); "Protokół z Zebrania Rady PKI odbytego 4 listopada 1978 w biurze PKI" (Minutes of the PAIRC Board meeting of November 4, 1978, in the PAIRC offices), PAIRC archives.

39. "Sprawozdanie Dyrektora Wykonawczego PAIRC na Zebranie Rady Dyrektorów w dniu 14 lutego 1978r." (Report of the PAIRC Executive Director for the Board of Directors Meeting of February 14, 1978), PAIRC archives in New York.

40. *Ibid.*

41. "Minutes of the Meeting of the Polish American Immigration and Relief Committee, Inc., held on February 17th 1979, at the Polish Soldier's Home, 17 Irving Place, New York, NY," PAIRC archives in New York.

42. Letter of F. Zon to the PAIRC, Boston, September 21, 1978 (the letter was attached to the Committee's Activity Report for 1979); PAIRC archives in New York.

43. W. Malinowski to the PAIRC Board, South River, NJ, August 19, 1978, PAIRC archives in New York. S.G.1.

44. [S.Gierat], "Polsko-Amerykański Komitet Imigracyjny," *Kombatant w Ameryce*, nr. 2 (80), June 1976, 12.

45. "Sprawozdanie z wyjazdu do Europy od 1 IX 1979, do 15 IX 1979, Janusza Krzyżanowskiego, Wiceprezesa Polskiego Komitetu Imigracyjnego" (PAIRC Vice President Janusz Krzyżanowski's Report on his trip to Europe September 1, 1979, to September 15, 1979), PAIRC archives in New York.

46. *Ibid.*; Letter of Dr. Ludwik Frendl from Munich to F. Proch, July 31, 1979, Committee report of February 3, 1979.

47. Proposed agreement prepared and sent by PAIRC First Vice President Janusz

Krzyżanowski to the president of the KPK, April 2, 1979, in the PAIRC report for 1979, PAIRC archives in New York.

48. The full text of the Refugee Act of 1980 was also published in: *Immigration and Nationality Act with Amendments and Notes on Related Laws*, Committee on the Judiciary, House of Representatives, United States, U.S. Government Printing Office, Washington, 1980, 171–177; *Country Reports on the World Refugee Situation: Statistics. Report to the Congress for Fiscal Year 1985*, (Washington, 1984), i.

49. Immigration and Naturalization Service, *Worldwide Guidelines for Oversees Refugee Processing*, Washington, 1983, 7–17.

50. *Immigration and Nationality Act with Amendments and Notes on Related Laws*, Committee on the Judiciary, House of Representatives, United States, U.S. Government Printing Office, Washington, 1980, 172.

51. United States Department of State, Bureau for Refugee Programs, *Orientation Manual*.

52. United States Department of State, Bureau for Refugee Programs, *Orientation Manual*, 25.

53. *Country Reports on the World Refugee Situation: Statistics*, Report to the Congress For Fiscal Year 1985, Washington, 1984, i.

54. *Ibid.*, 32.

55. United States Department of State, Bureau for Refugee Programs. *Orientation Manual*, 25.

56. *Refugee Resettlement Program. Report to the Congress. January 31, 1982*, 61.

57. "Austria Cites Doubling in Number of Polish Refugees in Last Year," *The New York Times*, April 7, 1981.

Chapter XII

1. Letter of SWAP Commandant E. Kaleniak to PAIRC of February 19, 1980, PAIRC report for 1980, PAIRC archives in New York.

2. Report on the PAIRC meeting of July 28, 1980, PAIRC archives in New York.

3. "Sprawozdanie z podróży do Europy odbytej w dniach od 5-go do 27-go sierpnia 1980 w imieniu Rady Nadzorczej Polskiego Komitetu Imigracyjnego w Nowym Jorku" (Report from trip to Europe made from August 5 to 27, 1980, on behalf of the Board of Trustees of the Polish American Immigration and Relief Committee in New York), 9. Report attached to the minutes of the Executive Committee of the PAIRC of December 6, 1980; PAIRC archives in New York.

4. *Ibid.*, 10–11.

5. *Ibid.*, 13–14.

6. Letter enclosed with documentation from the Committee's Board of Trustees meeting of June 6, 1981; PAIRC archives in New York.

7. "Minutes of the Meeting of the Board of Trustees of the Polish American Immigration and Relief Committee, Inc., April 4, 1981," PAIRC archives in New York.

8. "Minutes of the Meeting of the Executive Committee, May 12, 1981," PAIRC archives in New York.

9. "Annual Meeting and Annual Board Election of Polish American Immigration and Relief Committee, June [6] 1981," PAIRC archives in New York.

10. L. Łubieński to F. Proch, Munich, June 4, 1981, letter attached to the report from the PAIRC meeting of June 6, 1981; PAIRC archives in New York.

11. L. Frendl to F. Proch, April 9, 1981, letter attached to documentation from the June 6, 1981, meeting.

12. Letter of L. Frendl to F. Proch in New York, Munich, May 5, 1981, PAIRC archives in New York.

13. Letter of M. Trokenheim to L. Frendl in Munich, Stockholm, March 30, 1981; PAIRC archives in New York.

14. Minutes of the PAIRC board meeting of December 12, 1981, PAIRC archives in New York.

15. "Przybysze z Wiednia jednoczą się" (The Arrivals from Vienna Are Uniting), *Nowy Dziennik*, December 5–6, 1981; A very critical article about the work of the PAIRC was published by Andrzej Baranowski in *Nowy Dziennik*: "Emigranci" (The Emigrants), *Nowy Dziennik*, December 30–January 5, 1982/83; minutes of the PAIRC board meeting of December 12, 1981; PAIRC archives in New York.

16. Minutes of the PAIRC board meeting of March 20, 1982; PAIRC archives in New York.

17. "Sprawozdanie wiceprezesa wykon-

awczego J.Krzyżanowskiego na Roczne Zebranie Rady PKI w dniu 8 stycznia 1983." (Executive Vice President Janusz Krzyżanowski's report to the PAIRC annual Board meeting), PAIRC archives in New York.

18. Resolutions of a PNA board of directors meeting attached to a letter of Steve Rasiej to the Reverend John Karpiński, September 22, 1982; PAIRC archives in New York.

19. "FY 1983 Numerical Projections," attached to "Sprawozdanie wiceprezesa wykonawczego J.Krzyżanowskiego na Roczne Zebranie Rady PKI w dniu 8 stycznia 1983" (Executive Vice President Janusz Krzyżanowski's Report for the annual Board meeting of January 8, 1983), PAIRC archives in New York.

20. "Meeting Conducted on December 16, 1983, Polish American Immigration and Relief Committee, Inc.," PAIRC archives in New York.

21. "Problems Regarding the Admission of Polish Refugees to the USA," memorandum of Janusz Krzyżanowski of September 8, 1981, PAIRC archives in New York.

22. Janusz Krzyżanowski, "Refugees from Poland." Presented at European Refugee Conference in Geneva, November 29-30, 1983, PAIRC archives in New York.

23. "Polish American Immigration and Relief Committee, Meeting of December 14, 1984," PAIRC archives in New York.

24. Report on the Committee meeting of October 17, 1985; PAIRC archives in New York, report for the PAIRC annual board meeting of February 9, 1987; PAIRC archives in New York; "Budget Projection for FY 1988, PAIRC — Overview;" PAIRC archives in New York (which includes data for the two prior years).

25. Report on the committee meeting of October 17, 1985; PAIRC archives in New York. O. Konrad Hejmo, "Nowa emigracja i jej dramaty." (The New Emigration and Its Dramas) *Kronika Rzymska*, nr. 44-46, Rome, February-March-April 1986, 40-45; *Kultura*, nr. 9, Paris, 1986, 77-78.

26. "Statement by Janusz Krzyżanowski, Executive Vice President, Polish American Immigration and Relief Committee, for the House Sub-Committee on Immigration, Refugees and International Law, November 2, 1989," PAIRC archives in New York.

Chapter XIII

1. *U.S. Department of Justice, Immigration and Naturalization Service, 1992 Statistical Yearbook of the Immigration and Naturalization Service*, Washington, 1993, A.1-1–A1-21.

Chapter XIV

1. *World Refugee Report: A Report Submitted to the Congress as Part of the Consultations on FY 1993 Refugee Admissions to the United States, June 1992*, Washington, 127-128.

2. Peter Hoffer, "Austria to Tighten Policy on Refugees from East," *Washington Post*, Washington, May 5, 1988.

3. Minutes of the PAIRC meeting held on December 19, 1989, in its offices at 140 W. 22nd Street, New York, NY, PAIRC archives in New York.

4. Minutes of the PAIRC meeting of March 8, 1990, held in the PAIRC offices located at 140 W. 22nd Street, New York, NY, PAIRC archives in New York.

5. Minutes of the PAIRC meeting held on January 18, 1991, in the PAIRC offices located at 140 W. 22nd Street, New York, NY; PAIRC archives in New York.

6. Exchange of correspondence between PAIRC and the mother of K. S.; PAIRC archives in New York.

7. Minutes of PAIRC meeting held on April 19, 1991, in the PAIRC offices at 140 W. 22nd Street, New York, NY; PAIRC archives in New York.

8. Minutes of the PAIRC board meeting of November 14, 1991; PAIRC archives in New York.

9. Holiday appeal of the Rev. Msgr. Joseph Marjańczyk, president of the PAIRC board of trustees; PAIRC archives in New York.

10. Minutes of the PAIRC board of trustees meeting of May 19, 1997; Minutes of the Committee Council meeting of November 17, 1997; PAIRC archives in New York.

11. Exchange of correspondence of the

parents of Bogumił, Helena, and Marian Misiuk with the Committee in 1996; PAIRC archives in New York.

12. Letter of Iliona Polkowska of Jersey City to the Committee (undated, 1998); PAIRC archives in New York.

13. Minutes of the Committee council meeting of November 17, 1997; PAIRC archives in New York.

14. PAIRC archives in New York.

Bibliography

Archival Collections

Institute of National Remembrance (IPN), Cracow, Poland.
Press Collection
Jagiellonian Library, Cracow, Poland.
Collection of the Polish Immigration in North America at the Foundation for Recording of the Independence Movement.
Pilsudski Institute for Research in the Modern History of Poland, New York.
Rev. Felix Burant File.
Collection of the Polish National Alliance in New York.
Collection of the Polish-American Congress.
Collection of KNAP (Committee of Americans of Polish Descent in America).
Collection of the [Polish] Committee of National Defense.
Polish-American Immigration and Relief Committee in New York.
Minutes from the PAIRC board meetings.
Records of the PAIRC European branches.
Correspondence with U.S. branches and sections.
Selected files.
Society of Polish Veterans of W.W.II (SWAP), New York.
Personal files.

Printed Documents, Reports, Manuscripts, Typescripts

"Address by Senator Arthur H. Vandenberg upon the Occasion of the 40th Anniversary of the Polish Daily News." Hotel Book Cadillac, Detroit, MI, April 2, 1944.
"American Immigration Policy. Selected Statements." American Immigration Conference, New York, 1957.
Burant, Felix, Rev., "In Search of Milestones" (typescript at the PAIRC archives, New York).
_____. Memoranda by Rev. Col. Felix Burant, the chairman of the Immigration

Commission at the Convention of Polish American Congress at Philadelphia, PA, on May 29–31, 1948 (typescript at the Archives of PAIRC, New York).

_____. Statement of Rt. Rev. Msgr. Felix F. Burant, president of the Polish American Immigration Committee, before President's Commission on Immigration and Naturalization, October 1, 1952 (typescript at the PAIRC Archives).

_____. Statement of Rt. Rev. Msgr. Feliks F. Burant, president of the Polish Immigration Committee, Chaplain (Col.) USAR before Subcommittee on Immigration and Naturalization, June 10, 1953, regarding emergency immigration legislation (typescript at the PAIRC Archives).

Country Reports on the World Refugee Situation: Statistics Reports to the Congress for Fiscal Year 1985, Washington, 1984.

"Displaced Persons Act," Public Law 774 — 80th Congress, Chapter 647, 2nd session.

"Do Wszystkich Członków Polskich Sił Zbrojnych," London, 1946.

"Documents on Return of Poles to Poland," Polish Press Agency, Edinburgh, April 1946.

"Factual Report on the Plight of Displaced Persons in Germany. Observations made by a Delegation of U.S. Citizens on Behalf of the Polish-American Congress, Inc.," *Bulletin: Polish American Congress*, vol. 3, no. 6, Chicago, February 1947.

Foreign Relations of the United States (FRUS) Diplomatic Papers; The Conferences at Malta and Yalta, 1945, (United States Government Printing Office, Washington, DC, 1955).

Immigration and Nationality Act with Amendments and Notes on Related Laws. Committee on the Judiciary. U.S. House of Representatives. United States Printing Office, Washington, DC, 1980.

Immigration and Naturalization Service. Worldwide Guidelines for Overseas Refugees Processing. Washington, 1983

Krzyżanowski, Janusz. "Problems Regarding Admission of Polish Refugees to the USA." (Memoranda, typescript at the PAIRC archives.)

_____. "Refugees from Poland." Presented at European Refugee Conference in Geneva, November 29–30, 1983. Typescript at PAIRC archives.

_____. "Statement by Janusz Krzyżanowski, Executive Vice-President, Polish American Immigration and Relief Committee for the House SubCommittee on Immigration, Refugees and International Law," November 2, 1989. Typescript at the PAIRC archives.

"Pod Hasłem Jedności, Sprawozdanie ze Zjazdu Amerykańsko-Polskich Zrzeszeń na Wschodzie w New Yorku w dniach 11 i 12 marca 1944," Coordinating Committee of American-Polish Associations in the East, New York, 1944.

"Polish American Immigration and Relief Committee — Polski Komitet Imigracyjny — Charity Ball Book 1958, 20 września 1958, Hotel Plaza," New York, 1958.

Polski Komitet Imigracyjny w New Yorku, Działalność Komitetu w okresie od 4 lutego 1947 do 31 października 1949r, New York, 1948. Typescript.

Proch, Franciszek. Polski Komitet Imigracyjny — PKI. Polish-American Immigration and Relief Committee — PAIRC, lata 1946–1981. Typescript.

"Report to Byrnes in Paris," *Bulletin: Polish-American Congress*, vol. 3, no. 6, Chicago, February 1947.

Selected Readings on U.S. Immigration Policy and Law: A Compendium Prepared at the Request of Senator Edward M. Kennedy, Chairman, Committee on the Judiciary, United States Senate, for the use of the Select Commission on Immigration and Refugee Policy. Prepared by the Congressional Research Service, Library of Congress, Washington, DC, 1980.
Sprawozdanie Delegata na Europę Rady Polonii Amerykańskiej. American Polish War Relief, za okres 1941–1958. Geneva, 1958.
Sprawozdanie Zarządu Wykonawczego Poszczególnych Komisji i Komitetów oraz Biur w Chicago i Washingtonie na Trzecią Krajową Konwencję Kongresu Polonii Amerykańskiej w Atlantic City, N.J., w dniach 30–31 maja–1 czerwca 1952. Atlantic City, NJ, 1952.
Statistical Yearbook of the Immigration and Naturalization Service. Washington, 1993.
United States Department of State. Bureau for Refugee Programs. Orientation Manual.
United States Department of Justice. Immigration and Naturalization Service, 1992. Statistical Yearbook of the Immigration and Naturalization Service. Washington, 1993.
"Urzędowy Protokół Sejmu XXVIII Związku Narodowego Polskiego odbytego w dniach 10-go do 16-go września 1939, Book Cadillac Hotel." Detroit, MI, 1939.
Vandenberg, A.H., Jr., and J.A. Morris, eds. The Private Papers of Senator Vandenberg. Boston, 1952.
World Refugee Report. A Report Submitted to the Congress as Part of the Consultations on Fiscal Year 1993 Refugee Admissions to the United States, June 1992. Washington, 1992.
Zachariasiewicz, W. Executive Secretary of the Polish Immigration Committee, Survey of the Polish Refugee and Emigrant Centers in Europe. Typescript at PAIRC Archives, New York.

Press Articles, Books and Pamphlets

"Austria Cites Doubling in Number of Polish Refugees in Last Year." *The New York Times*, April 7, 1981.
Babiński G., & others, eds., "Poles in History and Culture of the United States of America": [scientific session, Warsaw 24–25 June 1976] / ed. Grzegorz Babiński, Mirosław Francić. Polska Akademia Nauk. Komitet Badania Polonii Zagranicznej, Wrocław, Kraków, 1979.
Baker, T. Lindsay. *Historia najstarszych polskich osad w Ameryce*. Ossolineum, Wrocław, 1981.
Baranowski, Andrzej. Emigranci, "Nowy Dziennik," New York, December 30–January 5, 1982.
Białasiewicz, W. *Pomiędzy lojalnością a porywem serc. Polonia amerykańska we wrześniu 1939 roku*. Chicago, 1989.
Bolek, Rev. F. *Who Is Who in Polish America. A Biographical Directory of Polish-American leaders and Distinguished Poles Residing in America*. New York, 1943.

Brożek, Andrzej. *Polish Americans*. Translated from Polish by Wojciech Worsztynowicz. Interpress, Warsaw, 1985.

Burant, Felix. "The Fruitful Years," in *Polski Komitet Imigracyjny. Dziewiąty Doroczny Bal w Dziesięciolecie Pracy na Rzecz Polskich Uchodźców, 28 września 1957 roku, Hotel Plaza*. New York, 1958.

_____. "In Memoriam. Late Rt. Rev. Msgr. Felix F. Burant, Pastor of St. Stanislaus Parish in New York, March 10, 1924 till August 25, 1964." New York, 1964.

_____. Ksiądz Burant nie żyje. "Nowy Świat." New York, August 26, 1964.

_____. *Pogrzeb Honorowego Kapelana ZNP Potężną Manifestacją Żałobną. Tysięczne Rzesze Polonii Złożyły Hołd ś.p. Prałatowi F.F. Burantowi*, "Czas." New York, September 4, 1964.

_____. *Srebrny Jubileusz Kapłaństwa Ks.Feliksa Buranta, 10 września 1944*. New York, 1944.

Cenckiewicz, Sławomir. *Tadeusz Katelbach. Biografia polityczna, 1897–1977*. Warszawa, 2005.

Chorzempa, Rosemary A. *Polish roots = Korzenie polskie*. Genealogical Publications, Baltimore, 1993).

Cieślik, Krzysztof. *Znani-nieznani: studia/Krzysztof Cieślik*. Marta Skwara, Jerzy Kazimierski, Szczecin 1997.

Coleman, Marion Moore. *Our Other World: A Polish Scrapbook*. Cheshire, CT: Cherry Hill Books, [post 1978].

Drozdowski, Marian Marek. *Ameryka Północna: studia Polska Akademia Nauk*. Instytut Historii: bibliografia drukow zwartych za lata 1944–1974.

_____. *Ameryka Północna: studia*. T. 1-2, Polska Akademia Nauk. Instytut Historii. Państwowe Wydawnictwo Naukowe, Warszawa, 1975, 1978.

_____. *Ameryka Północna: studia*. T. 2/pod red. Mariana Marka Drozdowskiego; Polska Akademia Nauk. Instytut Historii. 76.

Dworaczyk, Edward Joseph. *The Millennium History of Panna Maria, Texas: The Oldest Polish Settlement in America 1854–1966*. 1966.

_____. *The History of Panna Maria, Texas: The Oldest Permanent Polish Settlement in America 1854–1987*. Panna Maria Historical Society, 1987.

Eisenhower, Dwight. "Eisenhower Urges U.S. Admit 240,000 Above Alien Quota." The *New York Times*, April 23, 1953.

_____. "President Signs Bill for more Aliens," *The New York Times*, August 8, 1953.

Fijałkowski, Wiesław. *Polacy i ich potomkowie w historii Stanów Zjednoczonych Ameryki*. Wydawnictwa Szkolne i Pedagogiczne, Warszawa, 1978.

Fisher, Harold Henry. *America and the New Poland*. With the collaboration of Sidney Brooks. The Macmillan Co., New York, 1928.

Frajlich, Anna, ed. *Between Lvov, New York and Ulysses' Ithaca: Jozef Wittlin — Poet, Essayist, Novelist*. Department of Slavic Languages, Columbia University, New York, 2001.

Frank, L. *Auerbach Immigration Laws of the United States*. Indianapolis, 1955.

Galat, Henryk. *Wkład Polaków i Polonii w rozwój gospodarki, nauki i techniki USA*. Referat na sesję naukową Wkład Polaków i Polonii w rozwój Stanów Zjednoczonych, Warszawa, 24–25 czerwca 1976. Warszawa, 1976.

Gierat, Stanisław. Polsko-Amerykański Komitet Imigracyjny. "Kombatant w Ameryce," no. 2 (80), New York, June 1976.

Gordon, Ch. E. *Immigration and Nationality Law*. New York, 1979.
Haiman, Mieczysław. Historia udziału Polaków w amerykańskiej wojnie domowej. Chicago, 1928.
Hejmo, O.K. Nowa emigracja i jej dramaty, "Kronika Rzymska," no. 44–46, Rome, February-April 1986.
Hoffer P. "Austria to Tighten Policy on Refugees from East." *Washington Post*, May 5, 1988.
Hoskins, Janina W. *Polish Genealogy & Heraldry: An Introduction to Research*. Library of Congress, Washington, DC, 1987.
Hutchison, E.P. *Legislative History of American Immigration Policy, 1798–1965*. Philadelphia, 1985.
Iwańska, Alicja. *Potyczki i przymierza: pamiętnik 1918–1985* (Gebethner i Ska., Warszawa, 1993).
Jacobson, Matthew Frye. *Special Sorrows: The Diasporic Immigration of Irish, Polish, and Jewish Immigrants in the United States*. Harvard University Press, 1995.
Jezierski, Bronisław A. W obronie prawdy, czyli Zbiór artykułów przeciwko paszkwilom na naród polski i duchowieństwo w Polsce / napisał i zebrał Bronisław A. Jezierski.
Jurisson A., Rev. *Operation Good Samaritan: The Resettlement of Displaced Persons, 1949–1952*. New York, no date of publication provided.
Kamm, H. "A Confrontation on Refugees. South East Asian Nations Want to Know How Far West Will Go in Taking Their 325,000 Indochinese," *The New York Times*, June 28, 1979.
Kantor, Ryszard. *Między Zaborowem a Chicago: kulturowe konsekwencje istnienia zbiorowości imigrantów z parafii zaborowskiej w Chicago i jej kontaktów z rodzinnymi wsiami, Akademia Nauk*. Komitet Badania Polonii. Ossolineum, Wrocław, Kraków, 1990.
Kardela, Piotr. Polskę w sercu noszę. "Nowy Dziennik," New York, April 28, 2000.
_____. Stanisław Gierat 1903–1977. Działalność społeczno-polityczna. Szczecin, 2001.
Katelbach, Tadeusz. *Co przed 20 laty obiecywał Stevenson i Eisenhower*, "Dziennik Polski i Dziennik Żołnierza" London, October 28, 1972.
Kelly, Ch. B. *U.S. Immigration Policy. Analysis*. New York, 1979.
Kennedy, John F. *A Nation of Immigrants*. New York, 1963.
Kotlarz, Marek H. *Citizenship: Handbook* = Obywatelstwo: podręcznik: historia Stanów Zjednoczonych, struktura rządu — pytania i odpowiedzi, Konstytucja, Hymn: wersja angielsko-polska. "Exter," New York, 2001.
Kowalski, Stanisław J. *Jan Lechoń jako redaktor i publicysta w okresie Nowojorskim*, Redakcja Wydawnictw KUL, Lublin, 1996.
Krysiewicz T.T. *Polish Immigration Committee in the United States. A Historical Study of the American Committee for the Relief of Polish Immigrants: 1947–1952*. New York, 1954.
Krzeptowska-Jasinek, Maria. Podhalanie w Chicago. "Iskry," Warszawa, 1990.
Krzyżanowski, Janusz. Żołnierski program walki o Wolną i Niepodległą Polskę. Przemówienie wygłoszone 15 sierpnia na Święcie Żołnierza Polskiego na Polance Sokolej w Sommerville, N.J., "Nowy Świat," New York, August 31, 1957.
Kubiak, Hieronim, ed. Polonia amerykańska: przeszłość i współczesność/pod

red.Hieronima Kubiaka, Eugeniusza Kusielewicza i Tadeusza Gromady/. Polska Akademia Nauk. Komitet Badań Polonii. Wrocław, Kraków, 1988.

Kuzniewski, Anthony J. *Faith and Fatherland: The Polish Church War in Wisconsin, 1896–1918*. University of Notre Dame Press, Notre Dame, London, 1980.

Ławrowski, Andrzej. *Polacy w dziejach Stanów Zjednoczonych*. Krajowa Agencja Wydawnicza, Warszawa, 1977.

Lehman. "Citizens to Press for New Alien Act. Substantial Revision Sought. Lehman Says He Reminds President of Pledges." The *New York Times*, January 12, 1954.

Matuszewski, Ignacy. *Teoria i praktyka*, "Dziennik Polski." Detroit, April 6, 1946.

Matuszewski, Ignacy. *Dlaczego nie chcą wracać*, "Dziennik Polski." Detroit, April 10, 1946.

Narell, Irena. *History's Choice: A Writer's Journey from Poland to America*. Oakland: Akiba Press, 1995.

Niemcewicz. *Julian Ursyn Niemcewicz, Listy z Ameryki do Adama Kazimierza Czartoryskiego (1798–1806)*. Wydawnictwo Uniwersytetu Mikołaja Kopernika, Toruń, 2003.

Orłowski, Józef Kazimierz. *Ignacy Jan Paderewski i odbudowa Polski*. T. 1-2, Chicago, 1940.

Pacyga, Dominic A. *Polish Immigrants and Industrial Chicago: Workers on the South Side, 1880–1922*. Ohio State University, Columbus.

PAIRC. "Group Is Created to Aid Polish Escapees." *Buffalo Courier Express*, May 13, 1958.

_____. "The Polish American Immigration and Relief Committee, Twelfth Annual Charity Ball, September 24, 1960, Plaza Hotel, New York." New York, 1960.

_____. "The Polish American Immigration and Relief Committee, Thirteenth Annual Charity Ball, Statler-Hilton Hotel, 33rd Street & 7 Avenue, New York City, November 4, 1961." New York, 1961.

_____. "The Polish American Immigration and Relief Committee, XXV Silver Jubilee Annual Charity Ball, Statler-Hilton Hotel, Saturday, November 24, 1973." New York, 1973.

Piechota, Magdalena. *Jaka Ameryka?: polscy reportażyści Dwudziestolecia międzywojennego o Stanach Zjednoczonych*. Wydawnictwo Uniwersytetu Marii Curie-Skłodowskiej, Lublin, 2002.

Piekoszewski, Jan. *Problemy Polonii amerykańskiej*. "Pax," Warszawa, 1981.

Pienkos Donald. *PNA: A Centennial History of the Polish National Alliance of the United States of North America*. East European Monographs, Boulder, New York, 1984.

Polish American Congress. "1944–1994; Polish American Congress. Anniversary Banquet, October 22, 1994." Buffalo, 1994.

Praga, Jacek. *Zjednoczenie Polaków w Ameryce 1952–2002*. Comandor, Warszawa, 2002.

"Przybysze z Wiednia jednoczą się," "Nowy Dziennik." New York, December 5–6, 1981.

Radzik, Tadeusz. *Polonia amerykańska wobec Polski: 1918–1939*. Lublin, 1990.

_____. *Stosunki polsko-żydowskie w Stanach Zjednoczonych Ameryki w latach 1918–1921*. Lublin, 1988.

Sandberg, Neil C. *Ethnic Identity and Assimilation: The Polish-American Community: Case Study of Metropolitan Los Angeles, New York [etc.]*. Praeger Publishers, New York, 1977.

Sosnkowski Kazimierz, Gen. "Gen. Sosnkowski Meets Ike," *Polish American Journal*, vol. XLI, November 15, 1952.
Stefanowicz, Zygmunt J. Szkice z Życia Polonii Amerykańskiej. "Epoka," Warszawa, 1985.
"St. Joseph's Home for Polish Immigrants, Church of St. Stanislaus B&M, 1874–1954," New York, 1954.
Strakacz, Sylwin. Jerzy, Za kulisami wielkiej kariery: Paderewski w dziennikach i listach Sylwina i Anieli Strakaczów, 1936–1939. Krakow, 1994.
Swastek, Jozef Wincenty. *The Formative Years of the Polish Seminary in the United States*. Orchard Lake, MI: Center for Polish Studies and Culture. Orchard Lake Schools, 1985.
Tomczykowska, Wanda. *A Guide to Polonica in the San Francisco Bay Area, San Francisco, CA*. The Polish Arts and Culture Foundation, 1994.
Wachtl, K. *Polonia w Ameryce*. Philadelphia, 1944.
Wałaszek, Adam. Świątynia imigrantów: tworzenie polonijnego Cleveland: 1880–1930. "Nomos," Krakow, 1994.
Wańkowicz, Melchior. De profundis ; Polacy i Ameryka. "Polonia," Warszawa, 1991.
Watt, Richard. *Bitter Glory: Poland and Its fate: 1918–1939*. Hippocrene, New York, 1998.
Weintraub, Wiktor. O współczesnych i o sobie: wspomnienia, sylwetki, szkice literackie. "Znak," Krakow, 1994.
Wlodarski, Szczepan. *The Origin and Growth of the Polish National Catholic Church*. The Polish National Catholic Church, Scranton, PA, 1974.
Wygoda, Jerzy. Impresje amerykańskie: Polonia Wschodniego Wybrzeża = *Impressions of America: Polonia of the Eastern Coast*. Rzeszów, 2000.
Wyman, M. *Europe's Displaced Persons, 1945–1951*. Philadelphia, 1989.
Wyrwa, Józef. *Pamiętnik partyzanta*. Chicago, 1951.
Wytrwal, Joseph Anthony. *The Polish Experience in Detroit*. Endurance Press, Detroit, 1992.
"Wysoki Komisarz Narodów Zjednoczonych; Urząd Przedstawiciela w Niemczech." Info pamphlet, no date or place of publication provided.
Zahariasiewicz, W. Szkice z dziejów Polonii Amerykańskiej 1945–1990; Polski Komitet Imigracyjny i Pomocowy (Polish American Immigration and Relief Committee), "Dziennik Związkowy," Chicago, September 29, October 1, 2000.

Index

ACRPDP 57
Act of December 8, 1942 16
Act of June 21, 1941 16
Act of March 3, 1875 14
Act to Amend the Immigration and Nationality Act of 1952 (PL 85-316) 129
Adamski, Reverend Peter 104
Adesko, Judge Thaddeus V. 106, 107, 108, 164
Adjudication Commission of the Bundesamt 124
Administrative Court in Ansbach 124
Advisory Committee for Voluntary Foreign Aid 57
Advisory Committee on Voluntary Aid in Washington 116
affidavit of support 53, 103
Afghanistan 3
agents of Communist Poland 120
Alaska 35, 36
Albany Medical College 143
Alexander Hamilton Hotel (in New Jersey) 110
Alien Enemy Act 14
Alliance College Fund 22
Allied occupation zones in Germany 19, 34
Allies 26, 27, 61, 91
Amberg 79
America 14, 21, 27, 35, 37, 38, 42,, 60, 61, 67, 74, 76, 90, 101, 111, 120, 123, 126, 128, 137, 156, 174, 185
American Armed Forces 31
American Army 72
American authorities 31, 32, 102, 177, 189
American Commission for the Relief of Polish immigrants, the 39, 53, 54, 136

American Committee for Resettlement of Polish Displaced Persons 57
American Council of Voluntary Agencies for Foreign Service 155, 158, 175
American Embassy in Taiwan 76
American federal government 208
American Friends Service Committee 28
American Fund for Czechoslovak Refugees 125, 131
American Immigration and Citizens Conference (Plaza Hotel, New York) 162
American Immigration and Citizenship Conference 158
American labor market 131
American occupation forces 35
American occupation zone 31, 35
American Press 19
American Relief for Poland, (ARP) 19, 23, 24, 25, 26, 27, 28, 38, 39, 41, 42, 47, 89, 105, 107, 115, 116, 120, 160
American Third Army 32
Anders, General 25, 101, 120
Andrzejewska, Charlotte 167, 178
Anfuso, Congressman Victor 69, 74
Annual Christmas Program for Poles in Western Europe 108
April 1935 Constitution of Poland 29
Arab-Israeli War in 1948 67
Arciszewski, Tomasz 84
Argentina 98, 99, 100, 137
Arnhem 148
ARP 19, 25, 26, 27, 28, 115, 116, 120
Articles of Faith 96
Arundel, Canada 63
Association of Polish Refugees in Germany 79
assurance of employment 53

239

Atkielski, Auxiliary Bishop R.R. of Milwaukee 88
Atkins, Senator Arthur V. 67
Atlantic Broadcasting Corporation 49
Atlantic Charter 31, 61
Atlantic City 47
Atlee 28
Augustdorf 79
Australia 46, 154, 159, 161, 179, 180, 191, 194, 200, 216
Australian authorities 191, 194
Australian Commission for Emigration Matters 179
Austria 26, 28, 34, 45, 49, 50, 52, 67, 70, 77, 78, 89, 91, 92, 98, 116, 117, 120, 122, 128, 131, 133, 134, 136, 137, 154, 156, 157, 158, 168, 171, 174, 176, 178, 179, 185, 186, 192, 194, 199, 200, 201, 202, 208, 209
Austro-Hungary 15, 16
Avenel, New Jersey 103

Babirecki, Leopold 85
Baciński, Rev. Piotr 12
Bad Godesberg 124
Balkan nations 69
Balko, Andrzej 167, 174, 176, 178, 190
Baltic states 31
Baltimore 45
Barabasz, Rev. Mieczysław 12
Bartosiewicz, Alfred J. 167
Barycza, J. 167
Basista, Feliks 107
Batory, MS 74, 75, 76
Battle of England 148
Bau, Zdzisław 100
Bayer, Judge Walter J. 40, 44, 84, 164
Bayor, Jerzy 113
Beck, Józef 167
Belarus 25
Belarussians 31
Belgium 86, 89, 91, 98, 117, 137, 157, 168, 171, 172, 177, 178, 179, 192, 197, 199, 200, 209
Benelux countries 122, 154, 156, 168
Berezka, Lidia 178, 209
Bereźnicki, Bogdan 105
Berlin Wall 209
Berling soldiers 78
Bernard, Dr. William 129
Bevin, Foreign Minister Ernest 28, 29
Biedrzycki, Pastor Ceslaus S. 71
Bielański, Jadwiga 106
Bierut 29

Bieżanowski, Jan 211
Bill of Rights 126, 183
blank assurance 53
Blech, Karl 208
Bobrek, Walter 167
Bogacki, Reverend Max T., of St. Adalbertus Basilica Church 104
Bogdanowicz, J. of Cleveland 104
Bona, Bishop S.V. of Wisconsin 88
Book Cadillac Hotel 21
Borawski, J. 84
Bór-Komorowski, Generał Tadeusz 84
Bornholm 76, 77
Borough of Manhattan 43
Boryka family 145
Boręcki, Walter 164
Boston 41, 45, 49, 51
Brazil 98, 137
Brewka, Michał and Stefania family 144, 145
Brezhnev Doctrine 158
British Columbia 15
British Empire 29, 30
British government 29, 30, 63
Bronkowski, Rev. Wincenty 12
Brooklyn 12, 41, 201
Brown, Richard 147
Brussels 116, 133, 168, 179, 194
Brzana, Bishop Stanisław of Buffalo 88
Brzezinski, National Security Adviser Zbigniew 3
Brzeźnicki, Jerry 105
Buche, John A. 178, 195
Budny, H. 146, 164
Budny family factory 112
Buenos Aires 99
Buffalo 80, 155
Burant, Rev. Msgr. Feliks 38, 40, 41, 44, 48, 49, 50, 51, 55, 57, 59, 60, 61, 64, 65, 66, 67, 68, 73, 76, 79, 81, 82, 83, 84, 86, 88, 94, 95, 96, 97, 98, 104, 196, 107, 136, 142, 152, 153, 146, 148, 152, 165, 215, 217
Bureau of Immigration 15
Burke, Karol 21, 34, 36
Byrnes, Secretary of State James 36

camp for foreigners: Nürnberg 124; Zirndorf 124
Canada 15, 20, 45, 98, 113, 137, 154, 155, 158, 161, 172, 180, 190, 191, 194, 200, 205, 216
Canadian authorities 194
Canadian government 114

Canadian Polonia 114
Canadian SPK convention in Montreal 113
Caracas, Venezuela 49
CARE 78, 79, 87, 105
Caritas 125, 174
Carlin 191
Carnival Ball of the Zjednoczenie Polaków w Ameryce in Perth Amboy 110
Carter, President Jimmy 171
Carusi, Ugo 58
Castro 130; takeover 130
Catholic Church in America 88
Catholic Relief Services — National Catholic Welfare Conference 147
Celler, Emanuel 74
Central and Eastern Europe 64
Central Board of Polish Supplementary Schools (in Chicago) 106
Central Europe 19, 61, 101; political changes 158
Central Welfare Committee 11
Centralny Związek Polaków we Francji 92
Chałko, Władysława 107
Charkov 26
Chęciński, Mr. and Mrs. S. and J. 108
Chicago 20, 21, 23, 24, 34, 57, 58, 61, 80, 87, 100, 106, 107, 155, 164, 196, 198, 201, 211
China 129
Chinese Exclusion Act 15
Chinese exodus to Hong Kong 129
Chomicka, K. 85
Chopin 100
Christians 35
Chrzanowski, Władysław 104
Church World Service 28
Chwastek, Edward 108
Chyliński, T.H. of Washington 120
Cielak, John 108
Cieślak, I. 85
Cimmer, Piotr 113
Cisek, Dr. Janusz 5, 6
Civic Self-Aid Society 25
Cleveland 80, 105
Clubs of Little Poland (in Chicago) 106
Cold War 9, 55, 68
Cologne 133
Colorado 198
Committee Day 110
Committee for a Free Europe 93
the Committee 12, 42, 44, 45, 46, 47, 48, 49, 52, 54, 55, 57, 64, 65, 66, 67, 68., 71, 73, 74, 76, 77, 78, 79, 80, 81, 82, 83, 84, 85, 86, 87, 88, 89, 92, 94, 95, 96, 97, 98, 99, 100, 101, 102, 103, 104, 105, 106, 109, 110, 111, 112, 113, 114, 115, 116, 117, 119, 120, 121, 122, 123, 124, 127, 131, 132, 134, 136, 137, 142, 143, 145, 147, 148, 149, 150, 151, 152, 153, 154, 155, 156, 157, 159, 160, 161, 162, 163, 164, 165, 166, 168, 169, 170, 171, 172, 174, 175, 176, 177, 178, 179, 180, 185, 186, 187, 188, 189, 190, 191, 192, 193, 194, 195, 196, 197, 198, 199, 200, 201, 202, 203, 209, 210, 211, 212, 213, 214, 215, 216, 217
Communism 3, 36, 61, 62, 66, 69, 76, 77, 92, 101, 102, 115, 117, 119, 127, 131, 132, 135, 136, 158, 159, 177, 181, 183, 207
Communist Poland 97, 102, 106, 136, 137, 142, 146, 150, 169, 172, 184, 206
Conference of Americans of Central and East European Descent 142
Conference on refugees in Washington, D.C. (1969) 157
Congress of the Polish Diaspora of the Free World 195
Congressional Subcommittee on Immigration and Naturalization 66
Connecticut 41
Connecticut Tobacco Operation 72
Constitution 124
Consulate General of the Republic of Poland 20
Coordinating Council for Amending the McCarren-Walter Immigration Law 69
Coordinator of Refugee Affairs 198
Copenhagen 116
Council of Polish Refugees in Sweden 94
Cuba 131, 193; refugees 130
Cuban Missile Crisis 130
Custer, Wisconsin 38
Ćwikliński, Captain J. 75, 76
Cytacki, Walter 33
Czarnyszewicz, Florian 99
Czas 114
Czechoslovakia 37, 120, 131, 156, 158, 195, 201
Czermański, Zdzisław 100

Dachan, M. 120
Dachau concentration camp 94, 165
Danish government 90
Dattner, Zofia 94, 152
Daum, Lucjan 112
Dec, Jan 152, 164
Dembski, Kazimierz 41
Democratic Party 126

Democratic Platform (1956) 126
Denmark 66, 89, 98, 117, 136, 137
De Notto, Aleksandra 166
Department of Labor 131
Department of State 24, 57, 64, 116, 147, 162, 197, 198
Department of the Treasury 15
Derwiński, Edward J. 108
Detroit 21, 80, 105, 155, 172
Dickerson, Jr., Ralph 214
discrimination against Poles 150
Displaced Persons Act of 1948 3, 45, 57, 59, 61, 62, 70, 136
Displaced Persons Act of 1949 50, 51, 53, 57, 58, 60
Displaced Persons Act, amendment of 1950 52
Displaced Persons Commission in Washington, D.C. 52, 54, 57, 58, 59, 60
Displaced Persons Committee 57, 58
Division of Refugee and Migration Matters, Department of State 147
Dobroski, Steve 71
Domański, Stanisław 86, 120
Dombek, Franciszek 111
Doscinski, John C. 71
Downstate Medical Center in Brooklyn 143
D.P. Act of 1948 52
DP camps 34, 36, 58, 79, 98, 127, 128, 144
D.P. Law 65
DPs, former 135
Draft Commission 61
Drexel University 176
Drozdowicz, Gertruda 106
Dubček, Aleksander 158
Dubicki, Editor Józef 81, 130
Duch, General Bronisław 20
Durska, Czesława 152
Düsseldorf 133
Dworzak, Rev. Józef 12
Dybowski, Zygmunt 105
Dymek, Frances 58
Dziady 159
Dziekanowski, T. Wieniawa 164
Dziennik Polski 32, 33
Dziennik Związkowy 108
Dziergowska, A. 85
Dziewulak, Wacław 166
Dziuban, W. 111
Dzwoniarek, Stanisław 108

earthquake victims in the Azores 129
East Central Europe 30, 81, 185; escapees from 172

East Europe 30; refugees 186
Eastern Europe 199
Eastern Hemisphere 131
economic refugees 127, 131, 199
Ecuador 98
Eibel, Ryszard 101
Eisenhower, President Dwight D. 61, 63, 64, 65, 66, 69, 70, 76, 89, 98, 101, 126, 127, 128, 129
Elizabeth, New Jersey 103
Ellis Island 13, 46, 47, 49
emigration to Australia 190
England 45, 53, 54, 66, 88, 137
Equitable Gas Light Company in New York 11
Ernie Pyle 40
escapees 66, 74, 75, 102, 115, 117, 127, 133, 135, 155, 161
Estonians 31
Europe 14, 27, 37, 45, 46, 49, 53, 54, 57, 64, 70, 79, 86, 89, 99, 115, 126, 133, 154, 155, 156, 157, 158, 160, 172, 175, 177, 180; refugee camps in 185
Exodus of Czechs and Slovaks 158

Fabian, Piotr 87
Falaise 148
Falcons 106, 109, 110
Family Unification Program 1
Far East 68, 70, 126
Farmer's Cooperative on Long Island 71
FBI 55
Federal Agency for Alien Matters 124
Federal Republic of Germany 65, 149
Federal Reserve Bank in Washington, D.C. 24
Felician Sisters of the Congregation of the Immaculate Conception from New Britain, Connecticut 12
Fifth Kresowa Division 108
Fifth Red Column 90
First Armored Division of General Maczek 108
First Judicial District of New York 42
First Uhlan Regiment 85
Florida 130, 143, 204
Ford, Gerald 66
Foreign Legion 99
Foreign Service 60
Formosa 75, 76
Frąckowiak, Jerzy 108
France 21, 26, 89, 92, 98, 117, 122, 137, 154, 156, 167, 168, 171, 172, 174, 177, 178, 179, 192, 199, 200, 202, 209

Frankfurt 116, 133, 195, 197
Frankfurt am Main 26
Free Europe Citizens' Committee 116
Free Poland, SS 128
Free World 119
French Revolution 14
Frendl, Dr. Ludwik 174, 178, 193, 194
Funseth, R., Undersecretary of State 198

Gauting 145
Gawlina, Archbishop Józef 94, 119
Gawrysiak, Wacław 113
Gazeta Katolicka 12
Gdańsk 40, 158, 159
Gdańsk, Gdynia, Sopot 181
Geneva 26, 116, 133, 149, 158, 172, 174, 178, 189, 191, 194, 197, 200
Geneva Convention 74, 91, 124
Gerety, Pierce J. 69, 70
German-Soviet War 30
Germans 32, 35, 67, 69, 124, 133, 149, 165
Germany 15, 16, 18, 19, 26, 27, 28, 30, 34, 35, 39, 40, 49, 50, 52, 60, 64, 65, 66, 70, 71, 73, 77, 79, 87, 89, 91, 95, 96, 98, 105, 113, 115, 116, 117, 122, 124, 125, 130, 133, 134, 136, 137, 145, 154, 156, 157, 158, 166, 167, 171, 174, 178, 194, 197, 198, 208, 209
Gierat, Stanisław 85, 86, 95, 164, 177
Gierek, Edward 159, 181
Giergielewicz, Tadeusz 109
Głos Polski 114
Głowacki, Józef 87
Goettingen 79
Golcz, Rev. Jan 12
Gombrowicz, Witold 99
Gomułka, W. 159
Gordon, Antoni 94
Górska, Hanna 113
Gorski, Edwin 201, 210, 213
Gotland 195
Gottwald, SS 76
Government of the Polish Republic in London 29, 61
Grabowski, Adalbert 209
Grabowski, Julian 113
Grabowski, Zygmunt 87
Graduate School of Economics in Warsaw 101
Graham, Congressman 74
Great Britain 19, 21, 28, 30, 45, 52, 57, 64, 67, 89, 90, 95, 98, 179
Greece 89
Green Ball 100

Greenpoint, Brooklyn 211
Grupa Techniczna 85
Grużewska, Wanda 167, 174, 178
Grzybowski, Bohdan 108
Guatemala 98
Gulags in Russia 97
Guzy, J. 167
Gwiazda, Andrzej 181
Gypsies 168

Halle 30
Hamburg 79, 202
Hamtramck Common Council 105
Hanover 79
Harcaj, Colonel 108
Harcaj, Wanda 108
Harriman, New York Governor Averell 94
Hart, Senator Philip 146
Hartford, Connecticut 72, 83, 111
Harvard University 176
Heller, Louis 74
Heydenkorn, Benedykt 114
Hitler 19, 50, 68; prison camps 163
Hodara, D. 195
Hodara, Paul 178
Holland 98, 137
Holy Rosary Parish in Passaic, New Jersey 152
Hong Kong 67, 131
House of Commons 28, 31
House of Representatives, the 60, 127
House Sub-Committee on Immigration, Refugees and International Law 203
Houston, Texas 174, 201
HR 411 60
HUD 204
Hull, Secretary of State Cordell 22
Human and Health Services 197
Humphrey, Senator 62
Hungarian Revolution of 1956 128, 129, 132, 142
Hungarians 128, 201, 208, 209, 215
Hungary 21, 26, 128, 168, 193, 195
Hunter, Douglas R. 178
Hussar-Litwińska, Krystyna 210

ICM/IOM 5
ICMC (International Catholic Migration Commission) 180
Idlewild Airport 97
Illegal aliens, transport of 205
Immigration Act of 1891 15
Immigration Act of 1917 15

Immigration and Nationality Act (PL 89-236) 131
Immigration and Nationality Act of 1980 3
Immigration and Naturalization Committee, presidential 64
Immigration and Naturalization Service (INS) 13, 46, 60, 67, 97, 99, 101, 142, 146, 155, 167, 169, 183, 194, 195, 197, 200, 204, 211
Immigration Committee in Canada 114
Immigration History Research Center 214
Immigration Nursing Relief Act of 1989 205
immigration of Poles to Sweden 193
immigration quota system 64, 127, 129
Immigration Reform and Control Act of November 6, 1986 204
Impellitteri, New York Mayor V.R. 76
In Search of Milestones 95
India 67, 137
Inglot, Piotr 108
Innes, Captain Robert G. 32
INS, unfavorable attitude toward Poles 142
Institute of Physical Medicine and Rehabilitation of New York University at Bellevue Medical Center in New York City 96
Intergovernmental Committee for Migration (ICM) 54, 123, 125, 144, 179, 180, 186, 191
International Catholic Migration Committee 123
International Organization for Migration (IOM) 54
International Refugee Agreement of 1951 124
International Refugee Organization 26, 28, 51, 52, 54, 57
Iran 67
Iranians 201
Iraq 3
Ireland 89, 98
Iron Curtain 27, 33, 50, 64, 65, 66, 89, 90, 92, 97, 98, 102, 115, 127, 147
Israel 67, 70, 126, 159
Italian Caritas (UCEI) 168, 179
Italian Ministry of the Interior 195
Italy 26, 28, 45, 50, 52, 85, 89, 98, 99, 134, 137, 154, 156, 157, 158, 168, 174, 175, 178, 179, 195, 200
Ives, Irving 74

J. Piłsudski Institute 210
Jabłoński, J. 162
Jackson Perkins Operation 72
Jamestown 2
Jankowski, Kazimierz 104
Jankowski, Stefan K., Esq. 120
Januszewski, Frank 33
Jarecki, Lieutenant Franciszek 76
Jarmicki, Z. 113
Jaroszewski, B. 105
Jaruzelski, General Wojciech 181, 201, 203, 207
Jarzębowska, Florence 49, 77, 94, 152
Jarzębowski, Kazimierz 49, 84
Jarzębowski, W. 120
Jarzyna, Witold 77
Jasinowska, M. 85
Jaskólski 49
Jaźwiński, Lieutenant Zdzisław 76
Jędrzejowski, Z. 120, 149, 167
Jersey City 172
Jerzmanowski, Erazm 11, 12
JFK Airport 188
John Paul II, Pope 6, 100, 173
Johnson, President Lyndon B. 130, 131
Joliet, Illinois 157
Jordanowski, Stanisław 164, 211
Josz de Dulmen, Mieczysław 174
Józef Piłsudski Institute in New York 5, 9, 85, 203, 214
Judiciary Commmittee of the House of Representatives 60
Jurewicz, Lt. Col. Jan 108
Justice Department 67
Juszczak, Dr. Albert 6

Kabacińska, Ewa 151
Kaczorowski, Ryszard 207
Kafka-Kowal, Kaye 162, 164
Kania, Józef 20, 23
Kania, Stanisław 181
Karpiński, Rev. Msgr. John J. 152, 156, 162, 163, 193, 216, 217
Karwacki, Rev. Marian 112
Kasprzak, S. 85
Katyń Graves 26
Katz, Abraham A. (Bronx county clerk) 42
Kawa, Jadwiga 201, 213
Keating, Senator Kenneth 146, 147
Kęcki, Michael 48
Kellog, F. (assistant secretary of state for migration) 162
Kennedy, John F. 66, 127, 129, 131, 147, 148, 149
Kenya 98
Kępa, Helena 107

Khomeini, Ayatollah 201
Kiejna, Wincenty 112, 164
Kieniewicz, Mr. and Mrs. T.E. 197
Kiszczak, General Czesław 203
Klamka, Jan 111
Klekotka, Rev. Peter J. 113
Klemp, Wojciech 84
Klimecki, Rev. Hieronim 11, 12
Klonowski, Auxiliary Bishop Henry T. of Scranton 88
Klub Weteranów im. Józefa Piłsudskiego in Elizabeth, New Jersey 103
Klucz, Rev. Józef 12
Kluczyński, John 108
Koch, Judge Edward R. 44
Kocjan, Maria 107
Kogut, Wanda 104
Kokot, Antoni 120, 167, 178
Kołakowski, Leszek 159
Kolkhozes 26
Koło Lotników 104
Kołodziejski, T.A. 113
Kombatant w Ameryce 177
Komitet Narodowy Amerykanów Polskiego Pochodzenia, (KNAPP) 23, 33, 104
Komitet Niesienia POmocy Uchodźcom Polskim w Yonkers 111
Komitet Opieki nad Uchodźcami Polskimi 114
Komitet Uchodźców 24
Kongres Polonii Amerykańskiej 23
Konikowska, Ewa 166
Konikowski, Zbigniew 195
Konopacki, C.A. 100, 101
Korab-Janiewicz, Henryk 85, 94, 164
Korea 61, 72
Korean War 58, 62
Kornwestheim 79
Korzińska, Ewa 189, 190
Kosciuszko Foundation in New York 6, 84, 94, 165
Kosowicz, Edward 47, 84
Kot, Professor Stanisław 25
Kotowska, Z. 85
Kowalczyk, Rev. Msgr. Franciszek 87, 152, 153, 155, 156
Kowalska, Maria 108
Kozioł, Walter 108
Koźmor, Edward 84
Kresy Wschodnie 78
Krol, Archbishop John 88
Królicki, Henryk 178, 197, 202
Kronika Rzymska 202
Krychowski, Tadeusz 114

Krzan, Dr. Feliks 108, 211
Krzyżanowski, Janusz 1, 9, 89, 114, 165, 177, 178, 179, 189, 190, 193, 195, 197, 200, 203, 210, 213, 214, 216, 217
Kubec, Rev. Gerwazy 40, 44, 83
Kultura 100, 202
Kurmel, Edward 152
Kusper, Stanley J., Jr. 108, 164
Kwiatkowski, Stanisław 113

Labor Service Companies of the U.S. Army 36, 71, 72, 82
Labowski, Michael 164
Ladies Circle of the SPK 201
La Guardia, Fiorello 20, 31
Landshut 79
Lasko, Evelyn 166
Laskowska, Z. 85
Latin America 131
Latvians 31, 37, 69
Law of 1924 16
League of Nations 33
Lebanon 98
Lechoń, Jan 100
Legal Services Corporation 204
Legion Młodych Polek 79, 108
Lehman, Senator Herbert H. 62, 69, 74
Lenard, Kazimierz 106
Lenin Shipyards in Gdańsk 181
Lewandowski, Robert 108
Lewis, Fulton, Jr. 101
Liga Kobiet w Nowym Jorku 79
Liga Morska 87, 108
Lintorf 79
Linz 116
Liptak, Stanisław 193
Lis, Bogdan 181
Liszka, Edward 83
Lithuania 24, 25, 64, 101
Lithuanians 31, 37
Litwińska, Krystyna 108
London 22, 30, 33, 84, 86, 178, 179
London Government of the Polish Republic 23
Long Island City 48
Long Island Operations 71
Lubicz, E. 85
Łubieński, Ludwik 113, 117, 119, 120, 150, 155, 194
Lubowiecki, Reverend Monsignor Edward 79
Łukomski, Kazimierz 106
Lutheran World Federation 145

Luxembourg 137
Łyczak, Adam B. 83

Machrowicz, Congressman Tadeusz 60
Maksymowicz, T. 162
Makulec, Rev. Ludwik 77, 84, 162, 164
Malczewski, F. (Nr. 20 block leader) 32
Malinowski, Rev. Jan 107
Malinowski, L.V. 84
Malinowski, Władysław 177
Manhattan 12, 41, 44, 191, 211, 214
March (1968) events in Poland 159
Mariental-Horts DP camp 137
Marjańczyk, P.A., M. Div., Rev. Msgr. Joseph A. 5, 6, 163, 210, 212, 213, 214, 217
Martial law in Poland 109, 181, 182, 197, 199
Marut, W. 164
Maryańska, M. 85
Masalska, Katarzyna 113
Massachusetts 41
Matuga, Edward 106, 107
Matuszewski, Ignacy 32, 33
May 3rd Parade (in Chicago) 108
Mazewski, Aloysius A. 172, 193
Maziarz, Chester 108
Mazowiecki, Tadeusz 206, 207
McCarren and Walter proposal 62
McCarren-Walter Immigration Act 62, 127
McMahon, Senator Brian 60
Medicaid 197
Mednoye 26
Merło, Stanisław 86, 118, 120, 157, 168, 179
Merta, SS 74
Mexico 15; immigrants from 171
Miami 130
Michalski, T.Z. 114
Mielec 181
Migoń, Anna 106, 107, 108, 144, 164
Migration and Refugee Committee 129
Millennium of Poland's Christianity 113
Milwaukee, Wisconsin 20
Misiuk, Bogumił 212
Mission to Charitable Organizations of the United States in Geneva 202
Mizwa, Stephen P. 84
Monte Cassino 148
Morawski, Ignacy 40, 113, 114, 152, 162, 163, 164, 165
Morocco 98
Morris Street 12

Morskie Oko picnic area (in New Jersey) 110
Moscow 92
Moskal, Edward 214
Mroziński, Rev. Mieczysław 40, 44, 84
Munich 79, 116, 120, 133, 166, 174, 175, 178, 189, 194, 195, 197, 202, 209
Murmansk 25
Murthy, R. (exec. VP of the AICC) 162
Muskie, Secretary of State Edmund 3

Nadarzyn 208
Nansen Medal 63
Nansen passports 33
Napoleonic campaign 14
Narodowiec 92
Narvik 148
National Academy of Sciences 143
National Catholic Welfare Conference (NCWC) 41, 42, 49, 51, 53, 73, 79, 88, 116, 121
National Committee for Resettlement of Foreign Physicians 143
National Lutheran Council 28
NATO 66, 67, 68, 70, 92, 95, 182
NCRC 49
NCWC (Migration Refugee Services) 54
Near East 27, 45, 99, 151
Die Neue Zeitung 31
New Emigration Self-Help Society (in Chicago) 106
New Jersey 41, 86, 87, 164
New Orleans 45, 49
New York 1, 20, 23, 31, 38, 40, 46, 49, 51, 88, 89, 101, 107, 113, 117, 123, 130, 153, 171, 172, 178, 179, 180, 187, 188, 189, 193, 195, 196, 197, 204, 210
New York Polyclinic Medical School and Hospital 143
New York Times 36, 101, 186
New York World's Fair 20
New Zealand 161, 194
Newark-Irvington, New Jersey 110
Newark, New Jersey 72, 85, 103, 109, 212
NKVD 24, 25
Noris, J. 116
North Korea 76
Norton, Mary 74
Norway 66, 89, 98
Nowak, Edmund 107
Nowak, Jan 119
Nowak, Rev. Stanisław 13
Nowy Świat 19, 40, 41, 44, 51, 83, 85, 101, 152

Nurkiewicz, Ignacy 34, 36, 84
Nürnberg 116
Nürnberg-Zirndorf 133
Nyssa river 63

Obremski, Attorney S. 84, 94
Oder river 63
Office of Refugee Resettlement, Department of Health and Human Resources 184, 185
Office of the Plenipotentiary for Refugee Affairs 208
Ognisko in Deggendorf 79
Oldenburg 79
Ontario 114
open-door policy 95
Operation Carrot 31
Operation Good Samaritan 28
Operation White Cygnets 28
Orchard Lake, Michigan 214
Osiński, General Aleksander 22
Ostsee, trip to 138, 139, 140, 141
Ottawa 114
Our Lady of Mount Carmel Parish in Bayonne, New Jersey 163

PAC 36, 50
Paderewski, Ignace Jan 11, 22, 23, 51
PAIRC 6, 7, 20, 23, 44, 45, 47, 49, 50, 51, 53, 54, 55, 57, 58, 59, 60, 62, 64, 65, 68, 71, 72, 73, 75, 76, 78, 79, 80, 81, 84, 85, 86, 87, 88, 89, 92, 94, 95, 96, 99, 101, 104, 105, 106, 107, 108, 109, 110, 111, 113, 114, 115, 116, 117, 118, 120, 121, 122, 123, 124, 125, 127, 128, 134, 135, 142, 143, 144, 145, 146, 147, 148, 150, 151, 153, 154, 155, 156, 157, 158, 159, 163, 164, 165, 167, 168, 169, 172, 174, 175, 178, 179, 180, 184, 185, 188, 189, 190, 191, 192, 193, 194, 195, 196, 198, 199, 200, 201, 202, 206, 210, 213
Palestine 70, 126
Palewicz, Edward 107
Palmer, Minister Stephen E. 178
Palski, B. 120
Pankiewicz, Emil 113
Pankowiak, Edward 106, 107
Papanek, Dr. 131
Papée, Kazimierz 158
Paratroopers Circle 164
Pargiełło, Jan S. 45, 84
Paris 22, 36, 86, 116, 133, 178
Parole 128, 131
Parolee Law 145

Paschek, P. 202
Pasco 85
Passaic, New Jersey 156
passport policy of the Polish Communist government 132
Paterson, New Jersey 110
Patrzycki, Rev. Jan 12
Pawłowski, J. 84
Pela, John 105
Pelc, Maksymilian 202
Pennsylvania 41
"Permit 26" 26
Perth Amboy, New Jersey 163
Philadelphia 45, 49, 50, 172, 176
Piasecka-Johnson Foundation, Barbara 187, 193
Piątek, Zbigniew 104
Piech, Julian 108
Piekutowska, M. 85
Piłat, W. 162
Pilch, Wanda 85
Piskor, M. 85
Piskorski, Florian 116
Pittsburgh 20, 87
PKWN 77
PL 414 62
Plainfield, New Jersey 103
PNA 21, 108
Podbielski, Zygmunt 144
Podoski, Józef 167, 168
Polak, Kazimierz 111, 164
Poland 20, 21, 32, 33, 40, 42, 43, 47, 50, 61, 65, 68, 70, 76, 78, 89, 92, 96, 98, 101, 131, 137, 142, 149, 158, 168, 177, 180, 181, 182, 183, 184, 185, 186, 189, 190, 192, 194, 198, 199, 200, 203, 206, 208, 215, 216, 217, 218
Poland's Way of the Cross 165
Polanie Club 104
Polanka Sokoła in Sommerville, New Jersey 89
Poles 31, 37, 52, 55, 60, 64, 67, 68, 69, 70, 71, 72, 74, 90, 91, 92, 99, 100, 121, 127, 131, 134, 135, 137, 142, 146, 165, 175, 193, 204, 208, 209
Polish American Ball 111, 112
Polish American Collection 214
Polish American community 18, 19, 20, 55, 57, 62, 68, 73, 76, 79, 86, 87, 90, 93, 95, 97, 103, 104, 106, 107, 109, 112, 153, 155, 159, 163, 170, 172, 175, 216, 217
Polish American Congress 18, 28, 33, 34, 47, 49, 55, 56, 57, 58, 59, 60, 68, 75,

84, 94, 106, 127, 142, 160, 164, 165, 166, 198, 201
Polish American Immigration and Relief Committee 1, 5 9, 10, 14, 15, 38, 47, 52, 70, 72, 75, 76, 77, 80, 97, 131, 136, 173, 216, 217
Polish American Immigration Committee 38, 40, 42, 149, 177
Polish American Inter-Organizational Council 23
Polish American Inter Party Council 23
Polish American media 107
Polish American Press 19
Polish American Relief Fund 23
Polish and Slavic Center in Brooklyn 6
Polish Armed Forces 29, 30, 45, 52, 65, 66, 67, 74, 77, 135
Polish Army 20, 26, 59, 65, 119, 195
Polish authorities in London 34
Polish Brazilian community 100
Polish camps 32
Polish Canadian Congress 49, 113, 114, 175, 180, 181
Polish children 148, 155
Polish clergy in Canada 114
Polish Communist government 102, 158
Polish Community Center (Yonkers) 111
Polish Consular Corps 152
Polish crisis (of 1981) 195
Polish Cultural Foundation, Clark, New Jersey 214
Polish Day of the Polish American Immigration and Relief Committee 109
Polish Depees 50
Polish Diaspora 74, 218
Polish Displaced Persons Committee 56
Polish Embassy of the Polish Government in Exile to the Holy See 92
Polish Embassy, Washington., D.C. 20
Polish Falcons Society in America — Sokolstwo Polskie w Ameryce 19, 20, 152
Polish government 22, 26, 29, 34, 63, 74
Polish Home [in Manhattan] 42
Polish Home Army 61, 96, 119, 164, 165
Polish Hour 49
Polish Immigration Committee Day 109, 110, 112
Polish Information Center, Havana, Cuba 49
Polish Information District Center 180
Polish Institute of Arts and Sciences 214
Polish Language Press Association 84
Polish Legion of American Veterans 39

Polish National Alliance 12, 20, 34, 39, 57, 58, 84, 203, 214
Polish National Defense Fund 23
Polish National Home 19, 112
Polish National Liberation Committee 78
Polish Pavilion at 1939 World's Fair in NY 39
Polish People's Army 76
Polish People's Republic 66, 75, 76, 77, 207
Polish physicians 143
Polish Press Agency in Edinburgh 29
Polish press 74, 86
Polish priests (in America) 88
Polish question 19, 23
Polish Republic 9, 18, 19, 20, 26, 50; Ministry of Labor and Social Welfare 25
Polish revolt in Poznań 128
Polish Roman Catholic Union of America 39
Polish Scouts 104
Polish Section of Radio Free Europe 151, 156
Polish students 117, 119
Polish II Corps 99
Polish Veteran Home 189
Polish veterans in Great Britain 70, 89, 94, 193
Polish Women's Alliance in Chicago 155
political escapees 134
political refugees 102, 123, 129, 136, 199
Polkowska, Ilona 213
Polkowski, Piotr 213
Polonia 3
Polska Rada Uchodźcza 90
Polska Robotnicza Kasa Pomocy 83
Polskie Stowarzyszenie Byłych Więźniów Politycznych Niemieckich i Sowieckich Obozów Koncentracyjnych w Ameryce 88, 165
Polskie Stowarzyszenie Kasy p.o. św. Jana Kantego 87
Polsko Amerykańska Robotnicza Kasa Pomocy 79
Pope John Paul II Foundation 6
Popławski, Feliks 83, 94, 152, 158, 162, 164
Poprzęcki, Karol 108
Portugal 26, 89
POW camps 27
Poznań events 215
Praca, SS 75, 76
Prague Spring 158
PRCUA 87, 108

Preisler, Ewa 167
Preisler, Michał 167
President's Committee for Hungarian Refugee Relief 128
Proch, Franciszek J. 94, 105, 152, 160, 164, 165, 166, 167, 171, 172, 175, 187, 191, 192, 193, 194, 198, 210
Przybyła 49
Ptak, Daniela 166
Puciński, Roman 108
Pulaski Day Parade in New York 39, 71, 80, 146, 154, 170, 201

Quota Law of 1921 15
quota mortgages 65
quota system 3, 62

Rachocki, S.L. 157
Rada Oświatowa Złączonych Towarzystw 83
Rada Polonii Amerykańskiej — American Relief for Poland 19, 22
Radio Free Europe 90
Radoniewicz, Zbigniew 108, 164, 210
Rahway, New Jersey 110
Raith, Msgr. Vincent 111
Rasiej, Kazimierz 191
Ravensbrück concentration camp 151
Rawski, Czesław 117, 119, 120, 152, 153, 165
Reagan, President Ronald 3, 184
Reception and Placement Program 184
Rector Street 12
Red Army 30, 31, 36, 40, 50
Red Cross 22, 26, 28, 30, 32, 76, 97
Red terror 119
Redfern, Dr. 24
Reduta Choir 103
Refugee Act of March 17, 1980 182, 183, 184, 204
Refugee Act of 1953 (PL 203) 67
Refugee and Migration Committee 128
Refugee Committee 106
Refugee Data Center in New York 202
Refugee Fair Share Law 129
Refugee Relief Act 69, 70, 90
Refugee Relief Program 69
refugees 55, 60, 65, 66, 68, 72, 81, 86, 89, 91, 92, 102, 111, 114, 115, 116, 121, 123, 124, 127, 129, 130, 131, 133, 134, 135, 136, 137, 142, 143, 145, 147, 148, 149, 150, 151, 154, 156, 158, 159, 168, 169, 171, 175, 185, 186, 194, 196, 198, 199, 200, 201, 206, 208, 209, 216

Regal, Dolores 164
Republic of Poland 15, 207
Republican Party 126
Resettlement Grants 192
Resettlement in Canada, South Africa, Australia, England, Sweden and Switzerland 143, 144
Resiak, Zenon 77
riots in Warsaw 159
Riverhead (NY) 71
Rockland County Growers Association 72
Rockland County Operation 72
Rogoyski, Roman 167
Romania 21, 26, 198, 199
Romanians 37
Romaszkiewicz, PNA President John 22
Rome 86, 92, 116, 133, 168. 194, 195, 202
Rooks, Julia 105
Rooney, Congressman John J., of New York 147
Roosevelt, Franklin Delano 21, 22, 62
Rostenkowski, D. 108
Round Table discussions in Poland 207
Rowny, Lt. Gen. Edward 3
Różański, Dr. Edward 108, 164
Różański, John 152
Rozmarek, Karol 34, 36, 57, 58, 59, 60, 78
Rozmarek, Wanda 57, 106
Rozmarek-Komosa, Marilyn 107
Rubin, Bishop Władysław 74, 158, 161
Rudnicki, Ryszard 193, 197, 209
Rusinek, J. 114
Rusk, Dr. Howard 96
Russia 15, 16, 25, 26, 36, 61, 66, 101, 198
Russian Jews 185
Rygiel, Aleksandra 108
Rynca, M. 85
Rząd Jedności Narodowej 28
Rzepecki, Chester 107
Rzetelski, Stanisław 164

Sadowski, Colonel M., in Toronto 114
St. Lawrence University 38
St. Mark's Place 19
St. Peter 62
Saints Cyril and Methodius Parish, Brooklyn 84
Salazar, Antonio de Oliveira 26
Salzburg 116, 133
Samopomoc Byłych Żołnierzy PSC Emigrujących do USA 88
Samopomoc Nowej Emigracji (NYC) 88
Sao Paulo 100

Sapieha, Paweł 156, 166, 172
Sawicki, General Florian 203
Sawko, Chester 108, 164
Scandinavia 195
Second Polish Republic 207
Second World War 37
Senate Subcommittee for Refugee Matters 146
September Ball (Perth Amboy) 110
September 1939 campaign 27, 39
Seym 203, 207
Shade Tobacco Growers Cultural Association 72
Shade Tobacco Operation 72
Sheehan, Michael 72
Sherman Hotel 108
Sieminski, Congressman A. 74
Siew 85
Sikorski, General Władysław 23
Sikorski–Majski Pact 25, 101
Siniewicz, H. 85
Skarb Narodowy 83
Skonieczny, Wacław 108
Skonieczny, Zbigniew 108
Skrzypczyński, Henry 107
Śląsk 181
Smith, Captain John 2
Smoleń, Rev. 110
Snell, John L. 18
Sobieski, SS 74
Social Security 185, 197
Society of St. Adalbert 111
Sodality of the Blessed Virgin Mary 119
Sokolstwo Polskie w Ameryce 87
Soldiers' Home 157, 187, 203
Solidarity 166, 181, 182, 184, 185, 186, 192, 198, 200, 215, 216
Sommerville (New Jersey) 110
Sosnkowski, General Kazimierz 63
Sosulski, W. 164
South Africa 155, 203
South America 46
South River, New Jersey 177
South Vietnamese government 171
Southeast Asia 171
Soviet Union 19, 26, 30, 31, 33, 37, 47, 50, 84, 156, 165, 182, 185, 203, 208
Soviet Special Services 31
Sowa-Sowiński, Zygmunt 100
Spain 89, 98
Spellman, Francis Cardinal 51, 95
SPK 86, 90, 91, 92, 99, 108, 113, 120, 164, 168, 177, 201, 202, 211
Springfield, Massachusetts 41, 49

Stachurski, William 84
Stalin 19, 25, 28, 30, 50, 69, 70, 76, 115, 118, 184
Stańczyk, Benjamin C. 105
Stars and Stripes 31
State Department 52, 96, 103, 121, 123, 128, 129, 154, 158, 172, 174, 175, 176, 182, 189, 201, 202, 206, 207, 209, 214, 216; Refugee Program Bureau 4
Statler Hilton Hotel in Buffalo 104
Statler Hotel in New York 47
Statue of Liberty 62, 76, 95, 131
Stein, Charles 175
Steiner, Vera 178
Stevenson, Governor Adlai E. 63
Stockholm 195
Stoke, R.R. 31
Stop Fire Company 84
Stowarzyszenie Byłych Więźniów Politycznych Niemieckich i Sowieckich Obozów Koncentracyjnych 105
Stowarzyszenie Polek w Stanach Zjednoczonych 105
Stowarzyszenie Polskich Kombatantów 82, 85, 86, 103, 165
Stowarzyszenie Samopomocy Nowej Emigracji 211
Stowarzyszenie Synów Polski 84, 86
Stowarzyszenie Uchodźców z Albany 103
Stowarzyszenie Weteranów Armii Polskiej 82, 152
Strakacz, Sylwin 51
Strezelecki, Rev. Jan 12
Strzępek, H. 85
Studziński, Rev. Józef 40, 44
Subcommittee on Refugees and Escapees of the Senate Committee on the Judiciary 145
Suchanek-Suchecki, Wacław 166
Suffern, New York 72
Suffolk County 71
Sukarno, President 129
Sułkowski, Edmund 201, 213
Sułkowski, Władysław 104
Suzin, D. 120
Svenska Dagbladet 195
Swanstrom, Msgr. (later Bishop) Edward E. 51, 128, 129, 147, 157
SWAP 105, 108, 111, 157, 164, 214
Sweden 66, 67, 75, 89, 90, 95, 98, 136, 137, 155, 174, 194 195, 196, 200
Świder, Rev. Zygmunt 12
Świdnik 181

Index 251

Święcicki, Marian 109
Świerzbiński, Joseph 152, 162, 163
Świetlik, Rev. Dr. Franciszek 23, 113
Swing, General 101
Świnoujście 156
Switzerland 89, 158, 172
Sygnarski, Zbigniew 166
Sykurski, Marian 96
Synowiecki, Adam (of Winnipeg) 114
Szafrański, C. 164
Szczecin 159, 181
Szczygielska, Franciszka 87, 210, 213
Szenderowicz, Mr. 178
Sznuk, Colonel Stefan (in Toronto) 114
Sztybel, Tadeusz 41, 83, 94, 136
Szuberla 49
Szubiński, Rev. Franciszek 40, 44, 84
Szulc, Tad 100
Szymanowicz, Helena 108
Szymczak, Matt 24

Tarnowski, Adam 33, 34
Tenze, American attorney 101
Tesny, Franciszka 105
Third Reich 19, 27, 50
Tobruk 148
Todt 28
Tolstoy Foundation 125, 167, 171
Tomaszewska, Barbara 196
Toronto 114, 180
Towarzystwo Dobroczynne Pań Polskich 111
Towarzystwo Samopomocy Obywatelskiej 24
Tracewicz, Dr. Elżbieta 188
Transcontinental Leather, Inc. 176
Travelers Aid Society 46
Travemunde-Priwall 137
Treiskirchen camp 190
Treiskirchen in Austria 125, 167, 194
Treister, R. 179
Trenton, New Jersey 110
Trieste, territory of 67, 168
Trockenheim, Marek 174, 195, 196
Truman, President Harry S 28, 61, 62, 68
Truszkowska-Marciak, Elżbieta 166
Turkey 67, 98
Twentieth Congress of the Union of Polish Workers' Parties in 1956 97
Twenty Eighth Convention of the PNA, 1939 21
Two Edwards radio program 47, 48
Tyma, J. 107
Tyme, Antoni 107
Tyszkiewicz, Michał 166, 172

Ukrainians 37
Umiński, John 104
Unia Polska w Stanach Zjednoczonych Ameryki Północnej 87
Union of Poles in Germany 94
Union of Polish War Refugees in Brussels 49
United Nations 33, 34, 36, 37, 96, 104, 129, 182, 204
United Nations High Commissioner for Refugees 116, 124, 135, 144, 149, 150, 155, 158, 166, 167, 168, 178, 208
United Poles in America 110
United Polish Workers' Party 159
United States 14, 15, 19, 20, 22, 26, 27, 28, 29, 30, 32, 35, 36, 37, 43, 45, 49, 50, 51, 52, 53, 54, 55, 56, 57, 58, 59, 60, 61, 66, 67, 68, 71, 72, 74, 75, 76, 77, 79, 86, 91, 96, 97, 98, 99, 100, 118, 123, 126, 127, 128, 129, 130, 131, 134, 136, 137, 137, 142, 144, 145, 146, 147, 148, 154, 155, 156, 157, 158, 159, 160, 161, 165, 166, 169, 170, 171, 175, 176, 177, 179, 182, `83, 184, 185, 186, 188, 189, 190, 191, 192, 195, 196, 197, 200, 201, 202, 203, 204, 205, 206, 212, 216
U.S. Army 39, 61
United States Committee for Refugees 129
U.S. Congress 14, 16, 35, 56, 57, 58, 60, 74, 127, 129, 153, 182, 184, 185, 201, 205
United States Coordinator for Refugee Affairs 182
United States Escapee Program (USEP) 92, 96, 116, 121, 143, 145, 154, 156, 158
U.S. House of Representatives 21
U.S. Immigration and Naturalization Service 55
U.S. Mission to Humanitarian Organizations in Geneva 175
U.S. Mission to International Organizations 178
U.S. Public Health Service 54
USRP (United States Refugee Program) 121, 172, 175, 191
U.S. Senate 21, 60, 62
United Ukrainian Canadian Relief Committee 125
United Way 191, 192, 213, 214
Universal Declaration of Human Rights 183
University of Buffalo School of Medicine 143
University of Minnesota 214

Urbaniak, Feliks 112
Uruguay 137

V-Day 65
Vandenberg, Senator Arthur 33, 34
Vatican 202
Venezuela 98
Vianna, SS 74
Vienna 116, 133, 167, 175, 176, 178, 189, 190, 191, 194, 202, 209
Vietnam 171
Vietnam War 62, 171
Vilnius 24, 25
Virginia Company of London 2
Visa Diversification Program 1
Visa 93 program 200
Vistula River 186
The Voice of Polonia 48

Wagner, New York City Mayor Robert 94, 153
Walentynowicz, Anna 181
Wałęsa, Lech 181, 207
Walter, Congressman Francis E. 60, 127
Walter-Kennedy proposal 127
Walters, Francis 74
War Relief Services — NCWC 54
Warlikowski, E. 164
Warsaw 28, 29, 75, 92, 142, 208
Warsaw Pact 158, 168, 195, 206
Warsaw Uprising of 1944 36, 39, 61, 96, 151
Washington, D.C. 22, 23, 34, 58, 86, 96, 152, 171, 172, 175
Wasilewska, Wanda 78
Wąsowski, Captain Leonard 75
Watson, B. (administrator of Security and Consular Affairs of the Department of State) 162
Wazeter, Francis 164
Wędrogowski, Piotr 74
Węgiel, B. 113
Węgrzynek, Janina 40, 41, 44, 84, 85, 94
Wełdycz, Zofia 166
Werner, Jerzy 189, 190, 191
Wesoły, Archbishop Szczepan 6, 148, 158, 160
West European nations 134, 146, 155
West Germany 67, 168, 192, 199, 200
West Point, U.S. Military Academy 48
Western Allies 31, 148
Western Europe 26, 27, 30, 37, 38, 52, 65, 66, 115, 122, 136, 144, 159, 169
Wiadomości codzienne 105

Wichrowski, Colonel Bolesław 58, 78
Widlicki, Jennie 164
Widlicki, Matthew 130
Wieniawa-Ślesiński, Dr. 99
Wierzyński, Kazimierz 100
Wilkes Barre, Pennsylvania 87
Williamsburg 142
Wilson, President Woodrow 23
Witanowska, Eleonora 166
Witanowski, Edward 47, 84, 94, 152, 201
Wize, Krzysztof 120
Wójcik, Rev. Jakub 12
Wojewódka, Deacon Bolesław 164, 213
Wołowska, Honorata 23
World War I 23
World War II 3, 11, 13, 16, 17, 18, 22, 23, 39, 66, 68, 84, 85, 89, 92, 120, 134, 162
World's Fair 121
Woźnicki, Bishop Steven of Detroit 88
WRY (World Refugee Year) 58, 104, 129, 134
Wuerzburg 79
Wujastyk, Stanisław 172, 174, 175
Wycisło, Bishop Aloysius of Chicago 49, 88
Wyrwa, Józef 61, 62
Wysocka, Barbara 104
Wyszński, Hieronim 111, 155, 158, 162, 163, 165, 210, 214
Wyszyński, Stefan Cardinal 97

Yalta 3, 30, 31, 32, 35, 37, 63, 68
YMCA 28, 92
Yolles, Piotr 41, 84
Ystad, Sweden 75, 156
Yugoslavia 26, 128, 131, 168

Zablocki, Congressman Clement 3
Zachariasiewicz, Władysław 9. 75, 76, 81, 84, 86, 89, 90, 91, 92, 94, 100, 101, 106, 107, 109, 113, 114, 116, 130, 133, 134, 135, 142, 143, 152, 157, 164, 210, 214, 217
Zahorska, Elżbieta 210
Zahorski, Witold 86, 118, 120, 148, 168, 210
Zakrzewski, Adolf 85
Zakrzewski, Zygmunt 105
Zaleski, Judge Henry 71, 145, 146, 152, 164
Zaleski, Jerzy 107
Zamek 108
Zamoyski, August 100
Żebrowski, Ruth 164
Zgoda 12
Ziemba, Carl 105

Zirndorf refugee camp 124, 125, 158, 167, 175, 178, 197, 202
Zjazd "Amerykańsko-Polskich Zrzeszeń na Wschodzie" 23
Zjednoczenie Polskich Uchodźców w Niemczech 86
Zjednoczenie Polskie in Norway 90
Zjednoczenie Polskie Rzymsko Katolickie (Polish Roman Catholic Union of America) 20, 23, 85, 87
Zjednoczenie Polskie w Ameryce 105
Zjednoczenie Polsko Narodowe 87
Złączone Towarzystwa 83
Żłobicki, Jerzy 167, 174

Żółtowski, Dr. Wincenty 11
Zon, Ludwik F. 176
Żuraw, SS 75
Związek Narodowy Polski 21, 85, 110
Związek Oficerów Marynarki Handlowej w Ameryce 88
Związek Polaków in Denmark 90
Związek Polaków w Ameryce 105, 163
Związek Polaków w Austrii 86, 92
Związek Polaków w Belgii 91
Związek Polaków w Niemczech 91
Związek Polek w Ameryce 23, 24
Związkowiec 114
Żyro, Czesław 108

www.ingramcontent.com/pod-product-compliance
Lightning Source LLC
Chambersburg PA
CBHW051217300426
44116CB00006B/603